D1710256

# The Dixie Limited

# The Dixie Limited

## Writers on William Faulkner and His Influence

Edited by M. Thomas Inge

University Press of Mississippi    Jackson

www.upress.state.ms.us

The University Press of Mississippi is a member of the Association of American University Presses.

Library of Congress Cataloging-in-Publication Data

Names: Inge, M. Thomas, editor.
Title: The Dixie Limited : writers on William Faulkner and his influence / edited by M. Thomas Inge.
Description: Jackson : University Press of Mississippi, 2016. | Includes bibliographical references and index.
Identifiers: LCCN 2015042758 (print) | LCCN 2016000498 (ebook) | ISBN 9781496803382 (hardback) | ISBN 9781496806758 (epub single) | ISBN 9781496806765 (epub institutional) | ISBN 9781496806772 ( pdf single) | ISBN 9781496806789 (pdf institutional)
Subjects: LCSH: Faulkner, William, 1897–1962—Criticism and interpretation. | Faulkner, William, 1897–1962—Influence. | Literature, Modern—20th century—History and criticism. | BISAC: LITERARY COLLECTIONS / American / General. | LITERARY CRITICISM / American / General.
Classification: LCC PS3511.A86 Z78195 2016 (print) | LCC PS3511.A86 (ebook) | DDC 813/.52—dc23
LC record available at http://lccn.loc.gov/2015042758

British Library Cataloging-in-Publication Data available

*Dedications may be out of style,*
*but she could never be.*
*For Donária,*
*with love.*

# CONTENTS

# ACKNOWLEDGMENTS

This book is the end result of over fifty years of intermittent research. As I worked on a series of essays and books about William Faulkner, his life and his legacy, I noticed the frequency with which other major and minor writers, several of them Nobel Prize winners, took note of his accomplishments. Many times it was in the form of a book review of a Faulkner novel, a comment in a personal letter or diary, or a general essay of appreciation. Most were complimentary and acknowledged the power of his influence on their own work. But Faulkner was sometimes seen as a negative influence or an insurmountable model to which they might aspire but never excel. A few rejected his work outright and viewed his technical complexity as an example simply of bad writing.

Thus I began to seek out comments on Faulkner on an occasional basis, combing through collections of published letters and documents, biographies, criticism, and bibliographies, looking for such references. I have been aided by many colleagues and friends in this search, especially the work of Thomas McHaney in his early invaluable essay "Watching for the Dixie Limited: Faulkner's Impact on the Creative Writer," in *Fifty Years of Yoknapatawpha*, edited by Doreen Fowler and Ann J. Abadie (Jackson: University Press of Mississippi, 1980), pages 226–47. All of my colleagues in Faulkner studies have been helpful from time to time, a partial list of which would include Ann Abadie, Marcel Arbeit, John E. Bassett, Hunter Cole, Martha E. Cook, Doreen Fowler, Constante Graba, Jan Gretlund, Robert W. Hamblin, Lothar Hönnighausen, Valeria Lerda, Giovanni Lowe, Pearl McHaney, David Minter, Mo Yan, Charles E. Peek, Francois Pitavy, Carl E. Rollyson Jr., Judith Sensibar, Tao Jie, Glennray Tutor, and Waldemar Zacharasiewicz. Several sadly are no longer with us: William Boozer, Cleanth Brooks, Michel Gresset, Paul A. Orlov, Noel Polk, Dorothy Scura, Joan Williams, and Thomas Daniel Young. I hope to be forgiven this partial list as a complete one would be too lengthy to include here. Brenda Harview lent her keen expertise to the project by creating the index.

All of the comments uncovered in my research could not be reprinted in this volume. The book would be too lengthy and expensive. Several items were excluded because the requested permission fee was too high for our budget, or because I received no response from the copyright holders. If I have overlooked anyone who holds a claim to material here who is not acknowledged, I would appreciate knowing about it so a correction can be made.

A special word of gratitude is due Randolph-Macon College where three successive presidents have generously allowed the use of time and support to see not only this book but many more through to publication: Ladell Payne, a master of Faulkner and southern literature himself; Roger Martin, an eminent historian; and Robert Lindgren, who has the magic touch for strengthening an already great college. Provost William Franz saved the day at a crucial point by finding the resources to help make this book possible, for which both the Press and I are grateful.

The dedication page attempts to express my inexpressible appreciation for the most important person in all that I do.

February 2016
M. Thomas Inge

# The Dixie Limited

# Introduction

While commenting on the problems of being an individual southern writer amid so many genuinely talented writers from that region in the last century, Flannery O'Connor once noted, "The presence alone of Faulkner in our midst makes a great difference in what the writer can and cannot permit himself to do. Nobody wants his mule and wagon stalled on the same track the Dixie Limited is roaring down."[1] Her railroading metaphor wittily captured much of the respect and unease the example of William Faulkner has brought the worldwide community of writers.

Few modern writers, except perhaps James Joyce, have had so profound an influence throughout the world as has William Faulkner. He has been called a "writer's writer," that is one who is held up as a preceptor and model for other writers to emulate. The novel has certainly not been the same since Faulkner, that much seems clear, and the intent here is to document some of the reasons by surveying the exact nature of what Faulkner has meant to his colleagues both in the United States and abroad.

Faulkner began to attract the attention of other writers at the very start of his career as a published novelist. In Nashville, Fugitive poet Donald Davidson, not yet a spokesperson for Agrarianism, reviewed Faulkner's first three novels for his prominent book page in the *Nashville Tennessean* newspaper. *Soldiers' Pay* (1926) he found to be the product of a skillful writer with "a fine power of objectifying his own and other people's emotions, . . . an artist in language, a sort of poet turned into prose." *Mosquitoes* (1927) he thought too much under the influence of James Joyce and too possessed with the grotesque, but admirable nevertheless for "the skill of the performance." As an emerging poet himself, with two volumes in print, these are the kinds of things another wordsmith would find noteworthy. Davidson would remain an admirer of Faulkner's genius with words, and with the appearance of *Sartoris* in 1929, he would proclaim Faulkner "the equal of any except three or four American novelists who stand at the very top."[2]

Such praise was not only regional however. Modernist poet Conrad Aiken, writing in the *New York Post* on *Mosquitoes*, provided a thorough analysis of both the charms and deficiencies of Faulkner's prose and, along the way, found him the equal of Hemingway in dialogue, "with something of Katherine Mansfield's sense of light and texture, and a good deal of [Aldous] Huxley's erudition."[3] This placed him in the company of some of the best known writers of the time, and in a later 1939 essay for *Atlantic* magazine, a penetrating defense of the complexity of Faulkner's style, Aiken placed him in the company of Henry James and Balzac as a brilliant stylist.[4]

Reviewing *Mosquitoes* for the *New York Herald Tribune*, playwright Lillian Hellman (who had enthusiastically read the manuscript for the publisher) likewise found Faulkner comparable to Huxley at his best, and at his worst under the influence of Joyce in overwritten passages. Mainly the novel demonstrated a genius found "in the writings of only a few men."[5] Of course, both Aiken and Hellman were transplanted southerners, the first from Savannah, Georgia, and the second from New Orleans, Louisiana, the exact states in which the first two novels were set respectively. They were thus able to exercise a kind of judgment about authenticity that other readers might not. But this was not why they were impressed with the works. Their independent critical judgments suggested that they were in the presence of a great writer and rival.

Just about all of Faulkner's contemporaries also knew they were in for major competition from the young Mississippi country boy with an unabridged vocabulary and undisciplined style. Beginning with *Sartoris*, to be followed shortly by *The Sound and the Fury* (1929), *As I Lay Dying* (1930), and *Sanctuary* (1931), as well as the other stellar works of the 1930s, including *Light in August* (1932) and *Absalom, Absalom!* (1936), anyone who cared about writing in America could hardly overlook or ignore his presence. Among the older generation of writers, Sherwood Anderson both praised and mentored Faulkner into print, and he would say in an essay for *American Mercury* in 1930, "The two most notable young writers who have come on in America since the war, it seems to me, are William Faulkner and Ernest Hemingway."[6] That is a coupling that would be frequently made, usually to the chagrin of the latter.

The leading lady of southern letters, Ellen Glasgow, repulsed by the gothicism and grim naturalism of many modern writers, rejected Faulkner as one of their number. In her essays and letters, she referred to "the fantastic nightmares of William Faulkner," "the sodden futilitarians and the corncob cavaliers of Mr. Faulkner," and "Faulkner's school of Raw-Head-and-Bloody-Bones" fiction.[7] Similarly, the genteel midwestern sensibility of Booth Tarkington found Faulkner little to his liking, sarcastically nominating him "our Leader and Hero," but after parodying his prose in a 1932 letter to historical novelist Kenneth Roberts, he would grudgingly admit, "Outside of being different with parenthesis and things now and then, and some traces of Stephen Crane, our leader is often satisfactorily confusing in ways that demonstrate greatness."[8]

The writers who rested most uneasily in light of his increasing reputation were those immediate contemporaries who were making a conscious bid for recognition as *the* major American novelist. Ernest Hemingway, the major contender, always taking on the competition in figurative boxing matches, was especially worried that Faulkner was the better writer. When Hemingway was not put out or responding nastily to some negative comment he thought Faulkner had made about his own writing, he was quite generous in his praise. Reacting in 1932 to a reviewer of *Death in the Afternoon* who had misunderstood a reference to Faulkner in that book, Hemingway wrote the *New Yorker* to assert, "I have plenty of respect for Faulkner and wish him all luck."[9] In an essay for *Esquire* in 1935, he mentioned with admiration Faulkner's *Pylon*, and in a 1946 interview he agreed that Faulkner was "the greatest living American writer."[10] Despite referring sarcastically to Faulkner's mythic county as "Octonawhoopoo" and "Anomatopoeio County," and to the writer as "Old Corndrinking Mellifluous," Hemingway greatly respected Faulkner's achievement, as Faulkner did his.[11] They were simply different kinds of writers with different artistic visions, and their public personae sometimes got in their way.

F. Scott Fitzgerald, who alternately found himself either being tutored how to write better or being disparaged by Hemingway, although he needed no lessons, held no public discourse with Faulkner and no sense of competition. They had met and seemed to respect each other, but when Fitzgerald was making notes or giving advice about writing, he often cautioned against Faulkner's influence. He warned John Peale Bishop, when reviewing his manuscript for *Act of Darkness*, that too often he "saw patterns in this book which derived background and drama from Faulkner," and while working on *Tender Is the Night*, he made a note for himself: "Must avoid Faulkner attitude and not end with a novelized Kraft-Ebbing—better Ophelia and her flowers."[12] He and Zelda frequently gave friends copies of *Sanctuary*, although one told Zelda "she couldn't sleep for three nights it gave her the horrors so terribly," and Scott reported in 1932, "Have been reading *Sanctuary* and *Little Lord Fauntleroy* together—chapter by chapter (this is serious) and am simply overwhelmed by the resemblance. The books are simply two faces of the same world spirit."[13]

Of course, neither Hemingway nor Fitzgerald were likely to be influenced very much by Faulkner, set as they were in their own aesthetic ways, but the influence did go the other way. In Faulkner's first two novels, techniques he had learned about style and authorial attitude from both writers are clearly evident, and the original title for *Soldiers' Pay*, "Mayday," had been used previously by Fitzgerald for one of his short stories. After Fitzgerald's death in 1940, and the temporary eclipse of his reputation, when asked to list the major American writers, Faulkner usually omitted Fitzgerald but consistently included Hemingway, although what he said nearly always got him in trouble.

It was, in fact, what Faulkner said specifically about Thomas Wolfe that got him into the most trouble with Hemingway. On more than one occasion that got into print, Faulkner ranked Wolfe above Hemingway among the current generation of writers, because Hemingway lacked the artistic courage of a Wolfe. As Faulkner later retold it:

I said . . . that among his and my contemporaries, I ranked Wolfe first
because we had all failed but Wolfe had made the best failure because
he had tried hardest to say the most . . . My admiration for Wolfe is
that he tried his best to get it all said; he was willing to throw away
style, coherence, all the rules of preciseness, to try to put all the experience of the human heart on the head of a pin, as it were. He may have
had the best talent of us, he may have been "the greatest American
writer" if he had lived longer.[14]

As for Wolfe's opinion of Faulkner, he had lived long enough to see
his major works into print but two years before his death made some
encouraging if condescending remarks about both Hemingway and
Faulkner to a newspaper reporter:

I have met both Hemingway and Faulkner and my own deep feeling
is that neither has begun to reach full maturity and that both will do
better books than they have done yet . . . I don't think [Faulkner] has
begun yet to use the whole range and sweep of his material, for here
is a man whose talent could play over all of life. I've read "The Sound
and the Fury" and "As I Lay Dying" and, of course, "Sanctuary." I've
no notion of how he will develop, but here is a man with too extensive
knowledge to deal merely with the horrible and the demented and the
macabre types of life . . . "The Sound and the Fury" was in many ways
a very wonderful book, and I doubt that a man of that imaginative
and inventive power can be held down . . . or restricted to one type of
story.[15]

Interestingly enough, it was the very thing that Faulkner admired
in Wolfe—the sweep and inclusiveness of human experience—that
Wolfe felt Faulkner lacked in his focus on those alienated from and
marginalized by society. But if Wolfe could not tell by then, having
read some of his best novels, that Faulkner was a great writer, then
he probably never would have recognized his worth. We do not know
if Faulkner ever saw these comments, but he did not retain his high
opinion and rudely told a reporter in 1957 that reading Wolfe bored
him.[16]

Two other names usually appeared in Faulkner's lists of great

American writers—John Steinbeck and John Dos Passos—but neither publicly reciprocated during his lifetime. In a letter to a friend in 1956, Steinbeck complained that receiving the Nobel Prize had ruined Faulkner:

> When those old writings boys get to talking about The Artist, meaning themselves, I want to leave the profession. I don't know whether the Nobel Prize does it or not, but if it does, thank God I have not been so honored. . . . Sure he's a good writer but he's turning into a god damned phoney.[17]

When he asked Faulkner for advice about visiting Japan to attend the P.E.N. Congress in 1957, and Faulkner replied with useful suggestions, there was no hint of such rancor in Steinbeck's very friendly letter of thanks. But then he probably had not seen Faulkner's comment made while he was in Japan in 1955: "Steinbeck is just a reporter, a newspaperman, not really a writer."[18] As for Dos Passos, it was not until after Faulkner's death that he wrote a eulogy in 1963 praising his story-telling abilities, his visual use of details, his "marvelously accurate observations," and his creation of real characters based on the truth of experience, "just as Homer made his goddesses and heroes real because he built them out of traits he knew in men and women."[19]

Women writers were usually not included in the famous Faulkner lists, although Willa Cather occasionally crept on, but there was one whom he should have mentioned because of her importance to establishing his reputation—Evelyn Scott. At the time recognized as the author of a powerful and complex novel about the Civil War, *The Wave*, and seemingly destined for greatness, she was asked to review the galley proofs for *The Sound and the Fury* by Faulkner's publisher in 1929. Her one-page response was so enthusiastic that she was asked to expand it into a pamphlet, which was to be issued along with the novel for book dealers and critics. In the six pages of text, Scott outlined the reasons why *The Sound and the Fury* was "a unique and distinguished novel," "an important contribution to the permanent literature of fiction."[20] Moving through the novel book by book, she displayed in these few pages a clearer understanding of the plot, structure, and themes of the novel than most of the critics in the decade to follow. There is no doubt that this boost from a writer of greater reputation than his own helped establish the seriousness of Faulkner's work in the eyes of the literary world, but there is no record of his having reciprocated with a thank you or a single compliment as her career degenerated, except to say on one occasion when asked to name any good women novelists, "Well, Evelyn Scott was pretty good, for a woman."[21] This was 1940, when Scott was alive and still publishing, but note the past tense and the condescending last phrase.

At least two other contemporary women writers went on record about Faulkner, although he is not known to have mentioned them. Katherine Anne Porter did not include him on her list of the true masters of fiction, but she did lecture about his novels in the late 1940s and 1950s, speak appreciatively of his humor as "one of the funniest men in the world," and praise "The Bear" as "a just about perfect" piece of fiction. In general she thought his work was too emotional and "Dionysiac" and wrote in a letter probably to Caroline Gordon in 1931 about *The Sound and the Fury*: "I have never seen such a cold-blooded assault on the nerve-ends, so unrepentant a statement of horror as that book. And such good bold sound writing."[22] In 1951, Porter sent Faulkner a fan letter, which he seems to have disregarded.

When *The Portable Faulkner* appeared in 1946, Caroline Gordon let her views be known in a front-page review for the *New York Times Book Review*, where she unhesitatingly declared him as a "major novelist" and "poet" in prose. When she put together in collaboration with her then husband Allen Tate the 1950 textbook, *The House of Fiction: An Anthology of the Short Story*, she called Faulkner a "master" of the form in his ability "to unite concrete historical detail with lyricism."[23]

Other novelists, playwrights, and poets across the nation found it necessary to weigh in with an opinion on the value of Faulkner's example as a creative writer. James T. Farrell thought he had already been overpraised in 1932 but was forced to recognize his "impressive stylistic competence and a considerable virtuosity in construction and organization."[24] Upon publication of *Absalom, Absalom!* in 1936, Wallace Stegner noted that the novel had confounded most critics because they were inept or lazy, and although Faulkner may not have entirely succeeded in his intention, "the new technique of this novel may prove to be a significant contribution to the theory and art of fiction."[25] Stegner would also write with appreciation in later reviews of Faulkner's uses of humor and his ability to create violence such that "reading him is like taking hold of an electrified fence."[26] In Paris, in 1934, Henry Miller tried to find a copy of *Sanctuary* to read because, he wrote Anaïs Nin, "I have a feeling that he is the only possible rival I have today in America," and in 1944 he would write publisher James Laughlin that Faulkner was one of "only two American writers, since Twain and Whitman, who give the real American feeling." Miller expressed a desire to meet Faulkner several times over the years, but apparently he never did, although he visited Eudora Welty in Mississippi.[27]

Playwright Laurence Stallings in 1935 felt that there were three Faulkners "struggling for possession of Faulkner's heart." One was a humorist, the second was a southern sentimentalist, and the third was an author of "prose engendering enormous technical friction," and possibly one of the three was a "genius."[28] When Thornton Wilder read both *Light in August* and *The Hamlet* in 1940, he oddly misread the first as a defense of lynching and the second a defense of unscrupulous acquisitiveness: "Again," he wrote in his journal, "the South's thin blood must prostate itself in envy and admiration before any expression of action, however base." Wilder did not pick up *Absalom, Absalom!* until nine years later and then at Cleanth Brooks's suggestion. He was sorry he did. Recording his response in a journal entry, he found that "the book runs the risk momently of collapsing into ignominious absurdity," and he thought he detected racist attitudes in Faulkner's treatment of miscegenation.[29]

Poet Stephen Vincent Benét was an admirer of Faulkner's ability to create "continuously interesting characters," especially the Snopes family, and the "hallucinative power" of his style, which kept "one reading like a man in the toils of nightmare, till the last page is turned."[30] Dorothy Parker thought he simply was "the greatest writer we have," and Wallace Stevens once noted that "For all his gross realism, Faulkner is a poet," but E. E. Cummings (whom Faulkner had imitated in a few of his early poems) was not impressed and wrote with his typical free-lance comic spelling that "all the Flakners in Mis-souriissippi" could not match one of Isak Dinesen's best stories.[31]

In the beginning, Winfield Townley Scott was not impressed ei-ther. When he was reviewing *The Sound and the Fury* in 1929 (Scott himself was only nineteen at the time), he called it a tiresome mod-ernist experiment that "tells us nothing," but he changed his attitude as he reviewed Faulkner over the years. By the time of *Absalom, Absa-lom!* in 1936, he regretted his earlier lapse in judgment and was read-ing with greater appreciation, and when *The Reivers* was published in 1962, he had only praise for Faulkner and predicted that his last novel would prove a "classic of American literature."[32]

A dominant school of southern authors had emerged alongside Faulkner and Thomas Wolfe in the form of a group of writers gath-ered at Vanderbilt University in Nashville, at first as poets publish-ing *The Fugitive* magazine, then as essayists on behalf of the cause of Agrarianism against Industrialism in their 1930 manifesto *I'll Take My Stand*, and finally as independent critics, novelists, and men of letters in and outside the South. While Faulkner looked askance at organized writers turned polemical spokespersons, they were largely supporters of his work and contributed to his growing reputation. Donald Davidson's early appreciative reviews of his novels have al-ready been mentioned, and the other leading lights would have their say.

In preparing an essay on modern southern literature for the *Vir-ginia Quarterly Review* in 1935, John Crowe Ransom found Faulkner one of "the most artful Southern writers," "a powerful man of ge-nius," and "the most exciting figure in our contemporary literature just now."[33] This was before he picked up *Pylon* to review it for the *Nashville Tennessean*. *Pylon*, he wrote, was "frenzied and bad; the wildest prose he has ever written," and he concluded, "it is such a bad book that it seems to mark the end of William Faulkner."[34] It didn't, of course, and much later by 1951 Ransom would return to a balanced opinion by noting the uneven quality of his prose but believing "his perfections are wonderful, and well sustained, and without exact precedent anywhere."[35]

Allen Tate would seldom write at any length about Faulkner, but when he did, he would say and reiterate unequivocally that he was "the most powerful and original novelist in the United States and one of the best in the modern world."[36] Of course, Faulkner was a perfect example for Tate of the power to be gained by writing under the inspiration of provincial tradition and regionalism. The two other associated novelists who wrote frequently and at great length about Faulkner were Andrew Lytle and Robert Penn Warren. Both were also teachers and critics of literature and examined Faulkner's novels with an analytical eye sharpened by the actual practice of writing their own successful fiction. Lytle's several essay reviews for the *Sewanee Review* are extended appreciations of the style, structure, and meaning of the fiction by a writer who was clearly for Lytle, as he calls him at one point, the "master."[37]

Through a series of book reviews for various periodicals beginning in 1932 up to his editing of an anthology of criticism on Faulkner in 1966, more than any other writer, Warren paid tribute to the master's accomplishment, perhaps best summarized in his review of *The Portable Faulkner* for the *New Republic* in 1946 (itself an important essay that would lay down the major lines of criticism to follow): "Here is a novelist who, in the mass of his work, in scope of material, in range of effect, in reportorial accuracy and symbolic subtlety, in philosophical weight, can be put beside the masters of our own past literature."[38] Warren learned much from Faulkner about ways to transpose his personal experience as a southerner into art and perhaps the debt was partly repaid when Faulkner may have borrowed something from him. Just as Warren was writing his review of *The Portable Faulkner*, Faulkner read *All the King's Men*, and in a letter to the publisher complimented the book but was especially moved by the Cass Mastern narrative within the novel.[39] Frederick R. Karl has suggested that it was his reading of Warren that caused Faulkner to follow the "Cass Mastern pattern" in most of his work after 1946.[40]

Outside the South and the United States, Faulkner's work and career captured early attention in England and France. British novelist Richard Hughes was responsible for initiating his European reputation. While visiting the states in 1929, he read copies of *Soldiers' Pay* and *Mosquitoes*, and the galley proofs for *The Sound and the Fury* supplied by the publisher. Once home, he encouraged his own publisher to issue *Soldiers' Pay*, for which he wrote the introduction calling Faulkner "the most interesting novelist in America." Hughes then encouraged the elderly novelist Arnold Bennett to review *Soldiers' Pay* and *The Sound and the Fury*. While Bennett found him "exasperatingly, unimaginably difficult to read," he thought he had a "great and original talent" and made the famous comment, "he writes generally like an angel."[41] The strength of Bennett's reputation was such that soon other novelists began to pay attention in England. L. A. G. Strong, for example, reviewed several of the novels and said that Faulkner filled him "with admiration and envy," and V. S. Pritchett would come to the considered conclusion that he was "the only substantial American novelist since Henry James."[42]

But the praise was by no means uniform. Rebecca West in 1931 thought "*Sanctuary* would seem a clear case of art that had lost its sense of values."[43] Edwin Muir found *As I Lay Dying* naïve and full of "signs of immaturity," and Graham Greene, about to publish his first major novel *Brighton Rock*, declared that Faulkner "isn't another Joyce . . . that Mr. Faulkner has not created a single character of recognizable humanity and that the intellectual content of his novel [*Absalom, Absalom!*] is about nil."[44] George Orwell, known for his love of lucid style, predictably rejected *The Hamlet* in 1940 as "fatiguing" and certainly not worth a second reading to understand it.[45] But one of the most damning assessments perhaps ever written about Faulkner came from Irish short-story writer Sean O'Faolain, who began carefully to follow Faulkner's career in 1935 and would conclude by 1953, in one of his Christian Gauss lectures at Princeton University, "He is an ingenuous man, of strong feelings, a dedicated sincerity and poor equipment: a maimed genius," or as he subtitled his paper, "More genius than talent."[46]

Faulkner's reception and influence in France would be more profound. The person mainly responsible for introducing him there was the critic and translator Maurice Edgar Coindreau, first with an essay in 1931, the translation of two short stories in 1932 ("Dry September" and "A Rose for Emily"), and then a series of highly competent translations of the novels, beginning with *As I Lay Dying* in 1934.[47] Immediately the emerging French writers responded. André Malraux wrote an admiring introduction for the French version of *Sanctuary*, where he outlined Faulkner's worldview, in which Destiny controlled man's fate, and concluded that "*Sanctuary* is the intrusion of Greek tragedy into the detective novel."[48] Jean-Paul Sartre, who was introduced to Faulkner's novels even before they were translated by his companion Simone de Beauvoir, undertook analyses of *Sartoris* and *The Sound and the Fury* and applauded in the first its humanism and in the second its use of the metaphysics of time: "Faulkner's vision of the world can be compared to that of a man sitting in an open car and looking backwards."[49] In a 1946 essay, Sartre detailed just how profoundly Faulkner "evoked a revolution" in French literature, especially through his innovations in "the method of reflecting different aspects of the same event, through the monologues of different sensitivities," and changing the "chronological order of the story" in behalf of "a more subtle order, half logical, half intuitive."[50] In a letter to Malcolm Cowley, Sartre wrote, "For the youth of France, Faulkner is a god."[51]

Albert Camus would especially be drawn to *Requiem for a Nun* and believing that in it Faulkner had created a "modern tragedy," he effectively proved it by translating and adapting the work for the European stage where it had a long and successful run.[52] On more than one occasion, when asked by an American for an opinion, including the week before his untimely death in 1960, Camus would say, "Faulkner remains for me your greatest living creator."[53] Even this he had topped earlier by reportedly saying, "Faulkner is the greatest writer in the world."[54] After Camus's death, Faulkner would write a tribute to him. The only dissenting voice in France may have been from the much older and established André Gide, who read *Light in August* in 1926 and noted in his journal, "I had hoped to be able to admire it much more. Certain pages are those of a great book; lost in manner and device."[55] He was also reported to have said, "there is not one of Faulkner's characters who properly speaking has a soul." Faulkner always retained a good opinion of Gide, however, and called him a "very intelligent talent."[56]

If the French literary landscape had been radically altered by Faulkner, even more so was this true apparently in South America. The first translation of Faulkner to appear in Spain was a version of *Sanctuary* by Cuban novelist Lino Novás Calvo as early as 1934, and others would follow in both Spain and Argentina, including a

1940 translation of *Wild Palms* by Jorge Luis Borges of Buenos Aires. Borges believed "Faulkner was a writer of genius," but he was also "perverse" in his playing with time and using multiple narrators, which made reading him so difficult. Nevertheless he thought Faulkner was "not unworthy" of comparison with Shakespeare.[57] Of course, Borges's own erudite, labyrinthine "ficciones" owe little to Faulkner and create their own kind of difficulties for the reader. Borges's Guatemalan contemporary, Miguel Angel Asturias, put Faulkner "first" at the top of his list of favorite American novelists.[58]

With the next generation of South American writers, however, it is more than a matter of admiration. Carlos Fuentes of Mexico has reported, "When I first read Faulkner, I thought: 'I must become a writer.'" But he also felt strongly moved by his reading because of a kinship he detected in Faulkner's central theme of defeat:

> That is why we Latin Americans feel so close to Faulkner's works; only
> Faulkner, in the literature of the United States, only Faulkner, in the
> closed world of optimism and success, offers an image that is common
> to both the United States and Latin America: the image of defeat, of
> separation, of doubt: the image of tragedy.[59]

Fuentes's own concern in his work with the history of Mexico and its political and social problems, as well as his experiments with fragmented and nonchronological perspectives, are elements he owes to Faulkner's example.

Gabriel García Márquez of Colombia, who began reading Faulkner in 1949, would develop the affinity idea further, as when he observed, "I read Faulkner and found that his whole world—the world of the Southern United States which he writes about—was very much like my world, that it was created by the same people . . . One mustn't forget that Faulkner is in a way a Latin American writer. His world is that of the Gulf of Mexico."[60] García Márquez would claim that this was Faulkner's main influence on him, a confluence of spiritual kinship, but it is perfectly clear that he learned a good deal more: the creation of a fictional community to serve as a microcosm of an entire society, as well as his experiments with sentence structure, the fragmentation of time, and multiple narrators are merely the more obvious. It is indeed arguable that his 1967 masterpiece, *Cien años de soledad* (*One Hundred Years of Solitude*), could not have been possible without Faulkner's fiction to serve as inspiration and master instruction. García Márquez would state, "Faulkner is found in all the fiction of Latin America," and any number of writers have admitted this applies to them, including Juan Rulfo of Mexico, Julio Cortázar of Argentina, Mario Vargas Llosa of Peru, Juan Carlos Onetti of Uruguay, and José Donoso and Isabel Allende of Chile.[61] By liberating these writers, and many others, from the traditional themes and methods of narration, and paving the way for new techniques in dealing with time and history and modern tragedy, Faulkner helped generate what may be the most vital writing in the world at the century's end.

As a new generation of writers after Faulkner's emerged in the states, they too found their artistic and literary landscape considerably changed as a result of the large shadow cast by Faulkner. But it was a more diverse group now, with more African Americans and women than before. When fellow Mississippian Richard Wright published his first book in 1938, *Uncle Tom's Children*, he told an interviewer that Faulkner was one of his two favorite writers because "He is the only white writer I know of living in Mississippi who is trying to tell the truth (about the real South) in fiction."[62] *Native Son* attracted Faulkner's attention in 1940, and when *Black Boy* appeared in 1945, he sat down to write a letter to Wright commending his courage for saying what "needed to be said" about race relations in America, but he went on to express his preference for *Native Son*, because it was a more "artistic" statement on the level of general human experience.[63] Ten years later, he told a Japanese interviewer that Wright "wrote one good book and then went astray," because he failed to remain an artist first and a black activist second.[64] Wright had partly responded to this charge when Faulkner received the Nobel Prize in 1950 by writing a tribute in French in which he congratulated Faulkner for making art out of the material of regional experience: "Faulkner's greatness resided primarily in his power to transpose the American scene as it exists in the Southern states, filter it through his sensibilities and finally define it with words."[65] While there seems to be a meeting of the minds here, the truth is both followed separate missions as artists and writers.

In the same interview in which he mentioned Wright in Japan, Faulkner also noted, "Another [black writer] named Ellison has talent and so far has managed to stay away from being first a Negro, he is still first a writer."[66] Ralph Ellison's only novel, *Invisible Man*, had appeared three years earlier and was very Faulknerian in its uses of time, narrative consciousness, and surreal structure. But Ellison was always uneasy about Faulkner, and in an essay written in 1946 but not published until 1953, while he thought Faulkner had explored black experience "more successfully than anyone else," he also found "mixed motives" in his frequent use of black stereotypes. Nevertheless, he believed that Faulkner was "the greatest writer the South has produced."[67]

Among other black writers, Chester Himes said he always turned to Faulkner for inspiration when he was writing, because he felt that Faulkner's worldview was based on the absurdity of life, as was his own. Referring to his close relationship with Richard Wright, Himes once noted, "Faulkner had the utter influence over my writing, but Dick had influence over my life."[68] The younger and more radical James Baldwin had little patience for Faulkner, especially his gradualist attitude toward civil rights. For him, Faulkner was a mixture of contradictions and hypocrisy and embodied the confused paradox of being a southerner in the modern world. In more than one essay Baldwin would lay out his deep disappointment in Faulkner in no uncertain terms, as in his comments just five months before Faulkner's death:

> I respect Faulkner enough, for example, to be saddened by his pronouncements on the race question, to be offended by the soupy rhetoric of his Nobel Prize speech, and to resent—for his own sake—the critical obtuseness which accepted (from the man who wrote "Light in August") such indefensibly muddy work as "Intruder in the Dust" and "Requiem for a Nun."[69]

For Baldwin, Faulkner seemed to be a fallen idol who was unable to match his words with action, itself a profound form of respect.

Ernest Gaines found it possible to distinguish between Faulkner, the writer, and Faulkner the man who said inept things sometimes in interviews and public statements about race relations. Interestingly enough, Gaines did not turn to Wright, Ellison, or Baldwin to learn his craft, but to Chekhov, Turgenev, Joyce, Hemingway, Anderson, and especially Faulkner, the writer: "I think Faulkner has influenced me more than any other writer," he has said. Like Faulkner, Gaines has created a mythical community in his fiction, effectively recreated the rhythms of southern dialect, and addressed the themes of time and the past and their influence on the present moment. While his philosophy is different, these are things Gaines says he has learned from Faulkner.[70]

Among the women writers of the next generation who would speak up on behalf of Faulkner, most were southern, and perhaps the major voice was that of another Mississippian, Eudora Welty. She first began to read him when she was a student at the University of Wisconsin, from which she graduated in 1929. After her third book was out in 1943, she received a note from Faulkner asking about her work, which he would recall and compliment some fifteen years later at the University of Virginia. She also visited Faulkner in his home in the summer of 1949 through the auspices of a mutual friend.[71]

Welty would first venture into print in his defense against an unflattering review of *Intruder in the Dust* by Edmund Wilson that had appeared in the October 23, 1948, issue of the *New Yorker* and that suggested Faulkner's artistic development was hampered by his remaining "stubbornly" in Mississippi. In her letter in the January 1, 1949, issue, she asserted that Wilson was merely displaying his own provincialism and that writers are best judged by their accomplishments, not where they lived.[72] She went on to write a full appreciation of the novel for the *Hudson Review* that year in which she praised the energy, the humor, and the "intolerably unanalyzable and quite pure" style of the prose in *Intruder in the Dust*.[73] In other essays and reviews over the years, she would continue her soundly reasoned arguments that "above all present day story tellers, he is the one ahead of his time—the most astonishingly powered and passionate writer we have."[74] After his death, she would write, "His work is a triumphant vision . . . , an imagination that has shone incomparably the brightest in our firmament," and "No man ever put more of his heart and soul into the written word than did William Faulkner."[75]

Regarding his influence on her own work, she put it most pictur-
esquely when she said:

So often I'm asked how I could have written a word with William
Faulkner living in Mississippi, and the question amazes me. It was like
living near a big mountain, something majestic—it made me happy
to know it was there, all that work of his life. But it wasn't a helping or
hindering presence.[76]

She would go on to discuss how she had learned from him how to
capture the sounds and cadences of speech—"Faulkner did it perfectly"—and the ways to use locale and place in fiction, but beyond
these things, there was little influence, because "He wrote about a
much vaster world than anything I ever contemplated in my own
work."[77] Given the range of her own work, however, she was being
modest in that last statement, but she also clearly perfected her own
fictional voice. She is a good example of how to learn from and not be
intimidated by the presence of Faulkner.

The same can be said for Flannery O'Connor and others. While
she often issued denials in the spirit of humility—"I keep clear of
Faulkner so my own little boat won't get swamped," or "he makes
me feel that with my one-cylinder syntax I should quit writing and
raise chickens altogether"—O'Connor had her own distinctive vision and style, unmatched in its spiritual singularity and gothic bold-
ness, original and inimitable.[78] Carson McCullers went her own way
as well in her meditations on loneliness and isolation, and she had
nothing but good words for Faulkner's ability to achieve "a fusion
of anguish and farce that acts on the reader with an almost physical force."[79] Faulkner helped her win a Guggenheim fellowship in
1941 with a letter of recommendation (actually written by someone
else but signed by Faulkner like a blank check), and he said in 1958 at
the University of Virginia that "she's done some of the best work in
our time."[80] Another Mississippian, Elizabeth Spencer, wrote a full
essay on "Emerging as a Writer in Faulkner's Mississippi," in which
she concluded, "Faulkner was a lion in the path, menacing further
advance—or a bear in everybody's private wilderness," but "a good
many writers have found a way to borrow from this extraordinary

style of Faulkner's without sounding too much like the one who invented it," herself included.[81]

The one southern writer who seems to have found it hardest to get out from under the shadow of Faulkner was William Styron. This is partly because he had been deep into reading Faulkner when he wrote his first novel, *Lie Down in Darkness*, in 1951, which in turn demonstrated any number of affinities with *The Sound and the Fury* and *As I Lay Dying*. Faulkner read the book and thought it "showed promise," but he made no comment about the similarities.[82] Styron has himself admitted that he was imitating Faulkner at the start but then stopped and started all over again to escape the overwhelming influence. He would also argue, "I think that, whereas almost any fool could detect an influence of Faulkner in *Lie Down in Darkness*, I took the more obvious qualities of Faulkner, and was left with a book which had its own distinctive and original stance."[83] Styron would be known for some time, nevertheless, as imitation Faulkner, until he broke free of the reputation almost entirely with such original works as *The Confessions of Nat Turner* in 1967 and *Sophie's Choice* in 1979.

Shelby Foote, another Mississippian who was befriended by Faulkner, set about in the beginning of his career to write a series of novels and stories about a fictional Mississippi community interconnected in much the same way as the Yoknapatawpha cycle, which served to bring him the only reprimand of its kind on record. At the University of Virginia in 1957, Faulkner responded to a question about writers he thought worth reading: "There's a young man, a Mississippian, Shelby Foote, that shows promise, if he'll just stop trying to write Faulkner and will write some Shelby Foote."[84] Foote heeded his advice and turned to his Civil War narratives, both fictional and historical, to achieve a greater reputation, and he always praised the Faulkner canon as "one of the greatest bodies of work in all the world's literature."[85]

Walker Percy once said that "Faulkner has been both a blessing and a curse to the South—a blessing because he is probably the greatest American novelist of this century and a curse because he was so powerful and influential that many Southern writers, younger writers...have published as imitation Faulkners."[86] Doing something like that got Percy into trouble early on. When he had to produce a writing sample upon entering college, he submitted a piece in the style of *The Sound and the Fury* and was promptly placed in a remedial English class. As for his own writing, Percy said, "I'm probably least influenced by him than anyone else," although he saw his central character in *The Moviegoer* as an extension of one of Faulkner's: "In a way, Binx Bolling is Quentin Compson who didn't commit suicide."[87]

Peter Taylor believed that no one writing could escape the influence of Faulkner: "I think we all ought to get down on our knees every night and thank God for Faulkner. He is the master; he taught us all to observe our own world . . . What gets borrowed or stolen doesn't matter, because a good writer always adds something, makes his particular mark."[88] George Garrett agreed: "He has opened up new territories for all writers who have come and will come after him. He has changed our ways of thinking about the power and glory of fiction."[89] In an essay on "The Influence of William Faulkner," Garrett argued, "For myself, and for many of the young writers I know, he stands a master, an *example* from whom we can always learn. There is no sense of competition. Art is not a horserace."[90]

The new territories Faulkner opened up and the new ways of thinking extended far beyond the South and its writers. In reviewing one of his books, Nelson Algren also claimed him as his "master," and Kay Boyle spoke of the "fearless, gifted hand" of "the most absorbing writer of our time."[91] Poet Delmore Schwartz (the model for the character Van Humboldt Fleisher in Saul Bellow's *Humboldt's Gift*) wrote a lengthy appreciation of Faulkner for the *Southern Review* in 1941, and in 1955 an eleven-page exhaustive explication of *A Fable* to support his opinion that it was "a masterpiece, a unique fulfillment of Faulkner's genius which gives a luminous new meaning to his work as a whole," a conclusion shared by few others.[92] Thomas Merton thought "Faulkner was an outrageously and deliberately demanding writer . . . , a genius comparable to Melville, Hawthorne, Dickens, and Dostoyevsky," and looking for spiritual themes in his work, and paraphrasing Claude Edmonde Magny, noted "Faulkner works like a pre-historic Shaman who enmeshes the reader in numinous symbols and entrances him with sacred horror."[93] Absurd satirist Terry Southern wrote an appreciation of Faulkner's humor in *As I Lay Dying* as a "twenty-one-gun salute to the absurd."[94] Wright Morris published an appraisal of his technical virtuosity and engaging visual humor, but he also felt that "Faulkner's interest in technique is exhaustive, and often at the expense of his substance."[95]

There have been the dissenting voices, of course. When John Hawkes declared "I love Faulkner" in an exchange with John Barth, Barth replied, "I read Faulkner with proper astonishment and instruction when I was graduate student age. I do not remember him with great pleasure."[96] Truman Capote declared, in his first published interview, "I'm afraid of Faulkner, squeamish, really—I see him as a personal threat," and later in his career, "I find Faulkner's prose so cumbersome and tanglesome, the exact opposite of what I admire and try to do myself."[97] Vladimir Nabokov said in 1965 that he saw no way "Faulkner's corncob chronicles can be considered 'masterpieces.'"[98] It remained for Edward Dahlberg to offer perhaps the most savage attack on record, from which I will quote a few sample lines: "[T]he Popeye Faulkner novelist is a medieval corncob poet of everyday banalities that have a Rasputin odor . . . Faulkner the Nobel Prize winner, gives us a diseased world, a moldy poor white class—and all in the name of truth and humanity . . . Faulkner never bothered to learn how to write."[99]

Such opinions notwithstanding, so powerful is the Faulknerian influence that it continues to the present. One of the most popular contemporary writers is one more Mississippian who chooses not to write about the South or Mississippi, Richard Ford. Growing up in Jackson, he was aware of the spirit of Faulkner and the local reality of Eudora Welty, "whom I used to see," he says, "buying her lunch at the steam table at the Jitney Jungle grocery." He didn't begin to read Faulkner until college, especially *Absalom, Absalom!*, and luxuriated in the dazzling language, "Life, in words, geysering and eddying over each other." Thus it was, he says, that "if anything I read influenced me to take a try at being a writer—even on a midget scale—it was this pleasure I got from reading Faulkner."[100]

There is the case too of Toni Morrison, our most recent American Nobel Prize winner, who wrote her master's thesis on Virginia Woolf and Faulkner and has taught his works but who denies any direct influence on her fiction. She has been "fascinated by what it means to write" the way he did in *Absalom, Absalom!*, she says, but she feels her roots are more in a distinctive African American experience and culture. However that may be, critics are finding interesting parallels and reading the works of both together in ways to elucidate each other's vision and accomplishment.[101] There is a dialogue about race going on between them that is remarkably rational, intelligent, and enlightening.

Meanwhile the waves of Faulkner influence have begun to reach the shores of new parts of the world. South African playwright Athol Fugard says that Faulkner "convinced him he was on the right track by concentrating on the dramas of his own small world."[102] Japan's most recent Nobel Prize winner, Kenzaburo Oe, has proven himself a careful and articulate reader of Faulkner's fiction in his essays and comments, and as a writer has said, "Among the modern British and American writers, Faulkner is the one whom I have the strongest impulse to challenge."[103] Other Japanese writers have testified to his importance in their careers, including Takehiko Fukunaga, Yukio Haruyama, Otohiko Kagawa, Nobuo Kojima, Minako Ohba, Kazuko Saegusa, Hiroshi Sakagami, and Kenji Nakagami.[104] Even in China, one of the most respected contemporary authors, Mo Yan, has confessed that "Two particular works had the greatest impact on me. One was García Márquez's *One Hundred Years of Solitude*. The other was William Faulkner's *The Sound and the Fury*." While possessing his own style and point of view, established to escape the two sources of his inspiration, like both of them Mo Yan has proceeded to create a fictional world based on rural Shandong province very much in the grand Faulknerian manner.[105] Mo Yan joined Faulkner in a select circle of Nobel Prize winners in 2012.

This anthology of essays, articles, reviews, letters, and interviews arranged chronologically and published over the last eight decades by novelists, poets, and dramatists about Faulkner, his fiction, and the power of his accomplishment demonstrates how profound and far reaching his impact has been. Most speak about his technical virtuosity and aesthetic genius and how these have influenced their own practice as writers. Others express the difficulties of trying to escape his example in forging their own styles. A minority criticize him for what they see as artistic failures and poor writing. Such a variety of responses indicate, in any case, that Faulkner has been an unavoidable presence in his own time and after, and he will remain a permanent part of the literary landscape at home and abroad.[106]

*Notes*

1. Flannery O'Connor, *Mystery and Manners*, ed. Sally and Robert Fitzgerald (New York: Farrar, Straus & Giroux, 1969), 45.

2. Donald Davidson, "William Faulkner," *Nashville Tennessean*, April 11, 1926, Magazine Sections, p. 6; "The Grotesque," *Nashville Tennessean*, July 3, 1927, Magazine Section, p. 7. "Two Mississippi Novels," *Nashville Tennessean*, April 14, 1929, Magazine Section, p. 7. Reprinted in M. Thomas Inge, ed., *William Faulkner: The Contemporary Reviews* (New York: Cambridge University Press, 1995), 12–13, 20, 26–28.

3. Conrad Aiken, *A Reviewer's ABC* (New York: Meridian Books, 1958), 197–200.

4. Aiken, *A Reviewer's ABC*, 200–207.

5. Lillian Hellman, "Futile Souls Adrift on a Yacht," *New York Herald Tribune*, June 19, 1927, p. 9. Inge, *William Faulkner*, 19–20.

6. Sherwood Anderson, "They Came Bearing Gifts," *American Mercury* 21 (October 1930): 129.

7. Ellen Glasgow, "Heroes and Monsters," *Saturday Review of Literature* 12 (May 4, 1935): 3; *Letters of Ellen Glasgow*, ed. Blair Rouse (New York: Harcourt, Brace, 1958), 154, 143.

8. Kenneth Roberts, *I Wanted to Write* (Garden City, NY: Doubleday, 1949), 236–37.

9. *New Yorker*, November 5, 1932, pp. 74–75.

10. *By-Line Ernest Hemingway*, ed. William White (New York: Scribner's, 1967), 200; *Conversations with Ernest Hemingway*, ed. Matthew J. Brucolli (Jackson: University Press of Mississippi, 1996), 44.

11. Carlos Baker, *Ernest Hemingway: A Life Story* (New York: Scribner's, 1969), 495, 503, 532.

12. *The Letters of F. Scott Fitzgerald*, ed. Andrew Turnbull (New York: Scribner's, 1963), 365; Arthur Mizener, *The Far Side of Paradise: A Biography of F. Scott Fitzgerald* (Boston: Houghton Mifflin, 1951), 313.

13. *Correspondence of F. Scott Fitzgerald*, ed. Matthew J. Bruccoli and Margaret M. Duggan (New York: Random House, 1980), 270, 298.

14. Richard Walser, ed., *The Enigma of Thomas Wolfe* (Cambridge, MA: Harvard University Press, 1953), vii.

15. "An Interview with Thomas Wolfe," *Press Time: A Book of Post Classics* (New York: Books, Inc., 1936), 247–48. Originally published in the *New York Evening Post*, May 14, 1936.

16. *Lion in the Garden: Interviews with William Faulkner, 1926–1962*, ed. James B. Meriwether and Michael Millgate (New York: Random House, 1968), 267–69. Originally published in the *Washington Evening Star*, June 12, 1957.

17. *Steinbeck: A Life in Letters*, ed. Elaine Steinbeck and Robert Wallsten (New York: Viking, 1975), 529, 564–66.

18. *Lion in the Garden*, 91.

19. John Dos Passos, "Faulkner," *Occasions and Protests* (Chicago: Henry Regnery, 1964), 275–77. Also see Nancy St. Clair, "Dos Passos Lauds Faulkner in Talk," *Charlottesville Daily Progress*, February 9, 1963, p. 11.

20. Evelyn Scott, *On William Faulkner's "The Sound and the Fury"* (New York: Johnathan Cape and Harrison Smith, 1929), 5.

21. *Lion in the Garden*, 49. When the *Saturday Review of Literature* published an analysis of *Sanctuary* by psychoanalyst Lawrence S. Kubie in its issue of October 20, 1934, pp. 218, 224–26, Evelyn Scott wrote a response in the November 10 issue, pp. 272, 280, questioning Dr. Kubie's assessment of the character Popeye.

22. Jan Nordby Gretlund, "The Wild Old Green Man of the Woods: Katherine Anne Porter's Faulkner," *Notes on Mississippi Writers* 12 (Winter 1980): 67–79.

23. Caroline Gordon, "Mr. Faulkner's Southern Saga," *New York Times Book Review*, May 5, 1946, pp. 1, 45; Caroline Gordon and Allen Tate, *The House of Fiction: An Anthology of the Short Story with Commentary*, 2nd edition (New York: Scribner's, 1960), 331–34.

24. James T. Farrell, "The Faulkner Mixture," *New York Sun*, October 7, 1932, p. 29. Inge, *William Faulkner*, 83–84.

25. Wallace Stegner, "New Technique in Novel Introduced," *Salt Lake City Tribune*, November 29, 1936, p. 13-D. Inge, *William Faulkner*, 153–55.

26. Wallace Stegner, "The New Novels," *Virginia Quarterly Review* 16 (Summer 1940): 464–65; "Conductivity in Fiction," *Virginia Quarterly Review* 15 (Summer 1939): 446–47.

27. Henry Miller, *Letters to Anaïs Nin*, ed. Gunther Stuhlman (New York:

Putnam's, 1965), 130, 290, 294; *Henry Miller and James Laughlin: Selected Letters*, ed. George Wickes (New York: Norton, 1996), 29, 42.

28. Laurence Stallings, "Gentleman from Mississippi," *American Mercury* 34 (April 1935): 499–501.

29. *The Journals of Thornton Wilder, 1939–1961*, ed. Donald Gallup (New Haven, CT: Yale University Press, 1985), 18–21, 57–58.

30. Stephen Vincent Benét, "Flem Snopes and His Kin," *Saturday Review of Literature*, April 6, 1940, p. 7.

31. Dorothy Parker, "Best Fiction of 1957," *Esquire*, December 1957; Inge, *William Faulkner*, 464; *Letters of Wallace Stevens*, ed. Holly Stevens (New York: Knopf, 1966), 412; "E. E. Cummings: Twenty-Three Letters," ed. F. W. Dupee and George Stade, *Harper's Magazine*, March 1969, p. 78.

32. Winfield Townley Scott, "The Waning South," *Providence Journal*, October 20, 1929, Magazine Section, p. 27; "Faulkner, His Critics, and a Fresh Survey," *Providence Sunday Jounral*, November 22, 1936, Section VI, p. 8; "Faulkner," *Santa Fe New Mexican*, June 3, 1962, pp. 3, 8. Inge, *William Faulkner*, 37–38, 152–53, 528–29.

33. John Crowe Ransom, "Modern with a Southern Accent," *Virginia Quarterly Review* 11 (April 1935): 184–200.

34. John Crowe Ransom, "Faulkner, South's Most Brilliant but Wayward Talent, Is Spent," *Nashville Banner*, March 24, 1935, p. 8. Inge, *William Faulkner*, 120–21.

35. John Crowe Ransom, "William Faulkner: An Impression," *Harvard Advocate* 135 (November 1951): 17.

36. Allen Tate, "The New Provincialism," *Virginia Quarterly Review* 21 (Spring 1945): 262–72; "William Faulkner," *New Statesman*, September 28, 1962, p. 408.

37. Andrew Lytle, "Regeneration for the Man," *Sewanee Review* 57 (Winter 1949): 120–27; "The Son of Man: He Will Prevail," *Sewanee Review* 63 (1955): 114–37; *Sewanee Review* 65 (Summer 1957): 475–84.

38. Robert Penn Warren, "Not Local Color," *Virginia Quarterly Review* 8 (January 1932): 153–60; "The Snopes World," *Kenyon Review* 3 (Spring 1941): 253–57; "Cowley's Faulkner," *New Republic*, August 12, 1946, pp. 176–80, and August 26, 1946, pp. 234–37; "The Redemption of Temple Drake," *New York Times Book Review*, September 30, 1951, pp. 1, 31; Inge, *William Faulkner*, 343–46; *Faulkner: A Collection of Critical Essays* (Englewood Cliffs, NJ: Prentice-Hall, 1966).

39. *Selected Letters of William Faulkner*, ed. Joseph Blotner (New York: Random House, 1977), 239.

40. Frederick R. Karl, *William Faulkner: American Writer, A Biography* (New York: Weidenfeld & Nicolson, 1989), 746.

41. Richard Hughes, "Faulkner and Bennett," *Encounter* 21 (September 1963): 59–61.

42. L. A. G. Strong, *Spectator*, September 19, 1931, p. 362; V. S. Pritchett, "Time Frozen: *A Fable*," *Partisan Review* 21 (September–October 1954): 557–61; "That Time and That Wilderness," *New Statesman*, September 28, 1962, pp. 405–6.

43. Rebecca West, *Daily Telegraph*, October 2, 1931, p. 18.

44. Edwin Muir, *Listener*, October 16, 1935, p. 681; Graham Greene, "The Furies in Mississippi," *London Mercury* 35 (March 1937): 517–18.

45. George Orwell, "Fiction and Life," *Time and Tide*, November 9, 1940, p. 1097.

46. Sean O'Faolain, *Spectator*, April 19, 1935, p. 668; *The Vanishing Hero: Studies in the Novelists of the Twenties* (Boston: Little, Brown, 1957), 72–111.

47. Maurice Edgar Coindreau, "William Faulkner in France," *Yale French Studies* 10 (Fall 1952): 85–91.

48. André Malraux, "A Preface for Faulkner's *Sanctuary*," *Yale French Studies* 10 (Fall 1952): 92–94.

49. Jean-Paul Sartre, *Literary and Philosophical Essays* (New York: Criterion Books, 1955), 73–87.

50. Jean-Paul Sartre, "American Novelists in French Eyes," *Atlantic Magazine* 178 (August 1946): 114–18.

51. Malcolm Cowley, *The Faulkner-Cowley File* (New York: Viking, 1966), 21–22.

52. Albert Camus, *Lyrical and Critical Essays* (New York: Knopf, 1968), 311–21.

53. Albert Camus, letter, *Harvard Advocate* 135 (November 1951): 21; Ronald Donald Spector, "Camus' Illuminating Answers to Searching Questions," *New York Herald Tribune Book Review*, February 21, 1960, p. 1.

54. Joseph Blotner, *Faulkner: A Biography* (New York: Random House, 1984), 611.

55. André Gide, *The Journals of André Gide* (New York: Knopf, 1949), III: 341.

56. *Lion in the Garden*, 94.

57. Rita Guibert, *Seven Voices: Seven Latin American Writers Talk to Rita Guibert* (New York: Knopf, 1972), 100; Jorge Luis Borges, *An Introduction to American Literature* (Lexington: University Press of Kentucky, 1971), 48–49.

58. Guibert, *Seven Voices*, 154.

59. Luis Leal, "A Spanish-American Perspective of Anglo-American Literature," *Revista Canadiense de Estudios Hispánicos* 5 (October 1980): 71; Luis Harss and Barbara Dahmann, *Into the Mainstream: Conversations with Latin-American Writers* (New York: Harper & Row, 1967), 322; Alfred MacAdam and Charles Russ, "The Art of Fiction LXVII: Carlos Fuentes," *Paris Review* 82 (Winter 1981): 140–75.

60. Guibert, *Seven Voices*, 327.

61. Harley D. Oberhelman, "The Presence of Faulkner in the Writings of García Márquez," *Graduate Studies Texas Tech University* 22 (August 1980): 1–43.

62. *Conversations with Richard Wright*, ed. Keneth Kinnamon and Michel Fabre (Jackson: University Press of Mississippi, 1993), 10.

63. *Selected Letters*, 201.

64. *Lion in the Garden*, 185.

65. Richard Wright, "A Man of the South," *Mississippi Quarterly* 43 (Winter 1989–90): 355–57.

66. *Lion in the Garden*, 185.

67. *The Collected Essays of Ralph Ellison*, ed. John F. Callahan (New York: Modern Library, 1995), 86, 97.

68. Edward Margolies and Michel Fabre, *The Several Lives of Chester Himes* (Jackson: University Press of Mississippi, 1997), 101, 118.

69. James Baldwin, *Nobody Knows My Name* (New York: Random House, 1961), 117–26; "As Much Truth as One Can Bear," *New York Times Book Review*, January 14, 1962, pp. 1, 28.

70. *Conservations with Ernest Gaines*, ed. John Lowe (Jackson: University Press of Mississippi, 1995), 13, 25, 44–45, 90–92, 197.

71. *Conversations with Eudora Welty*, ed. Peggy Prenshaw (Jackson: University Press of Mississippi, 1984), 79, 322–23; Blotner, *Faulkner: A Biography*, 450; *Faulkner in the University*, ed. Frederick L. Gwynn and Joseph Blotner (Charlottesville: University of Virginia Press, 1959), 24.

72. Eudora Welty, "Department of Amplification," *New Yorker*, January 1, 1949, pp. 50–51. Inge, *William Faulkner*, 269–71.

73. Eudora Welty, "In Yoknapatawpha," *Hudson Review* 1 (Winter 1949): 596–98.

74. Eudora Welty, *Short Stories* (New York: Harcourt, Brace, 1949), 45.

75. Eudora Welty, "He Created Life in Fictional County," *Washington Post and Times Herald*, July 7, 1962, p. 2C; "Selected Letters of William Faulkner," *New York Times Book Review*, February 6, 1977, pp. 1, 28–30. A useful survey of her comments on Faulkner is found in Hunter Cole's "Welty on Faulkner," *Notes on Mississippi Writers* 9 (Spring 1976): 28–29.

76. *Conversations with Eudora Welty*, 80.

77. *Conversations with Eudora Welty*, 208, 220.

78. Flannery O'Connor, *The Habit of Being* (New York: Farrar, Straus & Giroux, 1979), 273, 292.

79. Carson McCullers, "The Russian Realists and Southern Literature," *Decision* 2 (July 1941): 15–19.

80. *Faulkner in the University*, 259.

81. *Faulkner and the Southern Renaissance*, ed. Doreen Fowler and Ann J. Abadie (Jackson: University Press of Mississippi, 1982), 120–37. See also Hunter Cole, "Elizabeth Spencer of Sycamore Fair," *Notes on Mississippi Writers* 6 (Winter 1974): 81–86.

82. *Faulkner in the University*, 13.

83. *Conversations with William Styron*, ed. James L. W. West III (Jackson: University Press of Mississippi, 1985), 6–7, 54–55.

84. *Faulkner in the University*, 50.

85. Shelby Foote, "Five Stories, One Novella and Crime Themes Comprise Faulkner's Newest Collection," *Delta Democrat Times* (Greenville, Mississippi), November 13, 1949, p. 18. Inge, *William Faulkner*, 287–89.

86. *Conversations with Eudora Welty*, 112.

87. *Conversations with Walker Percy*, ed. Lewis A. Lawson and Victor A. Kramer (Jackson: University Press of Mississippi, 1985), 10–11, 53, 300.

88. *Conversations with Peter Taylor*, ed. Hubert H. McAlexander (Jackson: University Press of Mississippi, 1987), 8, 82.

89. George Garrett, "Introduction," *Snopes* by William Faulkner (New York: Modern Library, 1994), xi.

90. George Garrett, "The Influence of William Faulkner," *Georgia Review* 18 (Winter 1964): 419–27.

91. Nelson Algren, "Faulkner's Thrillers," *New York Times Book Review*,

November 6, 1949, p. 4; Kay Boyle, "Tattered Banners," *New Republic* 94 (March 9, 1938): 136–37, Inge, *William Faulkner*, 177–79.

92. Delmore Schwartz, "The Fiction of William Faulkner," *Southern Review* 7 (Summer 1941): 145–60; "William Faulkner's *A Fable*," *Perspectives U.S.A.* 10 (Winter 1955): 126–36, Inge, *William Faulkner*, 401–10.

93. Thomas Merton, "The Sounds are Furious," *The Critic* 25 (April–May 1967): 76–80. See also Merton's "'Baptisms in the Forest': Wisdom and Initiation in William Faulkner," *Mansions of the Spirit: Essays in Religion and Literature*, ed. George A. Paniches (New York: Hawthorne Books, 1967), 19–44.

94. Terry Southern, "Dark Laughter in the Towers," *Nation* 190 (April 23, 1960): 348–50.

95. Wright Morris, *Earthly Delights, Unearthly Adornments* (New York: Harper & Row, 1978), 131–40.

96. Thomas LeClair, "Hawkes and Barth Talk about Fiction," *New York Time Book Review*, April 1, 1979, pp. 7, 31–33.

97. *Truman Capote: Conversations*, ed. M. Thomas Inge (Jackson: University Press of Mississippi, 1987), 12, 198.

98. Vladimir Nabokov, *Strong Opinions* (New York: McGraw-Hill, 1973), 57. (Thanks to Professor Charles Nicol for calling this to my attention.)

99. Edward Dahlberg, *Samuel Beckett's Wake and Other Uncollected Prose* (Elmwood Park, IL: Dalkey Archive Press, 1989), 67–74, 266–67.

100. Richard Ford, "The Three Kings: Hemingway, Faulkner, and Fitzgerald," *Esquire* 100 (December 1983): 577–87.

101. Carol A. Kolmerten, Stephen M. Ross, and Judith Bryant Wittenberg, eds., *Unflinching Gaze: Morrison and Faulkner Re-Envisioned* (Jackson: University Press of Mississippi, 1997), 3–16 and *passim*; Phillip M. Weinstein, *What Else But Love? The Ordeal of Race in Faulkner and Morrison* (New York: Columbia University Press, 1996).

102. John Battersby, "Athol Fugard: The Face of South Africa's Conscience," *Christian Science Monitor*, July 14, 1992, pp. 10–11.

103. Kenzaburo Oe, "Reading Faulkner from a Writer's Point of View," *Faulkner Studies in Japan*, ed. Thomas L. McHaney (Athens: University of Georgia Press, 1985), 62–75.

104. See their essays in *Faulkner Studies in Japan*, as well as *Faulkner: After the Nobel Prize*, ed. Michel Gresset and Kenzaburo Ohashi (Kyoto: Yamaguchi Publishing House, 1987), 326–36.

105. M. Thomas Inge, "Faulkner and Mo Yan: Influence and Conflu-ences," *Perspectives on American Culture: Essays on Humor, Literature, and the Popular Arts* (West Cornwall, CT: Locust Hill Press, 1994), 225–37. See also by M. Thomas Inge, "Mo Yan Through Western Eyes," *World Literature Today* 74 (Summer 2000): 501–6.

106. For an early important essay that covers a part of the same ground as this discussion, see Thomas McHaney, "Watching for the Dixie Limited: Faulkner's Impact upon the Creative Writer," *Fifty Years of Yoknapataw-pha*, ed. Doreen Fowler and Ann J. Abadie (Jackson: University Press of Mis-sissippi, 1980), 226–47.

An earlier version of this introduction appeared as an essay in *Faulkner: Achievement and Endurance*, Selected Papers, International Conference on William Faulkner, ed. Tao Jie (Beijing: Peking University Press, 1998), 46–81.

DONALD DAVIDSON

# "William Faulkner"

From *Nashville Tennessean*, April 11, 1926, Magazine Section, page 6.
Copyright © Donald Davidson. Reprinted by permission.

William Faulkner is a Southerner, and lives at Oxford, Mississippi. That is all I know of him, biographically speaking, except that he contributed to *The Double Dealer*, that New Orleans magazine which has succeeded in disclosing to the world many young writers of talent lying hidden in this part of the United States.

However, it is unnecessary to know anything about William Faulkner. He reveals himself quite clearly in his novel, *Soldiers' Pay*, as a sensitive, observant person with a fine power of objectifying his own and other people's emotions, and of clarifying characters so that they possess the "real life" within themselves which it is one of the functions of art to present. Furthermore, he is an artist in language, a sort of poet tuned into prose; he does not write prose as Dreiser does, as if he were washing dishes; nor like Sinclair Lewis, who goes at words with a hammer and saw. Take this bit of description:

> Solemnly the clock on the courthouse, staring its four bland faces across the town, like a kind and sleepless god, dropped eleven measured bells of golden sound. Silence carried them away, silence and dark that passing along the street like a watchman, snatched scraps of light from windows, palming them as a pickpocket palms snatched handkerchiefs. A belated car passed swiftly.

*Soldiers' Pay*, then, is such a book as John Dos Passos might have written if he had not visualized life as such a mixture of harsh planes, intersecting in viciously haphazard ways. And *Soldiers' Pay*, which deals with post-war people in a Southern town, is superior to Dos Passos's *Soldiers Three*, that much-talked-about war book, because it digs deeper into human nature.

Mr. Faulkner's title indicated the irony which he discovers in the post-war situation, that irony familiar to returned soldiers, who came back, sometimes broken and changed, to discover life moving as casually as ever in its old grooves, and people as much untouched by the war as by polar exploration. Such a discovery makes a man turn a little grim and bitter, but life goes on, with formidable fructifying and budding. People must still live, love, eat, dance, go to the movies, and therefore it is better not to remain grim and bitter. It is better to crack a joke, light a cigarette, and go about one's business. That is about what William Faulkner puts into his book.

The world of *Soldiers' Pay* is the post-war world, with a little Southern town given, let us say, as a typical specimen. Donald Mahon, a young aviator, returns to his place at a time somewhat indefinitely after the armistice. Although discharged from the hospital, he is a physical wreck, eyesight almost gone, feeble, useless limbs, a disfiguring scar across his face, just a hollow figure of a man with a mind hardly working. In effect, he comes back home to die. Around this central, inert figure, stopped midway in its experience of life, move all the persons of the book. Two people came with Mahon to see him safely home—Joe Gilligan, a typical soldier, buff, good-natured, careless, kind-hearted; Mrs. Powers, an intellectual, far-seeing young woman whose husband was killed in the trenches. There are also the town people: Cecily Saunders, the pert flapper to whom he was engaged; Rector Mahon, the dying man's father; Joe Jones, a sort of Latin scholar intensely resembling a Greek satyr in his insistent pursuit of fleshly pleasure; Emmy, the servant-girl, and various other minor persons. The story consists in the unfolding of the situation created by bringing all these people together. For example, Cecily Saunders is at first romantically intrigued by the idea of marrying a wounded hero. But when she sees Mahon's horrible scar, it turns her delicate stomach. No, she couldn't marry a man with such a disfigurement. Besides, she is really in love with young George Farr, who has been assiduously wooing her while the heroes were absent. Cecily agonizes and debates tremendously, with her shallow nature torn by contrary impulses. Finally, the generous Mrs. Powers relieves the situation by marrying Mahon. And at last Mahon dies anyway. There is also the tragic situation of the old rector, who thought his son was dead, and who, when he gets his son back, naively hopes for recovery. There is the tragedy of Emmy, the independent-minded servant girl who loved Mahon secretly. There is Jones, who goes after what he wants with deliberate hedonism. There is all the life of a Southern town, its secret as well as its obvious life, all the mingling of disillusionment and pagan recklessness that have characterized the post-war period.

It is, all in all, a powerful book, done with careful artistry and with great warmth of feeling. Mr. Faulkner is, as might be suspected, distinctly a "modern," and has used rather judiciously the special devices which Joyce and others have contributed to the technique of the novel. He has certain faults, such as a too inconsistent repetition of efforts which have an air of smartness rather than of fine art; he is too fond of phrases such as "faint lust"; he has too much of the current mania for depicting people "en deshabille"; he overemphasizes sensuousness, as many moderns do. But he also has a sense of humor, is fairly equable, and avoids the nervous distortion which gives to so many modern novels an effect very much like that of the modern paintings and statues regularly reproduced in the *Dial*. His book will baffle and perplex some people who read it. Or at least they will say they are baffled and perplexed, largely because they are disturbed at the very core of their being. Nevertheless, it is an interesting and even an exciting book for persons who read with discrimination. Mr. Faulkner will perhaps do better books later, but meanwhile he is to be congratulated on a fine initial performance, for *Soldiers' Pay* is, so far as I know, his first novel. And I realize even as I write, that I have not halfway conveyed the flavor of it.

# "Futile Souls Adrift on a Yacht"

From *New York Herald Tribune Books*, June 19, 1927, page 9.

Copyright © Lillian Hellman.

L ast year Mr. Faulkner wrote a novel called *Soldiers' Pay*. Many judicious readers thought it one of the few good books that came out of the war. Its tone was serious if its intent was ironic and its treatment imaginative. This year Mr. Faulkner has taken a quick turn, focusing his attention on an entirely different world. If his first novel showed more than the usual promise then this one, *Mosquitoes*, comes in time to fulfill it. But it must stand alone; a proof of the man's versatility.

It is perhaps unfair to any book, or at least unfair to an author's originality, should he have any, to compare his offering with another that has gone before. However, it remains one way to show excellence or demonstrate worthlessness. In 1923 Aldous Huxley wrote *Antic Hay*, which I think must still stand as the most brilliant book of the last few years. Since then, there has been a host of people who have followed, or attempted to follow, in his footsteps. In most cases their literary worth has been as ephemeral as it was temporarily interesting. If any of these books have approached *Antic Hay* any more closely than *Mosquitoes* it must by now be forgotten. Not that the plot or the people in *Mosquitoes* are similar to those in the Huxley book. As a matter of fact the novel more closely resembles *Those Barren Leaves* in structure, but in the brilliant result it stands closer to the better book.

*Mosquitoes* takes place on a yacht. Mrs. Maurier, a collector of famous people in her own home town of New Orleans, has arranged a boating party for the more artistic of her friends. They come, some of them, because they have nothing better to do, some of them because they are assured of food, some because they cannot help themselves. She has gathered Gordon, a sculptor; Mr. Taliafero, a gentleman who knows much about ladies' lingerie; a young niece and the niece's mechanically inclined brother; a Jew and his sister; Mark Frost, a poet. The niece has found somewhere in New Orleans a young man and a young lady who on that particular day have nothing much to do with themselves. The niece invites them along. They are so cheap, as human, as vulgar as any two she could have found, and yet they furnish the wine for the party. It is a mad trip, this boat ride; the niece is running off with the steward, an intellectual young lady pursuing the vulgar young man and most of the other gentlemen of the party keeping to their rooms for fear of the grapefruit that is served for every meal. Together these people are a fine combination of wit and sophistication and naïveté, but whatever their singularity, their problems, their frustration, are as important to you as if they were people who were more common. They are as tragic as other breeds are tragic, as authentic as your next door neighbor.

It is impossible to capture in a review of the humor, the delight of Mr. Faulkner's writing. It approaches in the first half a brilliance that you can rightfully expect only in the writings of a few men. It is full of the fine kind of swift and lusty writing that comes from a healthy, fresh pen.

Undoubtedly certain portions of it are overwritten, certain Joycean passages that have no direct place or bearing, parts that are heavy and dull with overloaded description. But it is not spoilt. If it contained only the fine last scene it would still be able to stand up.

If you have waited with some feeling akin to longing to read about a modern heroine who is plausible and sympathetic in her somersaults, or to watch a foolish and pathetic woman who has wealth and wants art, or perchance a decaying man who desires his youth; if you want a treat of really amusing conversation that depends upon its wit and not upon its flourishes; if you have waited to see these important matters done really well, then this is your book.

# "On William Faulkner's *The Sound and the Fury*"

New York: Jonathan Cape and Harrison Smith, 1929.

Copyright © Evelyn Scott. Reprinted by permission of the Scott Family,

with special thanks to Denise Scott Fears.

In this age of superlatives, one craves, despite one's disbelief in the supposed justification for censorships, a prohibition of some sort against the insincere employments of adjectives that, in an era of selection, carry rare meaning. One longs for measure in judgment. One desires above all a body of real criticism which will save the worthy artist from a careless allotment, before the public, with those whose object in writing is a purely commercial one. The sane critic, the critic who is careful of his words through his very generosity in recognizing valid talent, exists. But one doubts if the public in general has time to discriminate between the praise bestowed by such a critic, and the panegyrics of mere publicity. I want to write something about *The Sound and the Fury* before the fanfare in print can greet even the ears of the author. There will be many, I am sure, who, without this assistance, will make the discovery of the book as an important contribution to the permanent literature of fiction. I shall be pleased, however, if some others, lacking the opportunity for investigating individually the hundred claims to greatness which America makes every year in the name of art, may be led, through these comments, to a perusal of this unique and distinguished novel. The publishers, who are so much to be congratulated for presenting a little known writer with dignity of recognition which his talent deserves, call this book "overwhelmingly powerful and even monstrous." Powerful it is; and it may even be described as "monstrous" in all its implication of tragedy; but such tragedy has a noble essence.

The question has been put by a contemporary critic, a genuine philosopher reviewing the arts, as to whether there exists for this age of disillusion with religion, dedication to the objective program of scientific inventiveness and general rejection of the teleology which placed man emotionally at the center of his universe, the spirit of which great tragedy is the expression. *The Sound and the Fury* seems to me to offer a reply. Indeed I feel that however sophistical the argument of theology, man remains, in his heart, in that important position. What he seeks now is in a realization of the futility, up to date, of his search for another, intellectually appropriate embodiment of the god that lives on, however contradicted by "reason."

William Faulkner, the author of this tragedy, which has all the spacious proportions of Greek art, may not consider his book in the least expressive of the general dilemma to which I refer, but that quality in his writings which the emotionally timid will call "morbid," seems to me reflected from the impression, made to a sensitive and normally egoistic nature, of what is in the air. Too proud to solve the human problem evasively through any of the sleight-of-hand of puerile surface optimism, he embraces, to represent life, figures that do indeed symbolize a kind of despair; but not the despair that depresses or frustrates. His pessimism as to fact, and his acceptance of all the morally inimical possibilities of human nature, is unwavering. The result is, nonetheless, the reassertion of humanity in defeat that is, in the subjective sense, a triumph. This is no Pyrrhic victory made in debate with those powers of intelligence that may be used to destroy. It is the conquest of nature by art. Of rather, the refutation, by means of a work of art, of the belittling of the materialists; and the work itself is in that category of facts which popular scientific thinking has made an ultimate. Here is beauty sprung from the perfect *realization* of what a more limiting morality would describe as ugliness. Here is a humanity stripped of most of what was claimed for it by the Victorians, and the spectacle is moving as no sugar-coated drama ever could be. The result for the reader, if he is like myself, is an exaltation of faith in mankind. It is faith without, as yet, an argument; but it is the same faith which has always lived in the most ultimate expression of the human spirit.

*The Sound and the Fury* is the story of the fall of a house, the collapse of a provincial aristocracy in a final debacle of insanity, recklessness, psychological perversion. The method of presentation is, as far as I know, unique. Book I is a statement of the tragedy as seen through the eyes of a thirty-three-year-old idiot son of the house, Benjy. Benjy is beautiful, as beautiful as one of the helpless angels, and the more so slightly repellent earthiness that is his. He is a better idiot than Dostoyevsky's because his simplicity is more convincingly united with the basic animal simplicity of creatures untried by the standards of a conscious and calculating humanity. It is as if, indeed, Blake's Tiger has been framed before us by the same Hand that made the Lamb, and, in opposition to Blake's conception, endowed with the same soul. Innocence is terrible as well as pathetic—and Benjy is terrible, sometimes terrifying. He is a Christ symbol, yet not, even in the way of the old orthodoxies, Christly. A Jesus asks for a conviction of sin and a confession before redemption. He acknowledges this as in his own history, tempting by the Devil the prelude to his renunciation. In every subtle sense, sin is the desire to sin, the awareness of sin, an assertion in innuendo that, by the very statement of virtue, sin *is*. Benjy is no saint with a wounded ego his own gesture can console. He is not anything—nothing with a name. He is alive. He can suffer. The simplicity of his suffering, the absence, for him, of any compensating sense of drama, leave him as naked of self-flattery as was the first man. Benjy is like Adam, with all he remembers in the garden and one foot in hell on earth. This was where knowledge began, and for Benjy time is too early for any spurious profiting by knowledge. It is a little as if the story of Hans Andersen's Little Mermaid has been taken away from the nursery and sentiment and made rather diabolically to grow up. Here is the Little Mermaid on the way to find her soul in an uncouth and incontinent body—but there is no happy ending. Benjy, born male and made neuter, doesn't want a soul. It is being thrust upon him, but only like a horrid bauble which he does not recognize. He holds in his hands—in his heart—exposed to the reader—something frightening, unnamed—*pain!* Benjy lives deeply in the sense. For the remainder of what he sees as life, he lives as crudely as in allegory, vicariously, through uncritical perception of his adored sister (she smells to him like "leaves") and, in such emotional absolutism, traces for us her broken marriage, her departure forever from an unlovely home, her return by proxy in the person of her illegitimate daughter, Quentin, who, for Benjy, takes the mother's place.

Book II of the novel deals with another—the original Quentin, for whom the baby girl of later events is named. This section, inferior, I think, to the Benjy motive, though fine in part, describes in the terms of free association with which Mr. Joyce is recreating vocabularies, the final day in this life of Quentin, First, who is contemplating suicide. Quentin is a student at Harvard at the time, the last wealth of the family—some property that has been nominally Benjy's—having been sold to provide him with an education. Quentin is oversensitive, introvert, pathologically devoted to his sister, and his determination to commit suicide is his protest against her disgrace.

In Book III we see the world in terms of the petty, sadistic lunacy of Jason; Jason, the last son of the family, the stay-at-home, the failure, clerking in a country store, for whom no Harvard education was provided. William Faulkner has that general perspective in viewing particular events which lifts the specific incident to the dignity of catholic significance, while all the vividness of an unduplicable personal drama is retained. He senses the characteristic compulsions to action that make a fate. Jason is a devil. Yet, since the author has compelled you to the vision of the gods, he is a devil whom you compassionate. Younger than the other brothers, Jason, in his twenties, is tyrannically compensating for the sufferings of jealousy by persecution of his young niece, Caddie's daughter, Quentin, by petty thievery, by deception practiced against his weak mother, by meanest torment of that marvelously accurately conceived young negro, Luster, keeper, against all his idle, pleasure-loving inclinations, of the witless Benjy. Jason is going mad. He knows it—not as an intellectual conclusion, for he holds up all the emotional barriers against the reflection and self-investigation. Jason knows madness as Benjy knows the world and the smell of leaves and the leap of the fire in the grate and the sounds of himself, his own howls, when Luster teases him. Madness for Jason is a blank, immediate state of soul, which he feels encroaching on his meager, objectively considered universe. He is in an agony of inexplicable anticipation of disaster for which his cruelties afford him no relief.

The last Book is told in the third person by the author. In its pages we are to see this small world of failure in its relative aspect. Especial privilege, we are allowed to meet face to face, Dilsey, the old colored woman, who provides the beauty of coherence against the background of struggling choice. Dilsey isn't searching for a soul. She *is* the soul. She is the conscious human accepting the limitations of herself, the iron boundaries of circumstance, and still, to the best of her ability, achieving a holy compromise for aspiration.

People seem very frequently to ask of a book a "moral." There is no moral statement in *The Sound and the Fury*, but moral conclusions can be drawn from it as surely as from "life," because, as fine art, it is life organized to make revelation fuller. Jason is, in fair measure, the young South, scornful of outworn tradition, scornful indeed of all tradition, as of the ideal which has betrayed previous generations to the hope of perfection. He, Jason, would tell you, as so many other do today, that he sees things "as they are." There is no "foolishness" about him, no "bunk." A spade is a spade, as unsuggestive as things must be in an age which prizes radios and motor cars not as means, but as ends for existence. You have "got to show him." Where there is no proof in dollars and cents, or what they can buy, there is nothing. Misconceiving even biology, Jason would probably regard individualism of a crass order as according to nature. Jason is a martyr. He is a completely rational being. There is something exquisitely stupid in this degree of commonsense which cannot grasp the fact that ratiocination cannot proceed without presumptions made on the emotional acceptance of a state antedating reason. Jason argues, as it were, from nothing to nothing. In this *reduction ad absurdum* he annihilates himself, even his vanity. And he runs amok, with his conclusion that one gesture is as good as another, that there is only driveling self-deception to juxtapose to his tin-pot Nietzscheanism—actually the most romantic attitude of all.

But there is Dilsey, without so much as a theory to controvert theory, stoic as some immemorial carving of heroism, going on, doing the best she can, guided only by instinct and affection and the self-respect she will not relinquish—the ideal of herself to which she conforms irrationally, which makes of her life something whole, while her "white folks" accept their fragmentary state, disintegrate. And she recovers for us the spirit of tragedy which the patter of cynicism has often made seem lost.

# "Preface" to British edition of *Soldiers' Pay*

London: Chatto and Windus, 1930. Copyright © 1930 by the Estate of Richard Hughes. Reprinted by permission of Harold Ober Associates Incorporated.

The novel in America, at the moment, seems to have passed into a sort of interregnum. Generations change quickly there; and names only recently become really familiar in England—Lewis, Dreiser, Cabell, Wilder—seem there already to be looming with the vague bigness of the past, rather than an actual, growing stature of the present.

Nor has any whole new generation taken their place; only a few separate writers, first among them one immediately thinks of Hemingway. Indeed, for seriousness and purity, one has to think of him quite alone. But even Hemingway is more a short story writer than a novelist and even Hemingway, perhaps, has done now the work by which he is most likely to be remembered.

So that if I were asked who seems to me at the moment the most interesting novelist in America, I should not hesitate in naming one who is not only unknown in England but practically unknown in America also—William Faulkner. He is a Southerner, from Mississippi; and young, prolific, and unsuccessful.

"Physically, he is short in stature; but he is hardily constructed. His hair and eyes are very black. His nose, broken once, is aquiline, and his expression sharp and keen. He has ready wit, and is a brilliant and sure conversationalist, with the talent for inventing spontaneously extraordinary and imaginative stories." In his photographs his most expressive feature is his mouth.

Faulkner is a man who keeps outside the swirl of literary fashions and avoids literary people; he remains in his native state and (coming of an aristocratic family) follows the solid calling of house-painter; producing at the same time, out of the natural fecundity of his spirit, novel after novel to be dropped by hesitant publishers into an ungrateful world. It goes without saying that some are better than others: but he has written at present at least three books in the first class of contemporary work: yet none of them, until now, have been published in England.

*Soldiers' Pay*, the first to appear here, and also the first he ever wrote, comes as a fitting complement and wind-up to the literature of the War; for it deals with an aspect of the War previously practically untouched—namely, the Peace.

Its theme is the return of the solider, like an unwanted ghost, to the country he has "saved." The scene—the state of Georgia—is an unfamiliar one to most English readers, but not so unfamiliar as that they will expect; and even if it were more so, the theme would be the same in any setting. There is nothing in it that will seem foreign to anyone who is old enough to remember the years nineteen-nineteen and nineteen-twenty in England (or anywhere else, for that matter). The climatic episode of the dance, with the ex-service men huddled forgotten and disapproving in the corner, is tragic and vividly conceived: but it is, moreover, familiar enough.

After reading it, the somewhat similar last act of *The Silver Tassie* pales.

But *Soldiers' Pay* is more than just another (in the popular sense) "War Book." It is a tragic, fascinating, and beautiful story; told by a man who is a novelist to his finger-tips, not an amateur with a single unusual experience to relate; a man who writes because he *can*—and this point cannot be too strongly emphasized. It is not only an achievement, it is promising as well: and the promise is borne out by at least two other novels which Messrs. Chatto and Windus propose to issue shortly: by *Mosquitoes*, which is pure satirical comedy, and by *The Sound and the Fury*, a more ambitious and to my mind more impressive work than even *Soldiers' Pay*.

Reading them, one finds in Faulkner a man with an apparently in-exhaustible invention of incident and quickening sense of form, and containing in him the germs of an apparently inexhaustible number of characters peculiar without ever descending quite into the gro-tesque or the heroic: and one sees these characters, once they are alive, handled and moulded and propelled by a mind both highly and widely educated, combining humanity, emotion, and wit.

ARNOLD BENNETT

# Review of *Soldiers' Pay*

From *Evening Standard*, June 26, 1930, page 7.

Copyright © Arnold Bennett. Reprinted by permission of A. P. Watt

at United Agents on behalf of Jacques Eldin.

L ast year I made some fuss in this column concerning the young American novelist, William Faulkner, who had been mentioned to me in conversation by Richard Hughes, author of *High Wind in Jamaica*. No American, and even no American publisher, whom I asked about Faulkner had ever heard of him. I sent to New York for his books, but could get only one, *The Sound and the Fury*, and that not without difficulty. Strange that Americans have frequently to be told by Englishmen of their new authors!

The first printed fuss made about Theodore Dreiser's first book was made by an Englishman. *Sister Carrie* fell flat in the United States until a review of it by myself was republished there. Then American critics say that English critics sniff at American novels.

Now Faulkner is getting a show in England. His first book, *Soldiers' Pay*, has just been published here, with a preface by Richard Hughes. His second and third follow. *Soldiers' Pay* is labeled "Not a war-book." I call it a war-book. Its chief male characters are returned soldiers, and the whole story hinges on a terribly scarred aviator, who dies of war. Also war-scenes are directly described in the book, and very well described. Unless Faulkner runs off the rails, as some young men do, but as he probably will not, *Soldiers' Pay* will be an extremely valuable collector's item in twenty years' time. Faulkner is the coming of man. He has inexhaustible invention, powerful imagination, a wondrous gift of characterization, a finished skill in dialogue; and he writes, generally, like an angel. None of the arrived American stars can surpass him in style when he is at his best.

But praise of *Soldiers' Pay* must not be unreserved. It is a first book, and has the usual defects of a first book. It is clumsily constructed, being lopsided; the opening chapters, though admirable, are far too long. Faulkner is like Schubert was: he doesn't know when to stop. Further, the book is over-emphasized throughout. Also, some of the locutions are irritating: "His hands cupped her shoulder," "Jones released the fragile writing of her fingers." Etc. Faults of youth, minor and excusable.

A more serious fault, however, is that the book is difficult to read. Not as difficult as his second book, *The Sound and the Fury*, but still difficult. To read it demands effort. (The effort is adequately rewarded.) There is no excuse for this. The great masters are not difficult to read. You know what they mean, and in their passages of dialogue you know who is saying what. In too many novels of young authors a mathematical calculation, a counting of speeches, is needed to find out who is talking. A novel ought to be easy to read; it ought to please immediately. But too many young novelists seem to say: "Whether you like it or not, there will be some rough going in our books. Kant's *Critique of Pure Reason* is difficult, and our books will be difficult. We will not smooth your path. Indeed we intend to make your path as hard as we know how."

In this matter Faulkner is not guiltless. To get his full value involves some heavy work for the reader. But he is the most promising American novelist known to me; more promising than, for instance, Ernest Hemingway, author of the splendid *A Farewell to Arms*. He has in him the elements of greatness, and *Soldiers' Pay* contains quite marvelous pages.

# "Gentleman from Mississippi"

From *American Mercury* 34 (April 1935): 499–501. Copyright
© Laurence Stallings. Reprinted by permission of Sally Stallings.

I t is possible that one of the three writers struggling for possession of Faulkner's heart may be a genius. That writer is hard to distinguish because so much nonsense has been written about him, as every man of high talent provokes critical nonsense. For example, the short story "A Rose for Emily" is an immensely comic piece; but its significance can be left to those critics who wish to draw some sociological inference from every piece of fiction—even from the fact that once upon a time in Mississippi an old maid fed rat poison to her faithless lover. One hopes Faulkner lends no ear to the jitney sociologists who patronize him; for this truly comic side of his work is his best side, and the conversation of the bedraggled lily who ran the Memphis house—in *Sanctuary*—is downright genius. Faulkner has a whole gallery of tragic-comic figures from the back-waters of Huey Long's kingdom; but I think he would have peopled this gallery with similar studies had he been born in Swampscott. So much for the number one Faulkner.

There is a second Faulkner; and this second one has a yearning for the halcyon. Witness his recent story of the old pioneer woman who remembered the fine things brought on from the Old North State. That story had the gift of lending enchantment and grace to past things lovingly remembered. However, the natural animosities athwart our unseen frontiers have hailed his delineation of the more sullen streams of human conduct in Dixie as being the whole South itself. It is true that Faulkner has never done as well with his Gascons as with his Freudian clowns: witness his failure to make a fine novel out of *Sartoris*. Yet in a summary of all his work, it will be discovered that at least a third of Faulkner's writing is teeming with an affectionate regard for the ante-bellum gallantries of Thomas Nelson Page.

It is still another Faulkner who has written the new novel *Pylon*. This is the Faulkner who writes with a rush of prose engendering enormous technical friction which inexorably overheats the oil of the narration. There is always a great difficulty—at least for Faulkner—in this method of narration. I can only think, for a simile, of a jockey rating the pace when he is in at top weight and the distance is a mile-and-a-half. When Faulkner goes the full distance and writes a novel, he breaks with a great deal of smartness and the reader is instantly plunged into the shifting field of his rushing characters.

In *Pylon* these characters are typically Faulknerian in their curiously compelling sympathies which transcend a natural impulse of disgust. These are a barn-storming pilot, a parachute-jumper, and a woman shared by the two; there are also a little boy whose parentage was settled by a throw of the dice, a stupid mechanic, and a dipsomaniacal newspaperman. Faulkner is all eyes for the woman. She is the dark horse of the race, the unknown entry.

The barn-storming group is competing with a worthless old crate for a speed trophy at a New Orleans aviation meet (incidentally, Faulkner stubbornly persists in referring to the city as New Valois). Of necessity in the dash of the opening chapters, Faulkner cannot stop for a breather. And inevitably, he must pull up to do so later on; he must place and unmask his characters in their proper positions. Were it not for his superb technical facility as a writer, he would be out of the running at the first sudden check. *Pylon* is written in this manner of sprints and breathers. It is a strange, incalculable story which he has to tell, and he tells it for all he is worth, whipping heavily in the homestretch to bring the woman in under the wire. I put down the novel with the feeling that the thing has not come off, and yet with the curious satisfaction of a reader who has been incited to pity, to terror, and to laughter throughout.

*Pylon* has a wonderful feel of the aero about it. The speed-race around the closed course must be a first in the comparatively meager literature of the air, but it is all secondary to "a woman not tall and not thin, looking almost like a man in the greasy coverall, with the pale strong rough ragged hair actually darker where it was sunburned, a tanned heavy-jawed face in which the eyes look like pieces of china." It is this woman upon whom Faulkner lavishes his innate love of modernism which is never better exemplified than when he writes of airplanes. He has in other stories, such as "All the Dead Pilots," revealed this feeling before. One could almost say that so committed is Faulkner, a war pilot himself, to a zest for the empyrean, that he is only within those characters who, like Faulkner, have learned to spurn the earth. The sheer description of the air-race is superbly brilliant. The birdman's scorn of the earthbound is profoundly voiced, so profoundly that I believe the man will only rise above the limitations of the comic novelist by heeding this voice and giving himself over to it.

Faulkner's pilot and his parachute-jumper, who between them share the bovine woman dumbstruck by her two tramps of her bright blue sky, are themselves a group-hero of the age which the Wright brothers ushered in at Kitty Hawk. For those who love to discern symbolism in modern work, attention is drawn to the studious passion of Jiggs the mechanic for his boots. These boots are made for men of a pedestrian psyche, men earthbound and unwinged. Much of *Pylon* is told among the sodden morass which is the mind of Jiggs. The unconscious heroism of two boys throwing their lives away in provincial aviation meets is the quality the novelist is intent upon divining; it is rendered striking by the lack of divination which Jiggs brings to his task of overhauling valves and adjusting superchargers.

The desire of the hen-brained woman to fly, and to love carnally all men who fly, is not brilliantly wrought. Faulkner is hesitant in revealing in her the things which he has brought to her; had he let go at full rev he would have given his novel wings. She is of a piece with Faulkner's women characters—endowed with a grotesque motivation. She eludes recognition as a palpable character, shifting as Temple Drake changed in *Sanctuary*. Her last despairing curse as her lover breaks his ship in mid-air against the final pylon is hardly human, hardly understood. The little boy whose parentage must remain in question forever is an eaglet, and it suffices that he was sired by an eagle, and was born on a parachute pack. Yet these things are not shown clearly in the continuity of the novel, but are revealed in cutbacks which appear awkwardly and in spell-breaking pauses. Those who follow Faulkner, and like myself maintain an unflagging interest in the work of an artist, can dismiss such disappointing turns, and once more it is pleasant to adventure into the imagination of the curious gentleman from Mississippi.

# Review of *As I Lay Dying*

From *Listener*, October 16, 1935, page 681. Copyright © Edwin Muir.

The note on the dust-cover of *As I Lay Dying* says that it "has been long recognised in America as one of Mr. Faulkner's most powerful and remarkable works." We may probably assume, therefore, that it is one of his earliest novels; and indeed it shows many signs of immaturity, as well as simplicity, not achieved but unconscious, which tells us a great deal more about the fundamental elements of his work than his later novels do, with their smothering complication. The real subject of this story, simple to the point of desperation, is the corpse of a woman in late middle age. A truer title would have been "As I Lay Dead," but even that would give the story credit for more complexity than it has, for it is concerned not with death, but merely with the chemical changes which happen in a body after life has forsaken it. The "dying" is very quickly and perfunctorily got over, for what Mr. Faulkner—like the detective story-writer—is really after is the body, and the history he relates is the history of this body before it is finally shoveled underground and got out of the way. To have chosen such a curious theme, to have lingered over it with such professional solicitude, conscientiously and lovingly, must show the presence of a very deep-seated obsession. It may be objected that "Webster was much possessed by death" and that Donne was such another but death is a normal and indeed unavoidable subject of human thought, and, as Webster and Donne conceived it, was inseparable from life. To Mr. Faulkner, on the other hand, it is a sort of death absolute, or rather a sort of postmortem life, that has no connection with human life at all. We are told far more about Addie Bundren's corpse, for instance, than about herself. A vision of the horror of death such as Webster's depends for its power in his sense of life. But it may be said of this story of Mr. Faulkner that the most interesting character, or at least the character in which he shows most interest, is the corpse, not in its former incarnation as a human being with feelings, affections, and a soul, but simply in its dead, or rather gruesomely alive, state. What we are to deduce from such an obsession it is hard to say; for it is not a comprehensible obsession, like Webster's, but a blind one. The effect that this story produces is, in any case, one of self-indulgence, self-indulgence pushed to the point of keeping a corpse for nine days above ground on its journey to a distant town, saving it from a flood and then from a fire, reducing the family it left behind it to such a state that they end by confusing it with fishes and horses. Yet the effect is not horror but merely disgust, a much more cold and impotent emotion.

The story is interesting, nevertheless, as showing one of the probable reasons why Mr. Faulkner complicates his method of presentation so elaborately, and why his short stories are so much better than his novels. His technique is so complicated because there is something blind, something unaccounted for by his intellect, in his vision of the world, so that it can only take the form of a series of circular wanderings making towards a circumference which it can never reach. This probably accounts for the sulphurous and overcharged atmosphere in his novels, and the brilliance of the occasional flames, for they always appear against his background of impenetrable darkness. There are such flashes in this book, for instance in the scene describing the fire.

The flash is produced in the most wasteful and amateurish way possible, amid a terrific hubbub of adjectives and adverbs; but in descriptions such as this of physical events Mr. Faulkner has shown himself to be a remarkable writer. Little can be said for this story, however, except for a few isolated accounts of violent action.

# "New Technique in Novel Introduced"

From *Salt Lake City Tribune*, November 29, 1936, page 13-D.
Copyright © Wallace Stegner. Reprinted by permission of Page Stegner.

It is occasionally salutary for a reviewer to read other reviews of a book before he writes his own, if only for the caution it will give him about mistaking subjective judgments for truths. Where the book in question is difficult or involved or revolutionary in its approach, he will be astonished also to find how few critics are willing to let a writer do as he wishes, how few will judge a book on the standards it sets for itself instead of on standards the critic would impose upon it.

So, after reading half a dozen reviews of *Absalom, Absalom!* one is lead to preface all his utterances with "I suspect." I suspect, for example, that Clifton Fadiman's review in the *New Yorker* is not only impercipient and lazy, but silly as well. I suspect that three other reviews in reputable papers are at least impercipient and probably lazy. I suspect that the only review that does Faulkner's last book anything like justice is that by Bernard De Voto in the *Saturday Review.*

I suspect further that one cannot dismiss *Absalom, Absalom!* as 400 pages of turgid and invertebrate sentences about psychopathic ghosts. It is true that with isolated lyrical exceptions the experimental sentences do not come off; they are frequently not only invertebrate but downright bad syntax. The characters are admittedly ghostly and fleshless; the technique "cocks its snoot" at chronology and logic.

Granted one reviewer's charge that Faulkner writes his guts out trying to tell a simple story in the most complex way possible, there is still reason to believe that he probably knew what he was doing, and why he was doing it.

If Faulkner had wanted to tell simply the simple story of demonic Thomas Sutpen's rise from poor white to opulent planter, his matrimonial experiments with whites and Negroes, his desire for a son and a perpetuated name, and the final dissolution of that dream in a flaming house haunted by the whimperings of a half-wit mulatto who is the only survivor of the Sutpen blood, he could have told it as simply as that. The very fact that he didn't is proof enough that he didn't want to, that the manner is more important to him than the matter.

Instead of assuming the omniscience of motive and impulse and reaction that even the most realistic novelists in the past have felt obliged to assume, Faulkner presents his story through the mouths of seven different people, in what De Voto calls a "series of approximations." While there is plenty of character analysis here, it is frankly tentative, frankly the attempt of one character to understand another. The whole book, therefore, gives the impression of wavering uncertainty as Quentin Compson, Harvard freshman, tries to unravel the tangled threads of a tale which has reached him from a dozen incomplete sources, mutually contradictory in spots, filled with dark gaps where informants' knowledge gave out.

In other words, this novel, despite its shadowy, nightmarish quality, is in one respect the most realistic thing Faulkner has done. It reconstructs historical materials as any individual in reality has to reconstruct them—piecemeal, eked out with surmise and guess, the characters ghostly shades except in brief isolated passages. As in life, we are confronted by a story whose answers even the narrator does not know, whose characters he (and we with him) guesses at and speculates upon, but does not attempt to explain fully.

What Faulkner is actually saying, as explicitly if not as simply as it has ever been said, is that no man, novelist or otherwise, can know another except in the trivial superficies of his life; that the mind and emotions of another are mysteries as deep as the hereafter; that we arrive at our knowledge—or rather, our surmises—of other people through these approximations, these driblets of information from six or 600 sources, each driblet colored by the prejudices and emotions of the observer.

That is how we know Demon Thomas Sutpen, how we arrive at a conception of Miss Rosa and her thwarted emotional life; how we know what little we do of the motives of Henry Sutpen and of Charles Bon, who was to marry Judith's sister and whom Henry killed. We know as much as Quentin does, as much as Faulkner does; and at the end of the book Quentin and his roommate are frankly guessing, extemporizing, trying to piece out sections of the plot which are wholly dark, creating plausible but wholly imaginative characters to fill in the gaps, endowing them with motive and action to fit the few surviving facts.

Perhaps that is what the critics are howling about, that they don't know any more about these "psychopathic ghosts" than they do about the people they associate with every day. Accustomed to having our fictional characters complete, fully rounded, we feel cheated if an author rejects the omniscient lie at the basis of most fiction. Perhaps, too, Faulkner doesn't entirely succeed; certainly the style is tortured beyond what most readers will stand. But I suspect, and strongly, that the mere technique of this novel may prove to be a significant contribution to the theory of the art of fiction; and that *Absalom, Absalom!* will not be the last, or the best, to approach its materials in this way.

# "Tattered Banners"

From *New Republic*, March 9, 1938, pages 136–37. Copyright © Kay Boyle. Reprinted by permission of Ian von Franckenstein.

There are two Faulkners—at least to me there are two: the one who stayed down South and the one who went to war in France and mixed with foreigners and aviators; that is, Faulkner of the Sartoris saga (and the countless other savagely and tenderly chronicled documents of the South) and the Faulkner who wrote "Turn About," for instance, and "All the Dead Pilots" and *Pylon* with no perceptible cooling of that hot devotion to man's courage although the speech, the history, the conflict were no longer his strict heritage. I believe these two separate Faulkners (separated more by a native shyness of the foreigner than any variance in ideology or technique) possess between them the strength and the vulnerability which belong only to the greatest artists: the incalculable emotional wealth, the racy comic sense, the fury to reproduce exactly not the recognizable picture but the unmistakable experience, the thirst for articulation as well as the curiosity and the vocabulary—that rarity— to quench it. The weaknesses there are, the errors, the occasionally strained effects, are accomplished by the same fearless, gifted hand.

It is not difficult to reconcile the two Faulkners; perhaps as simple as recognizing that man is a good host or a good guest, but rarely both. On his own ground Faulkner was explicit, easy, sure; on someone else's he is a little awed, a little awkward, provincially aware of the chances he is taking. But I believe it is in the willingness to take these risks that Faulkner's whole future lies. That *The Unvanquished* happens to be one more chapter in the Sartoris saga is no valid de-

scription of it, nor that it is a book about the Civil War—a Civil War
in which the issue of black and white is lost in the wider issue not of
justice and tyranny, subjection and freedom, or even sin and virtue,
but merely of life and death. For one who loves Faulkner's work and
has followed it closely and impatiently, the difficulty lies in isolating
this book or any other book from the others and trying to say this or
that of it: his genius is not this book or perhaps any given book but
resides in that entire determined collection of volumes which reveal
him to be the most absorbing writer of our time. . .

It is, then, the sentimental and glamorous story of one old lady
who set out to find and ask a Yankee colonel to return to her a chest
of family silver tied with hemp rope, two darkies, Loosh and Phila-
delphy, and the two confiscated mules, "Old Hundred" and "Tinney";
and like a single and undaunted fife still playing, it is as well the essence of that war, a thing as intrinsically and nationally and gallantly
the South's as the revolution is France's and the rebellion Ireland's:
become now a legend, almost a fable of tattered banners, makeshift
uniforms, incredible courage and inhuman ferocity. It has those
weaknesses which can be found throughout Faulkner's work: the full-
length portraits which abruptly become caricatures not likenesses of
the living, the "ladies" without face or substance, the repetitions, the
maudlin lapses, the shameless voice of the evangelist declaiming in
solemn, flowery passages. But it has that fabulous, that wondrous,
fluxing power which nothing Faulkner touches is ever without. The
word for it may be glamor or it may be sentiment, but both these
words are mutable and I have used them here without contempt, ap-
plying them in their best sense as attributes to fact. They can confuse, they can disguise, but they can as well bring to the familiar a
heightened, an isolated and a therefore truer legibility. They were elements in that electric atmosphere and mystic climate in which Poe's
men and women lived and have survived and they are a vital part of
Faulkner's quicker, more comprehensive world. Faulkner and Poe,
set far enough apart in time, are strangely kin: unique in our history
in their immunity to literary fashion, alike in the fanatical obsession
with the unutterable depths of mankind's vice and even more with his
divinity.

If writing remains one of the Arts—with a capital A and be damned to the current mode of splitting it two ways in a poem or fresco on a wall—if its sensitive execution still demands the heart and the endurance which have kept artists lying prone on scaffoldings painting year in, year out, and if its success depends on its acceptance as convincing tragedy or comedy, then it can quite simply be said of Faulkner that he is the rare, the curious, the almost ludicrously authentic thing. In this book, as in his others, he writes with that "fierce desire of perfection" which contemporaries said Michelangelo evidenced when "flinging himself on the material of marble," vehemently seeking expression for "the human elements of fervor and tenderness."

# "On *The Sound and the Fury*: Time in the Work of William Faulkner"

From *Literary and Philosophical Essays* (New York: Criterion Books, 1955), 79–97. "À propos de le Bruit et la Fureur, la temporalité chez Faulkner" from Situations, tome I: Février 1938–septembre 1944, Nouvelle édition revue et augmentée par Arlette Elkaïm-Sartre en 2010, © Editions Gallimard, Paris, 2010.

The first thing that strikes one in reading *The Sound and the Fury* is its technical oddity. Why has Faulkner broken up the time of his story and scrambled the pieces? Why is the first window that opens out on this fictional world the consciousness of an idiot? The reader is tempted to look for guide-marks and to reestablish the chronology for himself:

> Jason and Caroline Compson have had three sons and a daughter. The daughter, Caddy, has given herself to Dalton Ames and become pregnant by him. Forced to get a hold of a husband quickly . . .

Here the reader stops, for he realizes he is telling another story. Faulkner did not first conceive this orderly lot so as to shuffle it afterwards like a pack of cards; he could not tell it in any other way. In the classical novel, action involves a central complication; for example, the murder of old Karamazov or the meeting of Edouard and Bernard in *The Coiners*. But we look in vain for such a complication in *The Sound and the Fury*. Is it the castration of Benjy or Caddy's wretched amorous adventure or Quentin's suicide or Jason's hatred of his niece? As soon as we begin to look at any episode, it opens up to reveal behind it other episodes, all the other episodes. Nothing happens; the story does not unfold; we discover it under each word, like an obscene and obstructing presence, more or less condensed, depending upon the particular case. It would be a mistake to regard these irregularities as gratuitous exercises in virtuosity. A fictional technique always relates back to the novelist's metaphysics. The critic's task is to define the latter before evaluating the former. Now, it is immediately obvious that Faulkner's metaphysics is a metaphysics of time.

> Man's fortune lies in his being time-bound.
> . . . a man is the sum of his misfortunes. One day you'd think misfortune would get tired, but then time is your misfortune . . .

Such is the real subject of the book. And if the technique Faulkner has adopted seems at first a negation of temporality, the reason is that we confuse temporality with chronology. It was man who invented dates and clocks.

> Constant speculation regarding the position of mechanical hands on an arbitrary dial which is a symptom of mind-function. Excrement Father said like sweating.

In order to arrive at real time, we must abandon this invented measure which is not a measure of anything.

> . . . time is dead as long as it is being clicked off by little wheels; only when the clock stops does time come to life.

Thus, Quentin's gesture of breaking his watch has a symbolic value; it gives us access to a time without clocks. The time of Benjy, the idiot, who does not know how to tell time, is also clockless.

What is thereupon revealed to us is the present, and not the ideal limit whose place is neatly marked out between past and future. Faulkner's present is essentially catastrophic. It is the event which creeps up on us like a thief, huge, unthinkable—which creeps up on us and then disappears. Beyond this present time there is nothing, since the future does not exist. The present rises up from sources unknown to us and drives away another present; it is forever beginning anew. "And . . . and . . . and then." Like Dos Passos, but much more discreetly, Faulkner makes an accretion of his narrative. The actions themselves, even when seen by those who perform them, burst and scatter on entering the present.

> I went to the dresser and took up the watch with the face still down. I tapped the crystal on the dresser and caught the fragments of glass in my hand and put them into the ashtray and twisted the hands off and put them in the tray. The watched ticked on.

The other aspect of this present is what I shall call a sinking in. I use this expression, for want of a better one, to indicate a kind of motionless movement of this formless monster. In Faulkner's work, there is never any progression, never anything which comes from the future. The present has not first been a future possibility, as when my friend, after having been *he for whom I am waiting*, finally appears. No, to be present means to appear without any reason and to sink in. This sinking in is not an abstract view. It is within things themselves that Faulkner perceives it and tries to make it felt.

> The train swung around the curve, the engine puffing with short, heavy blasts, and they passed smoothly from sight that way, with that quality of shabby and timeless patience, of static serenity.

And again,

> Beneath the sag of the buggy the hooves neatly rapid like motions of a lady doing embroidery, *diminishing without progress*[1] like a figure on a treadmill being drawn rapidly off-stage.

It seems as though Faulkner has laid hold of a frozen speed at the very heart of things; he is grazed by congealed spurts that wane and dwindle without moving.

This fleeting and unimaginable immobility can, however, be arrested and pondered. Quentin can say, "I broke my watch," but when he says it, his gesture is *past*. The past is named and related; it can, to a certain extent, be fixed by concepts or recognized by the heart. We pointed out earlier, in connection with *Sartoris*, that Faulkner always showed events when they were already over. In *The Sound and the Fury* everything has already happened. It is this that enables us to understand that strange remark by one of the heroes, "*Fui. Non sum.*" In this sense, too, Faulkner is able to make man a sum total without a future: "The sum of his climatic experiences," "The sum of his misfortunes," "The sum of what have you." At every moment, one draws a line, since the present is nothing but a chaotic din, a future that is past. Faulkner's vision of the world can be compared to that of a man sitting in an open car and looking backwards. At every moment, formless shadows, flickering, faint tremblings and patches of light rise up on either side of him, and only afterwards, when he has a little perspective, do they become trees and men and cars.

The past takes on a sort of super-reality; its contours are hard and clear, unchangeable. The present, nameless and fleeting, is helpless before it. It is full of gaps, and, through these gaps, things of the past, fixed, motionless and silent as judges or glances, come to invade it. Faulkner's monologues remind one of aeroplane trips full of air-pockets. At each pocket, the hero's consciousness "sinks back into the past" and rises only to sink back again. The present is not; it becomes. Everything *was*. In *Sartoris*, the past was called "the stories" because it was a matter of family memories that had been constructed, because Faulkner had not yet found his technique.

In *The Sound and the Fury* he is more individual and more undecided. But it is so strong an obsession that he is sometimes apt to disguise the present, and the present moves along in the shadow, like an underground river, and reappears only when it itself is past. When Quentin insults Blain,[2] he is not even aware of doing so; he is reliving his dispute with Dalton Ames. And when Bliad punches his nose, this brawl is covered over and hidden by Quentin's past brawl with Ames. Later on, Shreve relates how Blain hit Quentin; he relates this scene because it has become a story, but while it was unfolding in the present, it was only a furtive movement, covered over by veils. Someone once told me about an old monitor who had grown senile. His memory was that of a schoolyard and his daily walk around it. Thus, he interpreted his present in terms of his past and walked about his table, convinced that he was watching students during recreation.

Faulkner's characters are like that, only worse, for their past, which is in order, does not assume chronological order. It is, in actual fact, a matter of emotional constellations. Around a few central themes (Caddy's pregnancy, Benjy's castration, Quentin's suicide) gravitate innumerable silent masses. Whence the absurdity of the chronology of "the assertive and contradictory assurance" of the clock. The order of the past is the order of the heart. It would be wrong to think that when the present is past it becomes our closest memory. Its metamorphosis can cause it to sink to the bottom of our memory, just as it can leave it floating on the surface. Only its own density and the dramatic meaning of our life can determine at what level it will remain.

Such is the nature of Faulkner's time. Isn't there something familiar about it? This unspeakable present, leaking at every seam, these sudden invasions of the past, this emotional order, the opposite of the voluntary and intellectual order that is chronological but lacking in reality, these memories, these monstrous and discontinuous obsessions, these intermittences of the heart—are not these reminiscent of the lost and recaptured time of Marcel Proust? I am not unaware of the differences between the two; I know, for instance, that for Proust salvation lies in time itself, in the full reappearance of the past. For Faulkner, on the contrary, the past is never lost, unfortunately; it is always there, it is an obsession. One escapes from the temporal world only through mystic ecstasies. A mystic is always a man who wishes to forget something, his self or, more often, language or objective representation. For Faulkner, time must be forgotten.

> "Quentin, I give you the mausoleum of all hope and desire; it's rather excruciatingly apt that you will use it to gain the reduction ad absurdum of all human experience which can fit your individual needs no better than it fitted his or his father's. I give it to you not that you may remember time, *but that you might forget it now and then for a moment* and not spend all your breath trying to conquer it. Because no battle is ever won he said. They are not even fought. The field only

reveals to man his own folly and despair, and victory is an illusion of philosophers and fools."

It is because he has forgotten time that the hunted negro in *Light in August* suddenly achieves his strange and horrible happiness.

> It's not when you realize that nothing can help you—religion, pride, anything—it's when you realize that you don't need any aid.

But for Faulkner, as for Proust, time is, above all, *that which separates*. One recalls the astonishment of the Proustian heroes which can no longer enter into their past loves, of those lovers depicted in *Les Plaisiers et Les Jours*, clutching their passions, afraid they will pass and knowing they will. We find the same anguish in Faulkner.

> . . . people cannot do anything very dreadful at all, they cannot even remember tomorrow what seemed dreadful today . . .

and

> . . . a love or a sorrow is a bond purchased without design and which matures willynilly and is recalled without warning to be replaced by whatever issue the gods happen to be floating at the time . . .

To tell the truth, Proust's fictional technique *should have been* Faulkner's. It was the logical conclusion of his metaphysics. But Faulkner is a lost man, and it is because he feels lost that he takes risks and pursues his thought to its uttermost consequences. Proust is a Frenchman and a classicist. The French lose themselves only a little at a time and always manage to find themselves again. Eloquence, intellectuality and a liking for clear ideas were responsible for Proust's retaining at least the semblance of chronology.

The basic reason for this relationship is to be found in a very general literary phenomenon. Most of the great contemporary authors, Proust, Joyce, Dos Passos, Faulkner, Gide and Virginia Woolf have tried, each in his own way, to distort time. Some of them have deprived it of its past and future in order to reduce it to the pure intuition of the instant; others, like Dos Passos, have made of it a dead and closed memory. Proust and Faulkner have simply decapitated it. They have deprived it of its future, that is, its dimension of deeds and freedom. Proust's heroes never undertake anything. They do, of course, make plans, but their plans remain stuck to them and cannot be projected like a bridge beyond the present. They are day-dreams that are put to flight by reality. The Albertine who appears is not the one we were expecting, and the expectation was merely a slight, inconsequential hesitation, limited to the moment only. As to Faulkner's heroes, they never look ahead. They face backwards as the car carries them along. The coming suicide which casts its shadow over Quentin's last day is not a human possibility; not for a second does Quentin envisage the possibility of *not* killing himself. This suicide is an immobile wall, a *thing* which he approaches backwards, and which he neither wants to nor can conceive.

> . . . you seem to regard it merely as an experience that will whiten your hair overnight so to speak without altering your appearance at all . . .

It is not an *undertaking*, but a fatality. In losing its elements of possibility it ceases to exist in the future. It is already present, and Faulkner's entire art aims at suggesting to us that Quentin's monologues and his last walk *are already* his suicide. This, I think, explains the following curious paradox: Quentin thinks of his last day in the past, like someone who is remembering. But in that case, since the hero's last thoughts coincide approximately with the bursting of his memory and its annihilation, who is remembering? The inevitable reply is that the novelist's skill consists in the choice of the present moment from which he narrates the past. And Faulkner, like Salacrou in *L'Inconnu d'Arras*, has chosen the infinitesimal instant of death. Thus, when Quentin's memory begins to unravel its recollections ("Through the wall I heard Shreve's bed-springs and then his slippers on the floor hishing. I got up . . .") *he is already dead*. All this artistry and, to speak frankly, all this illusion are meant, then, merely as substitutions for the intuition of the future lacking in the author himself. This explains everything, particularly the irrationality of time; since the present is the unexpected, the formless can be determined only by an excess of memories. We now also understand why duration is "man's characteristic misfortune." If the future has reality, time withdraws us from the past and brings us nearer to the future; but if you do away with the future, time is no longer that which separates, that which cuts the present off from itself. "You cannot bear to think that someday it will no longer hurt you like this." Man spends his life struggling against time, and time, like an acid, eats away at man, eats him away from himself and prevents him from fulfilling his human character. Everything is absurd. "Life is a tale told by an idiot, full of sound and fury, signifying nothing."

But is man's time without a future? I can understand that the nail's time, or the clod's or the atom's, is a perpetual present. But is man a thinking nail? If you begin by plunging him into universal time, the time of planets and nebulae, of tertiary flexures and animal species, as into a bath of sulphoric acid, then the question is settled. However, a consciousness buffeted so from one instant to another ought, *first of all*, to be a consciousness and then, *afterwards*, to be temporal; does anyone believe that time can come to it from the outside? Consciousness can "exist within time" only on condition that it become time as a result of the very movement by which it becomes consciousness. It must become "temporalized," as Heidegger says. We can no longer arrest a man at each present and define him as the "the sum of what he was." The nature of consciousness implies, on the contrary, that it project itself into the future. We can understand what it is through what it will be. It is determined in its present being by its own possibilities. This is what Heidegger calls "the silent force of the possible." You will not recognize within yourself Faulkner's man, a creature bereft of possibilities and explicable only in terms of what he has been. Try to pin down consciousness and probe it. You will see that it is hollow. In it you will find only the future.

I do not even speak of your plans and expectations. But the very gesture that you catch in passing has meaning for you only if you project its fulfillment out of it, out of yourself, into the not-yet. This very cup, with its bottom that you do not see—that you might see, that is, at the end of a movement you have not yet made—this white sheet of paper, whose underside is hidden (but you could turn over the sheet) and all the stable and bulky objects that surround us display their most immediate and densest qualities in the future. Man is not the sum of what he has, but the totality of what he does not yet have, of what he might have. And if we steep ourselves thus in the future, is not the formless brutality of the present thereby attenuated? The single event does not spring on us like a thief, since it is, by nature, a Having-been-future. And if a historian wishes to explain the past, must he not first seek out its future? I am afraid that the absurdity that Faulkner finds in a human life is one that he himself has put there. Not that life is not absurd, but there is another kind of absurdity.

Why have Faulkner and so many other writers chosen this particular absurdity which is so un-novelistic and so untrue? I think we should have to look for the reason in the social conditions of our present life. Faulkner's despair seems to me to precede his metaphysics. For him, as for all of us, the future is closed. Everything we see and experience impels us to say, "This can't last." And yet change is not even conceivable, except in the form of cataclysm. We are living in a time of impossible revolutions, and Faulkner uses his extraordinary art to describe our suffocation and a world dying of old age. I like his art, but I do not believe in his metaphysics. A closed future is still a future. "Even if human reality has nothing more 'before' it, even if 'its account is closed,' its being is still determined by this 'self-anticipation.' The loss of all hope, for example, does not deprive human reality of its possibilities; it is simply a way of *being* toward these same possibilities" (Heidegger, *Zein und Zeit*).

*Notes*

1. The author's italics.

2. Compare the dialogue with Blain inserted into the middle of the dialogue with Ames: "Did you ever have a sister?" etc., and the inextricable confusion of the two fights.

# "Flem Snopes and His Kin"

From *Saturday Review of Literature*, April 6, 1940, page 7.

Copyright © Stephen Vincent Benét. Reprinted by permission

of Brandt & Hochman Literary Agents, Inc.

In the Snopes family, Mr. Faulkner has created what is probably the finest sub-human species in contemporary American literature. Compared to the Snopes, the Joads are the country-club set and Jeeter and his brood folks of high social consciousness, well adjusted to their environment. To create a set of characters with the acquisitiveness of the gypsy-moth and the morality of the swamp-moccasin, and to watch them writhing and squirming in their environment with blind ferocity of maggots, is in itself an achievement. It is an even greater achievement that the dark magic of Mr. Faulkner's style makes these creatures continuously interesting. Mr. Faulkner may be a great many things—he is seldom, if ever, dull. He can be clotted and confused, but his writing, at his best, has an hallucinative power which keeps one reading, like a man in the toils of a nightmare, till the last page has turned. In *The Hamlet*, his peculiar power is at its best. There are fewer of the long, winding sentences that strangle themselves to death in their own subordinate clauses—there is all of the earthy force that Mr. Faulkner can summon, like a spirit out of the ground, when he chooses to do so. Reading *The Hamlet* is like listening to the gossip of a country store, with its cruelty, its extravagance, its tall stories, and its deadly comment upon human nature—but a gossip translated, heightened, and made into art. It is, I suppose, an unpleasant book; it will be a repellant book to many readers. It is also, not always but frequently, superbly written. Nor is "unpleasant" the

first adjective this particular reviewer would think of. Mr. Faulkner is too good for that.

The story of *The Hamlet* is the story of the gradual sucking dry of Frenchman's Bend by Flem Snopes and his endless kin. In the rich, river-bottom country, Frenchman's Bend had been the original site of a vast pre–Civil War plantation. Used to a tradition of violence and to names like Armstid and Doshey, names "which could have come from nowhere since certainly no man would deliberately select one of them for his own," even to Frenchman's Bend the Snopes were a surprise and a portent. The big family in the country had been the Varners, corrupt enough but merry—lazyish overlords. They look important, but they had about the same resistance to the sucking acquisitiveness of Flem Snopes that the flesh of a squirrel has to the germs of tularemia. There was Flem and Mink and I.O., Ike the idiot, and the hideously untouched boy called Wallstreet Panic. They came out of nowhere. They settled on Frenchman's Bend and the Varners, like wasps on a burst pear, they got the store and the big house, the money and the women. They fought among themselves with the obscure brutality of bacilli—but, when they were through, it was time for Flem Snopes to move on to Jefferson, for he had eaten the heart out of Frenchman's Bend. I doubt if a more appalling portrait of the mean poor-white has ever been drawn. Yet it is drawn, particularly in the last section and the fantastic incident of the Texas ponies, with horrible veracity but also with the raw humor of the frontier. It may be observed that there is one man of relative good-will in the book, the sewing-machine-salesman, Ratliff. He doesn't, it is true, get anywhere in particular, but his disillusioned comment represents the defeated virtues of civilization—at least by comparison with the Snopes.

It would be easy to point out that Flem Snopes and his breed might well stand for the new barbarism we are all afraid of as easy as it is inadequate. I don't think that was Mr. Faulkner's point, he has drawn Flem Snopes and his bindweed family and done it a way that you will remember. This book contains one first class murder, an extraordinary tour-de-force in the portrait of the idiot, Ike, a mad treasure-hunt, a heroine, Eula Varner, so mammalian that she is practically a gland, a highly interesting sketch of a young man on the make, and other oddments and excitements. And all this material, the violence and the laziness, the nightmare and the tropic warmth of the deep South, is brought together and orchestrated by a masterly hand. Peasant humor and peasant horror—both are there. And, first, last, and always, Mr. Faulkner is a writer.

# "Fiction and Life"

From *Time and Tide*, November 9, 1940, page 1097 [excerpt].

Copyright © George Orwell. Reprinted by permission of Bill Hamilton as the

Literary Executor of the Estate of the late Sonia Brownell Orwell.

It is hard to know what to say about Mr. William Faulkner, who is generally spoken of as one of the most "important" of living American writers. He raises the question of whether a writer is to be taken seriously merely because he is "intellectual," i.e., because there is a great display of cerebration in his work. The following sentence, chosen at random, gives a fair enough idea of the style in which Mr. Faulkner chooses to write:

> He had to read in glasses now, leaving one class to walk blinking painfully against the light to the next, in the single unmatching costume he owned, through throngs of laughing youths and girls in clothes better than he has ever seen until he came here, who did not stare through him so much as they did not see him anymore than they did the poles which supported the electric lights which until he arrived two years ago he has never seen before either.

The whole book is written more or less in this manner, and a three-page paragraph of this kind of thing is, to put it mildly, fatiguing. The difficulty of reading it comes from the fact that Mr. Faulkner crams into each sentence thoughts which occur to him in passing but which have not necessarily much to do with the matter at hand. Like various other writers from Carlyle onwards, he is presenting the process of thought instead of the results. After a careful reading of *The Hamlet,*

I must record that I have quite failed to discover the plot of the story. All I can say with certainty is that it is about some people somewhere in the Southern States of America, people with supremely hideous names—names like Flem Snopes and Eck Snopes—who sit about the steps of village stores, chewing tobacco, swindling one another in small business deals, and from time to time committing a rape or a murder. A second reading—and to read a book of this length is several days' work—might extract something more definite, but it is my honest opinion that it would not be worthwhile.

# Journal Entries

From *The Journals of Thornton Wilder 1939–1961*, edited by Donald Gallup (New Haven, CT: Yale University Press, 1985), 18–19 (April 10, 1940), 20–21 (May 2, 1940), and 57–58 (November 6, 1949). Copyright © 1985 by the Wilder Family LLC. Reprinted by arrangement with the Wilder Family LLC and the Barbara Hogenson Agency, Inc. All rights reserved. Thanks to Tappan Wilder.

**WILLIAMSBURG, VA., APRIL 10, 1940.** Faulkner's *Light in August.*

So much that is splendid, but finally swamped and defeated in the emotional steam, the drive to cruelty, the confusion as to what is good and bad, the mix-up that arises from identifying the strong with the good; and the gentle with the bad. The image of the South, crying out in self-justification and self-condemnation, and all the twisted bitterness.

I am teased by one problem in it.

The surface is clear enough. The ambivalent hatred and adoration of the Negro; the impoverished Southern blood adoring the virility of the Negro. And the fatal envy-fascination of the Negro, which does not dare confess the envy-fascination, must take the indirect bypath of sadism: sexual envy becomes sexual sadism: the climax of the book is the castration of the half-Negro demon-hero Joe Christmas. Faulkner waits on that moment. He builds and builds the virility-hardness of Christmas, not by representing him as a sexual athlete, which would be too overt, but by rendering him and developing him hard under an unbroken succession of injustices and sufferings. Faulkner will not even allow him to be touched by the occasional alleviations of his misery; such as the attempts at kindness that come to him from

74

his adoptive-mother, Mrs. McEachern. W. F.'s attitude to woman is armed in neutrality—Lena's calm and fidelity and dogged search for her betrayer is a force dependent on her pregnancy; at times her characterization is about to advance to that of all-wise, all possessing earth-mother, but always it falls short and she too wears an ominous character, as though, in Byron Bunch, she is Woman that uses and victimizes men. (Two of the women in the book, Mrs. Armstid, who is grudgingly kind to Lena, and Miss Burden, are repeatedly called man-like.) Note the close: Christmas's mutilator, a little military-adoring small-town fascist. He carries a gun, even under disapproval of the sheriff. Faulkner tries to make fun of him, but his admiration for that gun and that belief in order and punishment sneaks out, and finally Faulkner confers upon him the glorious act of the book: the mutilation of the Negro.

The puzzle is Hightower; ex-minister, betrayed by his wife, touched with two fanaticisms, flabby, obese, given to reading the "sapless, lustless" Tennyson. Even more painful to him than the disgrace of his wife and his expulsion from the church was the letter he wrote to an institution for delinquent girls saying that henceforth he could now donate to them half of his little patrimony-income. All his conversation with Byron Bunch (so like those in the novels of Henry James, full of charged allusive indirect concern over how others will "feel" about what happens or may happen) are full of some vast emotion and moral weight disproportionate to the effect that these matters could ever have on him. I think that the answer to this is that for Faulkner, Hightower stands a symbol for the South. Hightower's other fanaticism is an episode in his grandfather's life ("the most important day of his life, the only day he ever really lived, took place thirty years before he was born"): his grandfather was killed on horseback in a gallant cavalry raid, here in Jefferson, where he had come to burn up the store of General Grant. The other thing about Hightower is the implication of impotence. The delinquency of his wife is justified in one place by the phrase "he either could not or would not satisfy her," and W. F. goes on to say that his excitement about the grandfather's cavalry raid was the injustice or burden which his wife had to bear. The closing ferocious scene of the book takes place in Hightower's house, Hightower having done what he could to prevent it.

So the humiliation of the once gallant South is represented in sexual terms; the Negro's strength is perpetually before their eyes to remind them of their loss. All novels of the South (save *Gone with the Wind!*) must be lynching novels, like this: only so can the South enjoy a triumph; and the triumph must be not the killing but the emasculation of the Negro.

*N.B.* Christmas's paramour and victim was not a Southern white woman, but a Yankee. Even Faulkner could not bear to make her a Southerner.

*N.B.* There is something very adolescent about W. F.'s preoccupation with the sexual life of his characters: Balzac must tell the financial status of each of his characters; W. F. must tell how his spend their nights—and particularly adolescent in the recurrent necessity to inquire how they *first* know sex.

ST. AUGUSTINE, [FLA.,] MAY 2, 1940. On Faulkner's *The Hamlet.*

The tribe of the unscrupulous Snopeses gradually move in on a farm community and like locusts gradually possess the land; at the end of the book, having risen to power in Frenchman's Bend, they move on toward the larger town of Jefferson.

Everywhere the admiration for low cunning; more than that, the author's admiration for anything—unqualifiedly—that succeeds. The Snopeses gain their first foothold merely by terrifying the community with the report that they are barn-burners. W. F. is thinking of Hitler, but the larger demonstration seeps away in his more detailed illustration, and it is best that it does. W. F.'s admiration of virility has been absorbed into an admiration for "getting on."

Ratliff, the one admirable character, an itinerant sewing-machine peddler, watches, comments, reflects. He even does some kind deeds—incredible ones: his taking into his sister's home the wife and children of a Snopes who has been murdered, the wife being a former lumber-camp prostitute; his restoring from his own pocket five dollars which a Snopes had tricked from a farmer's wife. But at the end of the book, W. F. turns on Ratliff, too, and shows him greedily digging for buried treasure (yet "Have I come to this?"), and shows him gulled by a Snopes.

This same motif we saw in *Light in August*. Though W. F. can surround the man of reflection with a temporary wistful prestige, in the end he must be immolated before some agent of force or cunning. Again the South's thin blood must prostrate itself in envy and admiration before any expression of action, however base.

But what curious reflection these men of reflection have: elliptical, wry, sarcastic, wrapped up in a super-subtle tangled syntax—W. F.'s fancy overwriting.

Devious—so is the method whereby even the facts of the narrative are communicated to the reader. In one passage we pass from the thoughts of a man being murdered to those of his murderer without transition. The *he* must serve both; the reader must return and reread a page and a half to disentangle the event. Surely this practice of indirection is related to W. F.'s insecurity in his emotional relation to his characters: he admires his "bad" characters but dare not avow it, and one small part of his mind despises them; he despises his "good" characters, yet wishes he could admire them.

The real immaturity in an author is the transparency with which he betrays this approval or disapproval of his characters—doubly immature when the approvals and disapprovals are thus mixed and impure—not because all ethical judgment is difficult, but because the author's emotional nature is at war with itself.

This is W.F.'s sentimentality: not only the uprush of emotional identification with the act of violence or guile, but the "messing up" of its statement, so that the admiration merely shows "around the corner"—as he thinks—but all the more overtly.

HAMDEN, [CT.,] NOVEMBER 6, 1949. Faulkner's *Absalom, Absalom!*

Cleanth Brooks having told me this is the best of Faulkner's, I have bought it and read it for the first time.

Written in quivering emotion and recounted, by refraction, by a series of narrators, all of them—except Quentin's father—in a state of quivering emotions, the book runs the risk momently of collapsing into ignominious absurdity. "Outrage" and "outraged" are the motif-words of the book and the author himself seems to be in a state of staggered outrage: that this vast iniquity had taken place in the land (the land whose other possession was the highest conceivable adherence to honor and pride and chivalry), and that the consequences of the iniquity were like the ancient concept of fate and retribution.

It has then the character of an "epic," the role of the supernatural being played by this operative doom. And the incongruity that ultimately saps its power is that we are all too aware that the author by reason of his state of quivering and outraged emotion is not capable of viewing the evils with that wide and removed view which alone can compass the actions of gods and man. It is as though we were hearing the fall of the House of Atreus told by a voice that was feverish and shrill, scandal-mongering-nosey, and a little prurient.

Just as *Light in August* trembled with anticipated horror and ecstasy toward the castration of a Negro, so *Absalom, Absalom!* does a frenetic dance about a finally impeded incestuous coupling of a white girl and her partially Negro half-brother—having previously fainted with outrage at three miscegenations: Thomas Sutpen and the mother of Clytemnestra (*sic!*) Sutpen; Thomas Sutpen and his first wife and Charles Bon and his New Orleans mistress.

The incongruity (the agitated narrator and the vast subject) betrays the author into grandiloquence. It would be rash to say, without having reread the others, that it is Faulkner's most grandiloquent book. This dizzying rhetoric rises to its most fantastic pitch when it approaches the subject of sex. . . . The one thing an author is not allowed is to look at the tragic background of life and the constitution of human nature for evil and absence of spirit *with surprise,* for surprise denotes that he is newly come from a conviction that it was otherwise. It is in this sense that Faulkner and the South are unequipped for tragic matter. They were first surprised to discover that they *were* guilty, and with that comes the green adolescent surprise that the human race can be indicted for guilt. It is surprise, therefore, that takes pleasure—the wrong kind of pleasure—in contemplating violence and lust. It is at once consolation and absolution to cry out in horror, to say nothing of a sort of relish in the abasement.

But this is a notable book. It marches to the terrific climax of its closing lines:

". . . Why do you hate the South?"

"I don't hate it," . . . *I don't hate it,* he thought . . . *I don't. I don't!* . . . *I don't hate it!*

The large articulated machinery of the plot does illustrate the motif that the institution of slavery set in motion its own retribution. The last lines are preceded by another theme, stated as though it were a baleful prophecy, that the descendants of miscegenation will gradually cover the country, and "conquer the Western hemisphere"—presumably as semi-idiots, like Jim Bond. That such descendants are assumed to be idiots or incapables is the Southerner's assumption. There is a sneer at George Washington Carver in the book.

CAROLINE GORDON

# "Mr. Faulkner's Southern Saga"

From *New York Times Book Review*, May 5, 1946, Section 7, pages 1, 45.

Copyright © Caroline Gordon.

Williiam Faulkner, alone among contemporary novelists, it seems to me, has the distinguishing mark of the major novelist: the ability to create a variety of characters. He is also a poet, or, as the Germans put it, a *dichter*. It is Malcolm Cowley's distinction to have presented in his preface to *The Portable Faulkner*, the first comprehensive survey of Mr. Faulkner's work that takes into account his symbolism. In 1939, a young Southern writer, Marion O'Donnell, published in the *Kenyon Review* an essay in which he traced in great detail an allegorical scheme in Mr. Faulkner's work. In his view, the Snopes, hillbillies who have moved in to town from the piney-woods section and have become horse traders, ginners, merchants, and finally bankers, represent the forces of corruption at work within the South.

The Sartoris, Millard, Compson, and other families stand for the old order. Their powerlessness to avert disaster, partly through the combination of circumstances and partly through their own weaknesses, is best symbolized by Colonel Sartoris, who, coming back from the Civil War with a citation of bravery at the hand of General Lee, turns politician and degenerates into such a forensic old windbag that his son, Bayard, finds himself unwilling to avenge his death. So far as I know, these two critics are the only ones who have read Mr. Faulkner's work in the way I think he wants to be read: seeing in it not a series of novels with sociological implications, but a saga, a legend that is still in the making.

"I call it a legend," Mr. Cowley says, "because it is obviously no more intended as an historical account of the country south of the Ohio than *The Scarlett Letter* was intended as a history of Massachusetts or *Paradise Lost* as a factual account of the Fall."

Mr. Cowley thinks of Mr. Faulkner as an epic poet or a bardic writer in prose, whose books form a number of interconnecting cycles. "Just as Balzac, who seems to have inspired the series, divides his 'Comedic Humaine' into Scenes of Parisian Life, Scenes of Provincial Life, Scenes of Private Life, so Faulkner might divide his work into a number of cycles—one about the planters and their descendants, one about the townspeople of Jefferson, one about the poor whites, one about the Indians (consisting of stories already written but never brought together), and one about the Negroes." The whole, according to Mr. Cowley, forms a record of the adventures of people who live in a mythical kingdom which Mr. Faulkner himself calls "Yoknapatawpha County" ("William Faulkner, sole owner and proprietor") and all the books in the saga are parts of the same living pattern.

It is this pattern and not the printed volumes in which part of it is recorded, that is Faulkner's real achievement. Its existence helps to explain one feature of his work: that each novel, each long or short story, seems to reveal more than it states explicitly and to have a subject bigger than itself. All the separate works are like blocks of marble from the same quarry, they show the same veins and faults of the mother rock. Or else—to use a rather strained figure—they are like wooden planks that were cut, not from a log but from a still living tree. The planks are planed and chiseled into their final shapes, but the tree itself heals over the wound and continues to grow.

William Faulkner was born at New Albany, Miss., on Sept. 25, 1897. His family soon removed—as one of his own characters might put it—to the county seat, Oxford, where William, the oldest of four brothers, attended the public schools, but without graduating from high school. He served in the Royal Flying Corps during the First World War and returned to Oxford to become a student at the University of Mississippi, since veterans could then matriculate without a high school diploma. Mr. Cowley records that he "neglected his class work and left without taking a degree. He has less of a formal education than any other good writer of his time," Mr. Cowley adds, "except Hart Crane—less even than Hemingway, who never went to college, but who learned to speak three foreign languages and studied writing in Paris under the best masters. Faulkner taught himself, largely, he says, by 'undirected and uncorrelated reading.'"

Mr. Faulkner's first novel, *Soldiers' Pay*, which reflected to some extent his experience as a flier, was published in 1926. It was followed by *Mosquitoes*, a satire on artistic life in New Orleans, which shows little promise of what is to come. In 1929, he published *Sartoris*, a novel of uneven merit, in which members of the Sartoris family, who will figure in later books, appear. It was followed by fifteen other books in which the same characters appear, disappear, and reappear in ever widening circles. Of them all, *Sanctuary* is the only one that received wide distribution. In 1945, Faulkner's seventeen books were out of print, some of them unobtainable in second-hand book stores.

One of the masters whom Faulkner evidently studied in his "undirected and uncorrelated reading" is Flaubert. He handles details with Flaubertian precision. It is perhaps no accident that the American writer achieved his first fame in the same way that the great French writer did, through the public's appetite for erotic detail and, in Mr. Faulkner's case, through the Eastern critics' desire for examples of Southern degeneracy. Mr. Cowley thinks that the story of Temple Drake and Popeye has more meaning than appears on a hasty first reading—"the only reading that more critics have been willing to give it." "Popeye," he says, "is one of several characters in Faulkner's novels who represent the mechanical civilization that has invaded and conquered the South. *Sanctuary* is not a connected allegory, as one critic explained it, but neither is it an accumulation of pointless horrors. It is an example of the Freudian nightmare turned backwards, being full of sexual nightmares that are, in reality, social symbols."

Mr. Cowley has made his selection for *The Portable Faulkner* with a view to giving a general panorama of life in the mythical Yoknapatawpha County, "decade by decade, from the days when the early settlers first rode northward along the Natchez Trace." There are no complete novels but there are two stories of almost novel length:

"The Bear," in my opinion as good a story as has been written by any American—and "Spotted Horses." Among the notable shorter pieces are: "Percy Grimm," the story of a man who asked only to live and die uniformed and regimented—"I created a Nazi before I ever heard of Hitler," Faulkner says of him, "Red Leaves," the story of a Negro slave of a Chickasaw chief who tried to escape being sacrificed on his master's grave, and "Was," which exhibits a brand of frontier humor reminiscent of Mark Twain.

The selections from the novels, the section from *The Wild Palms* called "Old Man," and the chapter entitled "A Wedding in the Rain" from *Absalom, Absalom!* are complete in themselves yet they retain what Mr. Cowley calls "the unity of the Faulkner legend." But the reader who makes Mr. Faulkner's acquaintance only in *The Portable* will hardly be aware of the full scope of his talent, for he will not have had an opportunity to observe the brooding intensity with which, in the full-length, moving backward and forward in time, he hovers over a theme—presenting the experiences of the characters from every conceivable angle, as a man in a lifetime of recollection might suck the marrow out of some event of his youth.

He will also not have had a chance to discover Mr. Faulkner's worst faults: an obscurity that comes partly from over-ambition and partly from succumbing to his own rhetoric, and an occasional weakness of structure. *Absalom, Absalom!* the story of Thomas Sutpen, the mountain boy, who being sent to the back door of a Tidewater mansion by a Negro servant resolved to acquire a mansion as large as the one he had been denied entrance to, with its concomitant land and slaves, has perhaps the strongest, most coherent structure; but *As I Lay Dying* seems to me the most perfect in proportion, presenting in a many-faceted design the lives of all the members of the Bundren family.

Mr. Faulkner's stories, as Mr. Cowley says, have "the quality of being lived, absorbed, remembered, rather than observed." It is, indeed, as if the author had squatted among the blue jeans that ring a Southern court house on Saturday afternoons and regarded natural objects long enough for them to take on other than their pristine shapes. One of Flem Snopes's wild calico ponies rushes past. The man leaping to catch it realizes, as if for the first time in his life, how long a horse's head is and, as the butt of his pistol hammers its nose, how hard the skull is.

The saw which Addie Bundren's son, Cash, uses to saw the planks of her coffin buzzes as insistently as the lathe which Binet kept turning in the courtyard when Emma Bovary, clutching Rodolphe's letter in her hand, looks down and sees the pavement rushing up to meet her. A little boy totes a monstrous catfish home and, cleaning it, finds it "as full of blood and guts as a hog." A log, rearing up suddenly out of a swollen current, confounds the men who are trying to carry a coffin across the river.

The solidity and immediacy of such details stand Mr. Faulkner in good stead when he will suddenly expand some image so that it seems to take in the whole of life. The saw, rasping on through scene after scene, of *As I Lay Dying* becomes a symbol of the discords of human life. The fish, "bleeding quietly in a pan," reveals to the boy what he could not have guessed from his elders' whispered comments: the fact that mortals must die. The log, rearing up, assumes in the eyes of the dazed and thwarted men such supernatural proportions that for an instant it stands "upon that surging and heaving desolation like Christ."

The Faulkner characters, like his incidents, stand for more than themselves. It is no accident that he continually uses words like "grave, absent, bemused" to describe them. They move rapt in the contemplation of their individual fates. At some time—early, like Thomas Sutpen, or late, like Joe Christmas—they leave everything else and go to meet it.

He has another characteristic which often marks the major novelist: compassion for all created beings. This compassion sometimes has subliminal objects. "The Long Summer" portrays the love of an idiot boy for a cow. The story, in spite of its Gothic language, is classical in feeling. The cow grazes, Io-like through windy leaves. He weaves a chaplet of flowers for her brow; and, when she is taken from him, squats, holding the crudely carved, wooden cow that has been given him for a toy, moaning. Mr. Faulkner is as tender toward man raising himself from all fours as when he walks up right.

The American author whom Mr. Faulkner most resembles is Hawthorne, in Mr. Cowley's view. "They stand to each other as July to December, as heat to cold, as swamp to mountain." And Hawthorne, he points out, had much the same attitude toward New England as Mr. Faulkner has for the South. ("New England is quite as large a lump of earth as my heart can really take in.")

As Mr. Cowley expresses it: "Like Faulkner in the South, he applied himself to creating its moral fables and elaborating its legends, which existed, as it were, in his solitary heart. Pacing the hillside behind his house in Concord, he listened for a voice: you might say he lay in wait for it, passively but expectantly, like a hunter behind a rock, then, when it had spoken he transcribed its words—more slowly and carefully than Faulkner, it is true, with more form and less fire, but with the same essential fidelity."

It is this fidelity to a voice, a voice which speaks of more than human endeavor, that makes the similarity between the two writers, I think. Mr. Faulkner's characters, like Hawthorne's, seem emanations from the land. It is fortunate for Mr. Faulkner's genius that he was born in northern Mississippi, a land he describes in *As I Lay Dying* as a country "where everything hangs on too long. Like our rivers, our land: opaque, slow, violent, shaking and creating the life of man in its implacable and brooding image."

No land less implacable and brooding could have given him his spiritual geography. As Hawthorne's imagination was colored by the dark, narrow houses on the somber streets of Salem, so is Mr. Faulkner's as tuned to the savage springs, the even more savage droughts of the upper Delta. He writes like a man who so loves his land that he is fearful for the well-being of every creature that springs from it.

# "The Private World of William Faulkner"

From '48, 2 (May 1948), 83–84, 90–94. Copyright © Roark Bradford.

William Faulkner is a Southern Democrat, a literary figure, and a legend. It is as difficult to disassociate him from his home town of Oxford, Mississippi, as it is to fix him and his work in time. There is Faulkner and there is Oxford. It is yesterday and tomorrow; it is before the Civil War and a hundred years hence; it is always now, with the Sartoris family and their friends struggling with the ramifications of genealogy and land titles and what to do when the fox gets a man down wind.

Some of the more serious appraisers of literary figures have called William Faulkner the second milestone in the development of American letters—Mark Twain being the first to emerge from the cross currents that became American culture. They point out that while Twain caught the bumptious humor of America's energetic growth, Faulkner is catching the unsubstantial threads of its tragic disintegration.

The Faulkner legend is the inevitable outcome of Faulkner's aversion to personal exploitation. "Because I write," he says, "doesn't make what I eat for breakfast or think of the international situation a matter of news or public concern." He thinks present methods of advertising—"selling something you haven't got to someone who doesn't want it"—are obscene. "I don't hold with bad manners, under any circumstances," he says. Faulkner never discusses for publication either himself or his work, and he never reads criticism of his books.

And so, the boys in the newsrooms have set to work unhampered by facts.

He is a Southern Democrat, which merely means that he is an individualist. He is not what is called a rugged individualist, although Bill Faulkner can be rugged enough when the occasion arises. His individuality, both in his life and in his writing, requires no adjective. It is part of his breeding, background, and nature.

The spirit of individuality asserted itself publicly early in Faulkner's career. Like so many other Southern boys who wanted to do things, it was necessary for Bill to support himself while he struggled through his apprenticeship. He got the job of postmaster at the University of Mississippi post office, but his duties began to interfere with his writing. His letter of resignation to the Postmaster General is one of the brighter items on file in Washington.

"As long as I live under the capitalistic system," he wrote, "I expect to have my life influenced by the demands of moneyed people. But I will be damned if I propose to be at the beck and call of every itinerant scoundrel who has two cents to invest in a postage stamp. This, sir, is my resignation."

Being averse to publicity does not make Faulkner a freak or an eccentric. You have to understand Oxford and Faulkner together and that each is a part of the other to appreciate why Faulkner refuses to be publicized.

He lives in a big white house on the edge of Oxford with his wife and his teenage daughter. The house is set in thirty-five acres of ground. There are dogs, horses, cows, hogs, and cats. There are Negroes, ranging in age and importance from Uncle Ned, who was personal attendant to Bill's grandfather and father, to Pom, who functions as houseboy when not in school. Uncle Ned rules the whole complex life of the farm. Every living creature on the place, human and brute, falls into the spirit of whatever project he plans.

There are lots of dogs around—blooded pointers, fine Dalmatian, a dachshund, and a few feists which once wandered up, made friends with Uncle Ned, and become a permanent part of the establishment. There is a fine Persian cat and a short-haired cat that dropped in one day and took up residence. There is also daughter Jill's pet saddle horse.

Recently, Uncle Ned decided to school a couple of half-breed hound dogs in trailing possums. The old man had managed a trade for a possum. He penned him up in the barn. When the air got right, the possum would be set free and the half-hounds taught to trail it.

"One morning, just before daylight," Bill related, "the household was awakened by the damnedest ruckus you ever heard. I slipped on my robe and ran out to see what the trouble was. The possum had broken out of the cage and tried to escape. But he didn't get more than a couple of hundred yards before he had to take to a tree.

"When I got there, every dog on the place, the two cats, and Jill's horse had formed a circle around that possum, holding him up the tree. The dogs were yipping fit to wake the dead. The two cats were yowling as loud as they could, and the horse was glaring defiantly at the possum. Pretty soon, Uncle Ned came, fussed at the dogs and cats, and put the possum back in his cage."

I liked the picture of all the animals entering into the spirit of Uncle Ned's scheme, although I knew that only dogs with hound blood would, instinctively, trail a possum. Possibly the other dogs would follow for the mere excitement of a chase. The cats, I figured, were added by Bill just to round out the picture, and the horse—"Do you mean," I said, with what I considered a sly sarcasm, "that the horse wasn't whinnying?"

"Of course not," Bill answered. "It just isn't in the nature of a horse to whinny when he trees a possum."

Oxford is different from many other small Southern towns. Like some of them, it is situated in the heart of poor, hillside farming country and is surrounded by poor people, black and white, whose lives are made bleak by the constant struggle for a livelihood. Yet, Oxford is the site of the University of Mississippi, an institution that has built a fine tradition of culture. The State of Mississippi has allocated to its other colleges the duties of teaching the technical trades that have swamped most centers of learning, and has kept "Ole Miss" remarkably free from the trade-school brand of education. In turn, the university has created a kind of erudite dignity which rises above the blatant, scheming, angle-figuring self-aggrandizement by which aggressive people are seeking life's fulfillment. This influence has been felt in the town and surrounding country, and the effect of it on the unlettered poor whites often produces strange phenomena.

Discussing politics with me, a farmer once told me proudly: "Old Bilbo lived long enough to fix that fellow Taft's clock, when he said Taft was like a baby mawkin' bird, all mouth and no bird! 'Y God. Pericles might'a said hit purtier, but he couldn't 'a said hit no truer!"

Only a character from a Faulkner tale or a Faulkner world could, believably and logically, speak of Pericles and Bilbo in the same sentence. Perhaps it is the impact of these two extremes of culture, unsoftened by an appreciable middle ground, that gives Faulkner his feeling for the tragic, and for the grisly humor with which he relieves it. It is not, however, that time stands still either for Faulkner or for the university; both exist in the timelessness of the arts. Each has something to give in the way of beauty, and neither will be distracted by current fads.

But press agents must work. A man who writes novels that astound and startle, and frequently confuse, ought to be Grade-A copy. Yet, Faulkner puts out no copy. The result is that a rumor grows into a story, a fact quickly expands into a legend.

Among these legends that have grown up about Faulkner is the one that he is a prodigious drunk. Like most Southerners, Bill likes an occasional drink of good whisky. Probably during his fifty-odd years he has lost a couple of weekends, now and then. Now, in a morality of calomel, corn whisky, and the Old Time Religion, Bill is not considered a heavy drinker. Yet, most of the yarns that have grown up about him have to do with Herculean binges.

One tale that is fairly indicative of the crop concerns Faulkner's first experience as a Hollywood writer. He was one of the first big names to be employed in the movie capital, and the moguls wanted to do the thing up right. They selected Nunnally Johnson, who is both a writer and a Southerner, to be the link between moviedom and this strange wild man who wrote about idiots, folks getting raped with corncobs, and people having their coffins built as they lay dying.

Johnson decided that the way to handle Faulkner was to overwhelm him with Hollywood grandeur and with the czar-like importance of an executive. To this end, he took the biggest and most elaborate office in the studio. The room was a hundred feet long, with three levels of floor. On entering, one had to walk the full length of the room, through long-napped green carpet, then descend two flights of marble steps to arrive eventually before the broadest and shiniest desk in Southern California. It was calculated to be both impressive and disconcerting.

Promptly on schedule, Faulkner entered, and Johnson immediately began handling telephones, papers, and push buttons. Faulkner walked through the carpet nap and down the steps, slowly, casually, like a man who had a heap of walking to do and was in no particular hurry to get it done. At the desk he removed his hat and held it in his left hand.

"Are you Mr. Johnson?" he asked.

"I am. Are you Mr. Faulkner?"

"I am."

There was an awkward silence. During this silence, Faulkner fished into his hip pocket, took out a pint of whisky, and began uncorking it. This act was complicated by the fact that the bottle had been sealed with heavy tinfoil. Bill dropped his hat on the floor and went to work with both hands. In the process, he cut his finger on the tinfoil. He attempted to staunch the flow of blood by wetting the wound with his tongue, but it was too deep a cut for that. Next, he looked around for a suitable drip pan. The only thing in view was the hat at his feet. Holding the bleeding finger over the hat, he continued to work, methodically and silently, until the bottle was finally uncorked. He then tilted it, drank half its contents, and passed it to Johnson.

"Have a drink of whisky?" he offered.

"I don't mind if I do," said Johnson, finishing off the pint.

This, according to the legend, was the beginning of a drunk which ended three weeks later, when studio sleuths found both Faulkner and Johnson in an Okie camp, sobered them up, and got them to work.

I for one have made no effort to verify this story; I am not a man to spoil a good tale with statistics. One Faulkner story, however, I did spoil. It was not a very good story, but it had had wide circulation. It is also about Faulkner's first Hollywood writing experience:

After a couple of weeks, according to this story, Faulkner felt ill at ease in his work. He suggested to his boss that he be allowed to do his writing at home. The boss, having visions of Faulkner in a hotel room banging away at his typewriter, said that would be all right. When they next heard from Faulkner he was in Oxford, Mississippi, two thousand miles from Hollywood. He had gone home to complete the assignment.

"I have heard that one," Bill said. "And since they told it, themselves, I don't suppose the truth will do anybody damage. Here are the facts:

"I was working with the brother-in-law of the head of the studio, and we were pretty friendly. But as soon as I had as much money as I wanted, I decided to quit. My friend urged me to remain until I had a lot of money.

"'I've got more money than anybody in Mississippi, now,' I told him. 'I won't ever need any more, I reckon.'

"'If you ever do,' said my friend, 'just let me know, and I'll get you back on the payroll.'

"I came home and went to work on my novel. But I had a few debts to settle, and what with one thing and another, my money began to run short. So I wrote to my friend to get me another job in Hollywood. This was late in November. The first week in December, I got a check from this man's brother—my regular salary, less 10 percent. This brother had just finished at Yale, and wasn't able to swing onto anything out there, so I suppose the family had set him up as an agent. Anyway, the checks came in every week, and I cashed them. This went on until about June, when they assigned me to work with Tod Browning. When I finished that assignment, I went off the payroll. And that," grinned Bill, "is the true story of how I worked in Oxford, Mississippi, for Hollywood."

Bill's younger brother, John, author of *Men Working* and *Dollar Cotton*, has probably contributed to the Faulkner legend.

"Old Bill," said John, "just naturally hates to see anybody make a fool of himself. After Bill had been writing a long time and nobody was paying much attention to him, he wrote *Sanctuary* and suddenly got famous all over the country. The editor of a big magazine decided maybe some of the stories he had refused might be a little better than he had thought, now that Bill was famous. So he came down to take another look.

"Bill was hospitable, but he wasn't interested in selling him the stories that had already been turned down. But word got around that a big magazine editor was in town, and everybody else had something they wanted to sell. Among these was a lady from the university who had a thesis. She got her thesis and a bottle of whisky and lured the editor out to the back porch. She'd give him a drink with one hand and try to sell him the thesis with the other.

"Well, sir, when old Bill walked out and saw what was going on, it made him so disgusted he just naturally took off his shoes and went to El Paso, Texas."

There is a sureness, an unswerving certainty, in Faulkner. He sees the play and he calls it exactly as he sees it. There is no false modesty, nor is there the slightest taint of egotism. What people think of him isn't important; what he thinks of other people is important. "It will be another fifty or a hundred years before my novels are enjoyed and appreciated," he said. "Right now, it is considered sissified and unmanly for folks to love the arts. That is because, at first, the men had to work all the time, and only the women had any time to take up artistic appreciation. That isn't necessary now, but the men had rather pretend they think art is unmanly than take the trouble to acquire an appreciation for it."

From the course which his most widely read novel, *Sanctuary*, followed, this view seems justified. *Sanctuary* catapulted him from obscurity into fame and notoriety, although it followed *The Sound and the Fury* and *As I Lay Dying*, both of which are rated as greater novels. Most American readers instantly associate the name of William Faulkner with the corncob episode in *Sanctuary*, and remember him for that alone. Yet some of Faulkner's most beautiful, most soul-searching passages, as well as some of his most ribald drollery, are contained in this novel. Feminine taste in the arts, it would seem, prefers a violently unusual form of vicarious rape to penetrating insight into tortured souls.

The younger psychologists are beginning to take up Faulkner's characters for study; but almost invariably they put them down again.

Their Messiahs, it seems, did not attempt a system which included the complicated mental make-up of the worn-out generations from Faulknerland. In another fifty or hundred years, perhaps, the psychologists will drop their Freud, Jung, or Adler systems and try to get at an understanding of how Pa Bundren, or *As I Lay Dying*, and a stinker to the ground, could be so shiftless in all things and at the same time so logically tenacious in getting his wife's body back to Jefferson.

In the meantime, Faulkner has novels to write, and he must keep at it. At the time of my visit, he had been working three years on his latest novel, and had completed five hundred pages of it. It will be a fable based on the interval between the Crucifixion and the Resurrection. A hundred years ago, or a hundred years hence, Pericles or Bilbo, a Sartoris or an Armstid, a Harvard graduate or a babbling Benjy, will all dovetail logically and beautifully into the Faulkner pattern.

VLADIMIR NABOKOV

# Letter to Edmund Wilson

November 21, 1948. Letter by Vladimir Nabokov from *Dear Bunny, Dear Volodya.*
Copyright © 1979, 2001 by the Estate of Vladimir Nabokov, used by permission
of The Wylie Agency LLC.

Dear Bunny,

I have carefully read Faulkner's *Light in August*, which you so kindly sent me, and it has in no way altered the low (to put it mildly) opinion I have of his work and other (innumerable) books in the same strain. I detest these puffs of stale romanticism, coming all the way up from Marlinsky and V. Hugo—you remember the latter's horrible combination of starkness and hyperbole—*l'homme regardait le gibet, le gibet regardait l'homme* [the man was looking at the gallows, the gallows was looking at the man]. Faulkner's belated romanticism and quite impossible biblical rumblings and "starkness" (which is not starkness at all but skeletonized triteness), and all the rest of the bombast seem to me so offensive that I can only explain his popularity in France by the fact that all her own popular mediocre writers (Malraux included) of recent years have also had their fling at *l'homme marchait, la nuit était sombre* [the man was walking, the night was dark]. The book you sent me is one of the tritest and most tedious examples of a trite and tedious genre. The plot and those extravagant "deep" conversations affect me as bad as movies do, or the worst plays and stories of Leonid Andreyev, with whom Faulkner has a kind of fatal affinity. I imagine that this kind of thing (white trash, velvety Negroes, those bloodhounds out of *Uncle Tom's Cabin* melodramas, steadily baying through thousands of swampy books) may be necessary in a social sense, but it is not literature, just as the thousands of stories and novels about downtrodden peasants and fierce *ispravniki* in Russia, or mystical adventures within the *narod* (1850–1880), although socially effective and ethically admirable, were not literature. I simply cannot believe that you, with all your knowledge and taste, are not made to squirm by such things as the dialogues between the "positive" characters in Faulkner (and especially those absolutely ghastly italics). Do you not see that despite the difference in landscape, etc., it is essentially Jean Valjean stealing the candlesticks from the good man of God all over again? The villain is definitely Byronic. The book's pseudo-religious rhythm I simply cannot stand—a phony gloom which also spoils Mauriac's work. Has *la grace* descended upon Mr. Faulkner too? Maybe you are just pulling my leg when you advise me to read him, or impotent Henry James, or the Rev. Eliot?

Sincerely yours,
Vladimir Nabokov

# "A Man of the South"

From *Mississippi Quarterly* 42 (Fall 1989): 355–57. [Originally published in French in *France-Etats-Unis* in December 1950.] Copyright © 1950 by Richard Wright. Reprinted by permission of John Hawkins & Associates, Inc., and the Estate of Richard Wright.

There was a time when Americans living abroad were ashamed of William Faulkner. Fiercely intent in presenting their country as the "most perfect democracy on earth," they believed that Faulkner's realistic and surprising descriptions were a betrayal, that the degradation he depicted so compellingly constituted a real lack of loyalty to the greatness and power of the American Republic.

Many naïve and self-conscious Americans had a hard time in the company of the French who praised Faulkner to the skies; those Americans could not help feeling that the French, whose subtlety is well known, were purely and simply making fun of them and found there a means of criticizing the United States. In fact, many one hundred percent Americans declared bluntly, "Faulkner does not represent us" or "Why does he consistently focus on pure degeneracy?"

It has taken a long time for Americans, suddenly confronted with the paramount reputation of Faulkner in Europe, to separate the astonishing genius of that man from the teeming jungle he was creating in one novel after another.

Only through reasoning were many Americans able to discover that Faulkner's greatness resided precisely in his power to transpose the American scene as it exists in the southern states, filter it through his sensibilities and finally define it with words.

Just as Poe's greatness had to be established by way of France into the American consciousness, it may be likewise with Faulkner whose greatness reverberates towards the shores of America.

A Frenchman remarked one day that American writers wrote in the same fashion as artists paint; in other words, that American literature was lacking in ideas and perspectives. Such an attack may be founded but there is in Faulkner's work an element that reminds one often of the painter more than the writer *per se*; and that is the purity of the artistic intention. I doubt seriously if Faulkner has ever written one line of what could be called propaganda. In fact I doubt if he would even know how. Simply to represent, in terms of form, color, movement, light, mood, and atmosphere has been the most notable hallmark of every Faulkner book from *Sartoris* to *Intruder in the Dust*.

The achievement of Faulkner is all the more arresting in that he is a southern white man, the product of a section of America which has withstood and nursed the stings of a Civil War defeat which it could never accept, and misinterpreted that defeat in the most infantile and emotional manner. The literature of the white South, as well as its public life, has been for almost a century under pressure as intense and cruel as that under which the Negro was forced to live; and it would be a grave mistake to feel that the Negro was the only victim of the white South's proud neurosis. The almost atavistic clinging to the "aristocracy of the skin," the reduction of all life's values to the protection of "white supremacy," crippled not only the Negro but the entire culture of the whites themselves. That is why there was never a symphony orchestra in the South until 1928; the tardy development of the social sciences in America can be traced to the South's abysmal fear of all facts relating to human relationships; and it was from the background of the fears of the South that sprang the fantastic behavior of the southern senators in the nation's capitol.

In the realm of artistic expression, the pressure to ensure conformity was almost as fierce as that which Russian Communists bring to bear upon their artists. Southern American art fell under the interdiction of "protecting the South's reputation," and no man save the hardiest dared challenge this standard. Talented and sensitive southerners fled the section, and those who remained brooded and accepted a scale of values which killed their souls.

But the South could not remain isolated forever; wars and convulsions of social change were bound to engulf it; industrialization induced such impersonal social relations that controls loosened and allowed a certain degree of negative freedom, and it was in this transition period of confusion that the genius of Faulkner leaped through and presented itself to a startled world.

The main burden of Faulkner's work is moral confusion and social decay and it presents these themes in terms of stories of violence enacted by fantastic characters. If Popeye, of *Sanctuary*, seems unreal and mechanical, it is because Faulkner cast him into a symbol of the rising tide of the soulless and industrial men who are beginning to swarm over the southern scene. If Joe Christmas, of *Light in August*, seems like a villain beyond redemption, it is because Joe Christmas represents the violence of the southern Negro reacting against social pressures too strong for him. And if other Faulkner characters exert frenzied efforts that lead to no end, as of the characters in *As I Lay Dying, Absalom, Absalom!*, and *The Unvanquished*, it is because so much of the South's energies, both of the blacks and whites, is spent fighting ghosts.

But, like all great art, the work of Faulkner cannot be restricted to merely the South when one attempts to unravel its implications. Southern American fear is no basically different from fear anywhere; and the obsessive compulsion to violence of the South obtains wherever men are men. Through that dialectical leap in meaning which art possesses, Faulkner, in showing the degradation of the South, affirmed its essential humanity for America and for the world. Happily, a Bilbo's hate-charged racist utterances will be forgotten, but Faulkner's gallery of characters will live as long as men feel the need to know themselves, as long as confused souls, needing repose and reflection, repair to books which form a reservoir of a nation's emotional experiences.

It was fitting that a recognition of Faulkner's labors should have been crowned with the Nobel Prize for Literature for 1950.

November 28, 1950

# "William Faulkner: The Novel as Form"

From *The Harvard Advocate* 135 (November 1951): 13, 24–26. Reprinted by permission of the Estate of Conrad Aiken and Joseph I. Killorin.

The famous remark made to Macauley—"Young man, the more I consider the less I can conceive where you picked up that style"—might with advantage have been saved for Mr. William Faulkner. For if one thing is more outstanding than another about Mr. Faulkner—some readers find it so outstanding, indeed, that they never get beyond it—it is the uncompromising and almost hypnotic zeal with which he insists upon having a style, and, especially of late, the very peculiar style which he insists *when he remembers*—he can write straightforwardly enough when he wants to; he does so often enough in the best of his short stories (and they are brilliant) often enough, too, in the novels. But that *style* is what he really wants to get back to; and get back to it he invariably does.

And what a style it is, to be sure! The exuberant and tropical luxuriance of sound which Jim Europe's jazz band used to exhale, like a jungle of rank creepers and ferocious blooms taking shape before one's eyes,—magnificently and endlessly intervolved, glisteningly and ophidianly in motion, coil sliding over coil, and leaf and flower forever magically interchanging,—was scarcely more bewildering in its sheer inexhaustible fecundity, than Mr. Faulkner's style. Small wonder if even the most passionate of Mr. Faulkner's admirers—among whom the present writer honors himself by enlisting—must find, with each new novel that the first fifty pages are always the hardest, that each time one must learn all over again *how* to read this strangely fluid and slippery and heavily mannered prose, and that one is even, like a kind of Laocoon, sometimes tempted to give it up.

Wrestle, for example, with two very short (for Mr. Faulkner!) sentences taken from an early page of *Absalom, Absalom!*: "Meanwhile, as though in inverse ratio to the vanishing voice, the invoked ghost of the man whom she could neither forgive nor revenge herself upon began to assume a quality almost of solidity, permanence. Itself circumambient and enclosed by its effluvium of hell, its aura of unregeneration, it mused (mused, thought, seemed to possess sentience as if, though dispossessed of the peace—who was impervious anyhow to fatigue—which she declined to give it, it was still irrevocably outside the scope of her hurt harm) with that quality even very attentive—the ogre-shape peaceful and now harmless and not even very attentive—the ogre-shape which, as Miss Coldfield's voice went on, resolved itself before Quentin's eyes the two half-ogre children, the three of them forming a shadowy background for the fourth one." Well, it may be reasonably questioned whether, on page thirteen of a novel, that little cordite bolus of suppressed references isn't a thumping aesthetic mistake. Returned to, when one has finished the book, it may be as simple as daylight: but encountered for the first time, and no matter how often reread, it guards its enigma with the stony impassivity of the Sphinx.

Or take again from the very first page of *The Wild Palms* this little specimen of "expositions": "Because he had been born here, on this coast though not in this house but in the other, the residence in the town, and had lived here all his life, including the four years as an intern in New Orleans where (a thick man even when young, with thick soft woman's hands, who should never have been a doctor at all, who even after six more of less metropolitan years looked out from a provincial and insulated amazement at his classmates and fellows: the lean young men swaggering in their drill jackets on which—to him—they wore the myriad anonymous faces of the probationer nurses with a ruthless and assured braggadocio like decorations, like flower trophies) he has sickened of it." What is one to say of that— or of a sentence only a little lower on the same page which runs for thirty-three lines? Is this, somehow perverted, the influence of the later Henry James—James the Old Pretender?

In short, Mr. Faulkner's style, though often brilliant and always interesting, is all too frequently downright bad; and it has inevitably offered an all-too-easy mark for the sharpshooting of such alert critics as Mr. Wyndham Lewis. But if it is easy enough to make fun of Mr. Faulkner's obsessions for particular words, or his indifference and violence to them, or the parrotlike mechanical mysticism (for it is really like a stammer) with which he will go on endlessly repeating such favorites as "myriad, sourceless, impalpable, outrageous, risible, profound," there is, nevertheless, something more to be said for his passion for overelaborate sentence structure.

Overelaborate they certainly are, baroque and involuted in the extreme, these sentences: trailing clauses, one after another, shadowily in apposition or perhaps not even with so much connection as that; parenthesis after parenthesis; the parenthesis itself containing one or more parentheses—they remind one of those brightly colored Chinese eggs of one's childhood, which when opened disclosed egg after egg, each smaller and subtler than the last. It is as if Mr. Faulkner, in a sort of hurried despair, has decided to try to tell us everything, every last origin or source or quality or qualification, and every possible future or permutation as well, in one terrifically concentrated effort: each sentence to be, as it were, a microcosm. And it must be admitted that the practice is annoying and distracting.

It is annoying, at the end of a sentence, to find that one does not know in the least what was the subject of the verb that dangles *in vacuo*—it is distracting to have to go back and sort out the meaning, track down the structure from clause to clause, then only to find that after all it doesn't much matter, and that the obscurity was perhaps neither subtle nor important. And to the extent that one *is* annoyed and distracted, and *does* thus go back and work it out, it may be at once added that Mr. Faulkner has defeated his own ends. One has had, of course, to emerge from the steam, and to step away from it, in order properly to see it; and as Mr. Faulkner works precisely by a process of *immersion* of hypnotizing his reader into *remaining immersed* in his stream this occasional blunder produces irritation and failure.

Nevertheless, despite the blunders, and despite the bad habits and the willful bad writing (and willful it obviously is), the style as a whole is extraordinarily effective; the reader *does* remain immersed, *wants* to remain immersed, and it is interesting to look into the reasons for this. And at once, if one considers these queer sentences not simply by themselves, as monsters of grammar or awkwardness, but in their relation to the book as a whole, one sees a functional reason and necessity for their being as they are. They parallel in a curious and perhaps inevitable way, and not without aesthetic justification, the whole elaborate method of *deliberately withheld meaning*, of progressive and partial and delayed disclosure, which so often gives the characteristic shape to the novels themselves. It is a persistent offering of obstacles, a calculated system of screens and obtrusions, of confusions and ambiguous interpolations and delays, with one express purpose; and that purpose is simply to keep the form—and the idea—fluid and unfinished, still in motion, as it were, and unknown, until the dropping into place of the very last syllable.

What Mr. Faulkner is after, in a sense, is a *continuum*. He wants a medium without stops or pauses, a medium which is always *of that moment*, and of which the passage from moment to moment is as fluid and detectable as in the life itself which he is purporting to give. It is all inside and underneath, or as seen from within and below; the reader must therefore be steadily *drawn in*; he must be powerfully and unremittingly hypnotized inward and downward to the image stream; and this suggests, perhaps a reason not only for the length and elaborateness of the sentence structure, but for the repetitiousness as well. The repetitiousness, and the steady iterative emphasis— like a kind of chanting or invocation—on certain relatively abstract words ("sonorous, latin, *vaguely* eloquent"), has the effect at least of producing, for Mr. Faulkner, a special language, a conglomeration of his own, which he uses with an astonishing virtuosity, and which, although in detailed analysis it may look shoddy, is actually for his purpose a life stream of almost miraculous adaptability. At the one extreme it is abstract, cerebral, time-and-space obsessed, tortured and twisted, but, nevertheless, always with a living *pulse* in it; and at the other it can be overwhelming in its simple vividness, its richness in the actual, as the flood scene in *The Wild Palms.*

Obviously, such a style, especially when allied with such a method, and such a *concern* for the reader, must make difficulties for the reader; and it must be admitted that Mr. Faulkner does little or nothing as a rule to make his highly complex "situation" easily available or perceptible. The reader must simply make up his mind to go to work, and in a sense to cooperate; his reward being that there *is* a situation to be given shape, a meaning to be extracted, and that half the fun is precisely in watching the queer, difficult, and often so laborious, evolution of Mr. Faulkner's idea. For, like the great predecessor whom at least in this regard he so oddly resembles, Mr. Faulkner could say with Henry James that it is practically impossible to make any real distinction between theme and form. What immoderately delights him, alike in *Sanctuary, The Sound and the Fury, As I Lay Dying, Light in August, Absalom, Absalom!,* and *The Wild Palms,* and what sets him above—shall we say it firmly—all his American contemporaries, is his continuous preoccupation with the novel *as form,* his passionate concern with it, and a degree of success with I which would clearly have commanded the interest and respect of Henry James himself. The novel as revelation, the novel as slice-of-life, the novel as mere story, do not interest him: these he would say, like Henry James again, "are the circumstances of the interest," but not the interest itself. The interest itself will be the *use* to which these circumstances are put, the degree to which they can be organized.

From this point of view, he is not in the least to be considered as a mere "Southern" writer: the "Southernness" of his scenes and characters is of little concern to him, just as the question whether they are pleasant or unpleasant, true or untrue. Verisimilitude—or at any rate, *degree* of verisimilitude—he will cheerfully abandon, where necessary, if the compensating advantages of plan or tone are a sufficient inducement. The famous scene in *Sanctuary* of Miss Reba and Uncle Bud, in which a "madam" and her cronies hold a wake for a dead gangster, while the small boy gets drunk, is quite false, taken out of its context; it is not endowed with the same kind of actuality which penetrates the greater part of the book at all. Mr. Faulkner was cunning enough to see that a two-dimensional cartoon-like statement, at this juncture, would supply him with the effect of a chorus, and without in the least being perceived as a change in the temperature of truthfulness.

This particular kind of dilution, or adulteration, or verisimilitude was both practiced and praised by James: as when he blandly admitted of *In the Cage* that his central character was "too ardent a focus of divination" to be quite credible. It was defensible simply because it made possible the coherence of the whole, and was itself absorbed back into the luminous texture. It was for him a device for organization, just as the careful cherishing of "viewpoint" was a device, whether simply or in counterpoint. Of Mr. Faulkner's devices, of this sort, aimed at the achievement of complex "form," the two most constant are the manipulation of viewpoint and the use of the flash-back, or sudden shift of time-scene, forward or backward.

In *Sanctuary*, where the alteration of viewpoint is a little lawless, the complexity is given, perhaps a shade disingenuously, by the violent shifts in time; a deliberate disarrangement of an otherwise straightforward story. Technically, there is no doubt that the novel, despite its fame, rattles a little; and Mr. Faulkner himself takes pains to disclaim it. But, even done with the left hand, it betrays a genius for form, quite apart from its wonderful virtuosity in other respects. *Light in August*, published a year after *Sanctuary*, repeats the same technique, that of dislocation of time, and more elaborately; the time-shifts alternate with shifts in the viewpoint; and if the book is a failure it is perhaps because Mr. Faulkner's tendency to what is almost a hypertrophy of form is not here, as in the other novels, matched with the characters and the theme. Neither the person nor the story of Joe Christmas is seen fiercely enough—by its creator—to carry off that immense machinery of narrative; it would have needed another Popeye, or another Jiggs and Shumann, another Temple Drake, and for once Mr. Faulkner's inexhaustible inventiveness seems to have been at fault. Consequently what we see is an extraordinary power for forming relatively *in vacuo*, and existing only to sustain itself.

In the best of the novels, however,—and it is difficult to choose between *The Sound and the Fury* and *The Wild Palms*, with *Absa-*

*lom, Absalom!* a very close third—this tendency of form has been sufficiently curbed; and it is interesting, too, to notice that in all these
three (and in that remarkable *tour de force, As I Lay Dying*, as well),
while there is still a considerable reliance obtained by a very skillful
fugue-like alteration of view-point. Fugue-like in *The Wild Palms*—
and fugue-like especially, of course, in *As I Lay Dying* where the shift
is kaleidoscopically rapid, and where, despite an astonishing violence
to the plausibility (in the reflections, and *language* of reflection, of the
characters), an effect of the utmost reality and immediateness is, nevertheless, produced. Fugue-like, again, in *Absalom, Absalom!* where
indeed one may say the form is really circular—there is no beginning
and no ending, properly speaking, and therefore no *logical* point of
entrance: we must just submit, and follow the circling of the author's
interest, which turns a light inward towards the center, but every moment from a new angle, a new point of view. The story unfolds, therefore, now in one color of light, now in another, with references backward and forward: those that refer forward being necessarily, for the
moment, blind. What is complete in Mr. Faulkner's patterns, *a priori*,
must, nevertheless, remain incomplete for us until the very last stone
is in place; what is "real," therefore, at one stage of the unfolding, or
from one point of view, turns out to be "unreal" from another; and we
find that one among other things with which we are engaged is the
fascinating sport of trying to separate truth from legend, watching
the growth of legend from truth, and finally reaching the conclusion
that the distinction is itself false.

Something of the same sort is true also of *The Sound and the Fury*—
and this, with its massive four-part symphonic structure, is perhaps
the most beautifully *wrought* of the whole series, and an indubitable
masterpiece of what James loved to call the "fictive art." The joinery
is flawless in its intricacy; it is a novelist's novel—a whole textbook
on the craft of fiction, comparable in its way to *What Maisie Knew* or
*The Golden Bowl*.

But if it is important, for the moment, to emphasize Mr. Faulkner's
genius for form, and his continued exploration of its possibilities, as
against the unusual concern with his violence and dreadfulness of
his themes—though we might pause to remind the carpers on this
score of the fact that the best of Henry James is precisely that group

of last novels which so completely concerned themselves with moral depravity—it is also well to keep in mind his genius for invention, whether of character or of episode. The inventiveness is of the richest possible sort—a headlong and tumultuous abundance, and exuberant generosity and vitality, which makes most other contemporary fiction look very pale and chaste indeed. It is an unforgettable gallery of portraits, whether character or caricature, and all of them endowed with violent and immediate vitality.

"He is at once"—to quote once more from James—"one of the most corrupt of writers and one of the most naïf, the most mechanical and pedantic, and the fullest of *bonhomie* and natural impulse. He is one of the finest of artists and one of the coarsest. Viewed in one way, his novels are ponderous, shapeless, overloaded; his touch is graceless, violent, barbarous. Viewed in another, his tales have more color, more composition, more grasp of the reader's attention than any others. [His] style would demand a chapter apart. It is the least simple style, probably, that was ever written; it bristles, it cracks, it swells and swaggers; but it is a perfect expression of man's genius. Like his genius, it contains a certain quantity of everything, from immaculate gold to flagrant dross. He was a very bad writer, and yet, unquestionably, he was a very great writer. We may say briefly, that in so far as his method was an instinct it was successful, and that in so far as it was a theory it was a failure. But both in instinct and in theory he has the aid of an immense force of conviction. His imagination warmed us to its work so intensely that there was nothing his volition could not impose upon it. Hallucination settled upon him, and he believed anything that was necessary in the circumstances."

That passage, from Henry James's essay on Balzac, is almost word for word, with scarcely a reservation applicable to Mr. Faulkner. All that is lacking is Balzac's greater *range* of understanding and tenderness, his greater freedom from special preoccupations. For this, one would hazard the guess that Mr. Faulkner has the gifts—and time is still before him.

# "Faulkner at Stockholm"

From *A Continuing Journey: Essays and Addresses* (Boston: Houghton
Mifflin Company, 1967), 163–67. [Written in 1951 and published in *The Harvard
Advocate* 135 (November 1951): 18, 43.] Copyright © 1967 by Archibald MacLeish.
Reprinted by permission of Houghton Mifflin Harcourt Publishing Company.
All rights reserved.

Ten years ago the responsibility of the artist was an unfashionable, not to say an improper, subject in American literary circles. Attempts to discuss it in the context of Hitler's war were received with hoots of derision. The writer had no responsibility for anything but the utter manner of his writing. What he wrote *about* was his own business, not to be judged by his contemporaries. Flaubert had been right: "The finest books are those that have the least subject matter . . . there are no such things as either beautiful or ugly subjects . . ." There was no such thing, for the artist at least, as a choice between Europe—the tradition of the freedom of the human spirit which Europe meant—and the suffocating evil which menaced it.

In the year just past, William Faulkner, accepting the Nobel Prize in Stockholm, and using that moment "as a pinnacle" from which to speak to younger writers throughout the world, took as the text of his sermon the writer's responsibility. He began with a definition of the subject—a categorical definition. There is only one thing worth writing about: "the problems of the human heart in conflict with itself." He went on to relate that election of subject to the tragedy of the time in which he–and each of us also—lives; the tragedy of "a general and universal physical fear so long sustained by now that we can even bear it." Unless a writer writes less of "the old universal truths," the old universal truths of the human spirit, "he will write as though he stood among and watched the end of man." For his own part, Faulkner said, "I refuse to accept this. I believe that man will not merely endure"–endure, that is, as "a puny inexhaustible voice" in a ruined world–"he will prevail. He is immortal, not because he alone among creatures has an inexhaustible voice, but because he has a soul, a spirit capable of compassion and sacrifice and endurance." And having thus defined the subject and related it to the time in which he lived, Faulkner concluded by affirming, in explicit and unequivocal words, the writer's responsibility, using, not that word, but the more direct and personal word, duty: "The poet's, the writer's duty is to write about these things. It is his privilege to help man endure . . . ."

This address was received, as the world knows, without audible protest from any quarter. Quite on the contrary, it was praised even by those who had previously been loudest in their contempt for its fundamental proposition. And the question naturally presents itself: Why?

The most obvious answer is Faulkner himself. Faulkner spoke at Stockholm not only with eloquence, but with an authority which the men of ten years ago did not begin to possess. There is no writer in English more widely or more truly esteemed than William Faulkner. His views, simply because they are in his views, are received with respect and examined with attention.

Another probable answer is to be found in the terminology Faulkner employs. His proposition, though it is derived from the tragedy of his own time, is of universal application and it is stated in universal terms: few literary controversialists would undertake to deny that the poet has a generalized duty to remind man "of the courage and honor and hope and pride and compassion and pity and sacrifice which have been the glory of his past." Had Faulkner advanced this same proposition in terms of a particular crisis, the effect might have been different. To say that the poet has a responsibility for the things of the human spirit, for the glory of the human past, in the face of a particular attack upon the human spirit by a particular enemy of the human spirit, brings the general truth to a specific application which certain minds will reject. And not only because it reduces the inoffensive generalization to a precise application which may be difficult but for another and more plausible reason.

A general duty to write of the things of the spirit is clearly compatible with that paramount loyalty to his own experience which every artist accepts by the acceptance of his art. A specific duty to take the side of man, the side of human spirit, at a *particular* moment of history, and in the face of a specific evil, is not so clearly compatible. It involves judgments of the world. There were writers, not so long ago, who regarded Fascism as something less than the spiritual destroyer which the world has discovered it to be, and there are doubtless writers now who do not see the present struggle between spiritual freedom and repressive authoritarianism as the critical battle for the human future in which others know themselves to be engaged.

A third explanation of the shift of sentiment is probably to be found in the changes in the world itself. The last ten years must certainly have been the longest in human history. Certainly they have been the most heavily freighted with menace and premonition. Faulkner's definition of the crisis in terms of physical fear may well be mistaken. It is interesting to notice that he alters it in the little Commencement Address he gave somewhat later. "What threatens us today," he there says, "is fear. Not the atom bomb, nor even fear of it . . . Our danger is not that. Our danger is the forces in the world today which are trying to use man's fear to rob him of his individuality, his soul . . . ." But however the crisis is defined—and most survivors of the decade of McCarthy will prefer Faulkner's second definition to the first—there can be no doubt that the sense of crisis has grown more urgent from year to year since the last war. Not only our bodies—perhaps least of all our bodies—but our civilization, the whole worth and meaning of our human lives, is in danger. And, face to face with that danger, the distinctions so laboriously established by the critic and the literary philosopher between life and poetry, between art and experiences, have dissolved into the unrealities out of which they were made. To *be* artist—precisely to *be artist*—a man must concern himself in our time with the things of the human spirit not only in their universal forms but in their specific, their present, agony. Like Tu Fu, he must be able to stare into the tragic face of his world and see "the bones behind those crumpled eyes."

These glimpses of reality which show the human truth behind the artifices of literary theory seem to occur in times like ours. The same Flaubert who dismissed the importance of the idea of the subject so easily in later years, wrote in 1851 to his friend Louis Bouilhet: "Beneath us the earth is trembling. Where can we place our fulcrum, even admitting that we possess the lever? The thing we all lack is not style, nor that dexterity of finger and bow known as talent. We have a large orchestra, a rich palette, a variety of resources. We know many more tricks and dodges, probably, than were ever known before. No, what we lack is the intrinsic principle, the soul of the thing, the very idea of the subject."

One can only be grateful that, a hundred years later, at another mid-century of the human spirit, a novelist of a comparable stature found his way to the same truth and had the courage to put it into words.

# "William Faulkner: An Impression"

From *The Harvard Advocate* 135 (November 1951): 17. Reprinted by permission of the Estate of John Crowe Ransom and Robb Forman Dew.

It is an admirable occasion, and I regret that I have to offer only an impression of William Faulkner's achievement, not a prepared and focused study of some of his fictions. I wish the occasion had come twenty years earlier, when a badly neglected author needed the appreciation of his compatriots; or perhaps it is better to say, when they needed to know their own author as well as foreign critics did, and to obtain for themselves the benefit of a full response to his power. But at least it is all the easier and more reasonable to honor him now.

My own impression has not changed a great deal during the years that followed my reading of *The Sound and the Fury*, *As I Lay Dying*, and *Light in August*. He has extended his range and still maintained his powers. In the later work as in the earlier there are some important fictions, and some lesser ones; his is one of those fertile talents which register with some unevenness from book to book. The early book in which the bravado seemed to me aimless virtuosity, and the feeling more cynical than pitiful, was *Sanctuary*. But Faulkner himself disparaged it immediately; and it is very curious now, and as if he had become quite self-conscious about his responsibilities as an author, that in his very latest work, *Requiem for a Nun*, he should write its sequel. The intent of the new book is, apparently, to redeem the girl Temple, to whom in the early book he had assigned only formal sanctuary in the convent; and it is to be accomplished by requiring her, in the context of all her bourgeois respectability, the fullest confession of her sins. But that does not produce much of a book. The affair is a poor theatrical one, and all Faulkner's talent cannot change it.

The books of this writer are unequal, and the style is less than consistently sustained. He is therefore not Ben Jonson, he is not even the indefatigable Shakespeare, he is John Webster,—if we look for his equivalent among the Elizabethan writers whom he resembles in the force of his horror, as in the rightness of his sense of human goodness, as in the gift a language which is generally adequate to the effects intended.

I would stand on the three early books which I have named as sufficient evidence of the narrative power and the detailed poetry of his creations. And since they are fictions, I suppose some of his analogues in this field need to be named. I think of Dostoyevsky, Melville, and D. H. Lawrence. Faulkner could never have done the like of *The Brother Karamazov*, however; he may know the depths of the human soul, but he has not had the advantage of the society of his literary peers discussing the realistic novel and performing it, nor that of intellectuals with their formidable dialectic, permitting him to give to his creation so vast and controlled a spread as Dostoyevsky did. He could not have done *Moby Dick*, and that is aside from the matter of whether he would quite have wished to do it; there is an encyclopedic virtuosity there, and surely at some of the great climaxes there is an academicism in the style, whereas Faulkner is not a man of great learning, and certainly his acquaintance with the academy did not adulterate the natural directness of his style. His power of language is brilliant and fitful like Lawrence's, but he is never negative (it is not in him to labor a hateful small prose); and his positive is simple and passionate (or Elizabethan), not complicated with modern theory. I am afraid these comparisons are much too quick and crude, since they seem absurd as soon as I read them; and I think the truth must be, really, that he is not quite like any other writer whom I can think of. Perhaps they will serve to remark at least the quality of those great writers with whom, if anybody, he seems to keep company best.

I am content to say, in the last resort, that there are imperfections in his work both large and small, to the extent almost of whole books sometimes, and perhaps of passages and sentences in most of the books. But his perfections are wonderful, and well sustained, and without exact precedent anywhere. If he were deliberately a "perfectionist," as are some highly prepared and articulate artists, his great gifts might have been paralyzed, or to some extent inhibited. To read him is to contemplate the common human behaviors under the aspect of magnificence. And I believe we are struck with shame when we are led to think about the poverty of our own perception of life. We feel that our education, our cultural habit, has immunized us from reality, and from passion. It is in the sense that he recovers us from an immense torpor that we are so much in his debt.

# "Faulkner and Desegregation"

From *Nobody Knows My Name* (New York: Vintage Books, 1961), 117–26. Copy-right © 1956 by James Baldwin. Copyright renewed. Originally published in *Partisan Review* 23 (Fall 1956): 568–73. Used by permission of the James Baldwin Estate.

Any real change implies the breakup of the world as one has always known it, the loss of all that gave one an identity, the end of safety. And at such a moment, unable to see and not daring to imagine what the future will now bring forth, one clings to what one knew, or thought one knew; to what one possessed or dreamed that one possessed. Yet, it is only when a man is able, without bitterness or self-pity, to surrender a dream he has long cherished or a privilege he has long possessed that he is set free—for higher dreams, for greater privileges. All men have gone through this, go through it, each according to his degree, throughout their lives. It is one of those irreducible facts of life. And remembering this, especially since I am a Negro, affords me almost my only means of understanding what is happening in the minds and hearts of white Southerners today.

For the arguments with which the bulk of relatively articulate white Southerners of good will have met the necessity of desegregation have no value whatever as arguments, being almost entirely and helplessly dishonest, when not, indeed, insane. After more than two hundred years in slavery and ninety years of quasi-freedom, it is hard to think very highly of William Faulkner's advice to "go slow." "They don't mean to go slow," Thurgood Marshall is reported to have said, "they mean don't go." Nor is the squire of Oxford very persuasive when he suggests that white Southerners, left to their own devices, will realize that their own social structure looks silly to the rest of the world and correct it of their own accord. It has looked silly, to use Faulkner's rather strange adjective, for a long time; so far from trying to correct it, Southerners, who seem to be characterized by a species of defiance most perverse when it is most despairing, have clung to it, at incalculable cost to themselves, as the only conceivable and as an absolutely sacrosanct way of life. They have never seriously conceded that their social structure was mad. They have insisted, on the contrary, that everyone who criticized it was mad.

Faulkner goes further. He concedes the madness and moral wrongness of the South but at the same time he raises it to the level of a mystique which makes it somehow unjust to discuss Southern society in the same terms in which one would discuss any other society. "Our position is wrong and untenable," says Faulkner, "but it is not wise to keep an emotional people off balance." This, if it means anything, can only mean that this "emotional people" have been swept "off balance" by the pressure of recent events, that is, the Supreme Court decision outlawing segregation. When the pressure is taken off—and not an instant before—this "emotional people" will presumably find themselves once again on balance and will then be able to free themselves of an "obsolescence in [their] own land" in their own way and, of course, in their own time. The question left begging is what, in their history to date, affords any evidence that they have any desire or capacity to do this. And it is, I suppose, impertinent to ask just what Negroes are supposed to do while the South works out what, in Faulkner's rhetoric, becomes something very closely resembling a high and noble tragedy.

The sad truth is that whatever modifications have been effected in the social structure of the South since the Reconstruction, and any alleviations of the Negro's lot within it, are due to great and incessant pressure, very little of it indeed from within the South. That the North has been guilty of Pharisaism in its dealing with the South does not negate the fact that much of this pressure has come from the North. That some—not nearly as many as Faulkner would like to believe—Southern Negroes prefer, or are afraid of changing, the status quo does not negate the fact that it is the Southern Negro himself who, year upon year, and generation upon generation, has kept the Southern waters troubled. As far as the Negro's life in the South is concerned, the NAACP is the only organization which has struggled, with admirable single-mindedness and skill, to raise him to the level of a citizen. For this reason alone, and quite apart from the individual heroism of many of its Southern members, it cannot be equated, as Faulkner equates it, with the pathological Citizen's Council. One organization is working within the law and the other is working against and outside it. Faulkner's threat to leave the "middle of the road" where he has, presumably, all these years, been working for the benefit of Negroes, reduces itself to a more or less up-to-date version of the Southern threat to secede from the Union.

Faulkner—among so many others!—is so plaintive concerning this "middle of the road" from which "extremist" elements of both races are driving him that it does not seem unfair to ask just what he has been doing there until now. Where is the evidence of the struggle he has been carrying on there on behalf of the Negro? Why, if he and his enlightened confreres in the South have been boring from within to destroy segregation, do they react with such panic when the walls show any signs of falling? Why—and how—does one move from the middle of the road where one was aiding Negroes into the streets—to shoot them?

Now it is easy enough to state flatly that Faulkner's middle of the road does not—cannot—exist and that he is guilty of great emotional and intellectual dishonesty in pretending that it does. I think this is why he clings to his fantasy. It is easy enough to accuse him of hypocrisy when he speaks of man being "indestructible because of his simple will to freedom." But he is not being hypocritical; he means it. It is only that Man is one thing—a rather unlucky abstraction in this case—and the Negroes he has always known, so fatally tied up in his mind with his grandfather's slaves, are quite another. He is at his best, and is perfectly sincere, when he declares, in *Harper's* "To live anywhere in the world today and be against equality because of race or color is like living in Alaska and being against snow. We have already got snow. And as with the Alaskan, merely to live in armistice with it is not enough. Like the Alaskan, we had better use it." And though this seems to be flatly opposed to his statement (in an interview printed in *The Reporter*) that, if it came to a contest between the federal government and Mississippi, he would fight for Mississippi, "even if it meant going out into the streets and shooting Negroes," he means that, too. Faulkner means everything he says, means them all at once, and with very nearly the same intensity. This is why his statements demand our attention. He has perhaps never before more concretely expressed what it means to be a Southerner.

What seems to define the Southerner, in his own mind at any rate, is his relationship to the North, that is to the rest of the Republic, a relationship which can at the very best be described as uneasy. It is apparently very difficult to be at once a Southerner and an American; so difficult that many of the South's most independent minds are forced into the American exile; which is not, of course, without its aggravating, circular effect on the interior and public life of the South. A Bostonian, say, who leaves Boston is not regarded by the citizenry he has abandoned with the same venomous distrust as is the Southerner who leaves the South. The citizenry of Boston do not consider that they have been abandoned, much less betrayed. It is only the American Southerner who seems to be fighting, in his own entrails, a peculiar, ghastly, and perpetual war with all the rest of the country. ("Didn't you say," demanded a Southern woman of Robert Penn Warren, "that you was born down here, used to live right here?" And when he agreed that this was so: "Yes . . . but you never said where you living now!")

The difficulty, perhaps, is that the Southerner clings to two entirely antithetical doctrines, two legends, two histories. Like all other Americans, he must subscribe, and is to some extent controlled by the beliefs and the principles in the Constitution; at the same time, these beliefs and principles seem determined to destroy the South. He is, on the one hand, the proud citizen of a free society and, on the other, is committed to a society which has not yet dared to free itself of the necessity of naked and brutal oppression. He is part of a country which boasts that it has never lost a war; but he is also the representative of a conquered nation. I have not seen a single statement of Faulkner's concerning desegregation which does not inform us that his family has lived in the same part of Mississippi for generations, that his great-grandfather owned slaves, and that his ancestors fought and died in the Civil War. And so compelling is the image of ruin, gallantry and death thus evoked that it demands a positive effort of the imagination to remember that slaveholding Southerners were not the only people who perished in that war. Negroes and Northerners were also blown to bits. American history, as opposed to Southern history, proves that Southerners were not the only slaveholders, Negroes were not even the only slaves. And the segregation which Faulkner sanctifies by references to Shiloh, Chickamauga, and Gettysburg does not extend back that far, is in fact scarcely as old as the century. The "racial condition" which Faulkner will not have changed by "mere force of law or economic threat" was imposed by precisely these means. The Southern tradition, which is, after all, all that Faulkner is talking about, is not a tradition at all: when Faulkner evokes it, he is simply evoking a legend which contains an accusation. And that accusation, stated far more simply than it should be, is that the North, in winning the war, left the South only one means of asserting its identity and that means was the Negro.

"My people owned slaves," says Faulkner, "and the very obligation we have to take care of these people is morally bad." "This problem is . . . far beyond the moral one it is and still was a hundred years ago, in 1860, when many Southerners, including Robert Lee, recognized it as a moral one at the very instant they in turn elected to champion the underdog because that underdog was blood and kin and home." But the North escaped scot-free. For one thing, in freeing the slave, it established a moral superiority over the South which the South has not learned to live with until today; and this despite—or possibly because of—the fact that this moral superiority was bought, after all, rather cheaply. The North was no better prepared than the South, as it turned out, to make citizens of former slaves, but it was able, as the South was not, to wash its hands of the matter. Men who knew that slavery was wrong were forced, nevertheless, to fight to perpetuate it because they were unable to turn against "blood and kin and home." And when blood and kin and home were defeated, they found themselves, more than ever, committed: committed, in effect, to a way of life which was as unjust and crippling as it was inescapable. In sum, the North, by freeing the slaves to their masters, robbed the masters of any possibility of freeing themselves of the slaves.

When Faulkner speaks, then, of the "middle of the road," he is simply speaking of the hope—which was always unrealistic and is now all but smashed—that the white Southerner, with no coercion from the rest of the nation, will lift himself above his ancient, crippling bitterness and refuse to add to his already intolerable burden of blood-guiltiness. But this hope would seem to be absolutely dependent on a social and psychological stasis which simply does not exist. "Things have been getting better," Faulkner tells us, "for a long time. Only six Negroes were killed by whites in Mississippi last year, according to police figures." Faulkner surely knows how little consolation this offers a Negro and he also knows something about "police figures" in the Deep South. And he knows, too, that murder is not the worst thing that can happen to a man, black or white. But murder may be the worst thing a man can do. Faulkner is not trying to save Negroes, who are, in his view, already saved; who, having refused to be destroyed by terror, are far stronger than the terrified white populace; and who have moreover, fatally, from his point of view, the weight of the federal government behind them. He is trying to save "whatever good remains in those white people." The time he pleads for is the time in which the Southerner will come to terms with himself, will cease fleeing from his conscience, and achieve, in the words of Robert Penn Warren, "moral identity." And he surely believes, with Warren, that "Then in a country where moral identity is hard to come by, the South, because it has had to deal concretely with a moral problem, may offer some leadership. And we need any we can get. If we are to break out of the national rhythm, the rhythm between complacency and panic."

But the time Faulkner asks for does not exist—and he is not the only Southerner who knows it. There is never time in the future in which we will work out our salvation. The challenge is in the moment, the time is always now.

# "Best Fiction of 1957"

From *Esquire*, December 1957 [excerpt]. Copyright © National Association for the Advancement of Colored People.

Now about those books we all want to give. For myself, to open the holiday exercises, I should dearly wish to send those I most love and respect William Faulkner's *The Town*. The only drawback to this otherwise smooth-flowing plan is that the beloved and venerated go buy and read every Faulkner book as soon as it comes out—which is among the reasons for my feeling toward them, and *The Town* must long have been on their bed tables. It is presumptuous to offer such small awards as these to the greatest writer we have (oh, all right, all right; to the man I believe to be the greatest writer we have, then), even if there were any room left on Mr. Faulkner on which to hang them. Nor can I say that this is William Faulkner's finest work, for his books are so variegated that comparisons among them are not possible. *The Town* comes after *The Hamlet* in his triptych of the horrible, evil, greedy, irresistible Snopes family, on their way to taking over full power in Yoknapatawpha County. I hope you will permit me to crawl back to those words I once said about this being no banner year for American novels. This is the year in which *The Town* appeared; I was a fool and a liar.

TERRY SOUTHERN

# "Dark Laughter in the Towers"

From *The Nation*, April 23, 1960, pages 348–50. Copyright © by the

Terry Southern Literary Trust, Nile Southern, Trustee.

Reprinted by kind permission of Nile Southern.

There's no doubt about it, the rarest Laughter is brewed in high places; it courses down the walls of civilization, stone by stone, brow by brow, slowing always, thinning, at last, to a trickle. "*I don't get it!*" shouts fierce Mister Dumbell and the howl is taken up by the querulous, those who know better, and *voila* . . . that faculty's development is boxed into another twenty-year septic tank. And yet the day God and Democracy folded in America, there was bound to be almost nothing left but Laughter. Laughter and Sex.

Laughter has always been a big thing, of course, but refinement of faculties, like any growth in the jungle, requires sustenance, and each flourishes at the expense of another—the overshadowed become stunted and die, or else must mutate into a new species. Now, of the four great emotions that grew in our garden—God, Democracy, Sex, and Laughter—it seems that two are already dead, the third is mutating in a curious way, and Laughter, the exotic perennial, appears to be in the bloom of a strange and startling second growth.

Nowhere is art forced to breed with such religious urgency and abandon as on the floor of a moral shambles; overnight new forms spring up, to appear like wildflowers in the splintered marble of a demolished drugstore. We find ourselves now standing on the threshold of a strong existentialist literature.

Just as formal Existentialism is a quasi-science of methodology—not concerned with asserting a standard of values but with determining the nature of the standards that actually prevail—so, a mature existentialist literature is one in which no standard of aesthetics (or communication) is presumed to obtain *prior* to the created work, but which may, possibly, be derived *from* it. What this involves primarily is the gradual discarding of the purely literary orientation from which most traditional literature is conceived and read, and the taking instead of life and imagination as the frame of reference. An example of this is Meursault's indifferent behavior (in *The Stranger*) at his mother's funeral. To an appreciation which derives mainly from a professed ethic, such as "Christianity," or from a literary orientation (i.e., comparing Meursault's behavior with that of other protagonists in the same circumstances) his behavior would appear to be "a mark against him," whereas, in fact, the actual effect achieved is quite the opposite. This author-reader responsibility, in character delineation, of sometimes deliberately reversing stock values that are suspected of being dead, would seem to be a vital one, because only through such experimentation (on the part of the author) and such openness (on the part of the reader) can the real, existing, values be separated from those which are merely hypothetical.

In primitive existentialist fiction (i.e., pre-French) there are elements of humor which, though cherished by certain intrepids, have heretofore resisted that kind of formalized understanding the academics traffic in. Prior to the general acceptance of the literary concept of "*the absurd*," the work of Kafka, for example, was unclassifiable; it stood apart, freakish and isolated, outside the historical scheme. It contained elements irreconcilable with even its most oversimplified definitions, e.g., "an allegory about anti-Semitism." Why then make K. out to be such an incorrigible donkey? *Why* were he and Frieda rolling around in that spilt beer on the floor of the Herrenhof? *Why the relentless dead-pan burlesque?* We are not laughing *with* K., nor *with* Kafka; if there is any laugh, it is *at* them. Now this is a deliberate form of humor, inexplicable except in terms of *the absurd*, or in another area of its development, *the grotesque*.

Let us consider briefly, in this later light, the sequence and tone of events in a well-known novel of 1929, Faulkner's own twenty-one-gun salute to the absurd, *As I Lay Dying*.

Addie Bundren, farm wife and mother, lies ill in bed, presumably dying. Outside the open window, her eldest son, Cash, is noisily constructing a coffin; from time to time Mrs. Bundren leans forward to see how the work is progressing. Beyond the bedroom screendoor, sitting on the porch, old Anse Bundren, her husband, discusses with two of their sons (Jewel and Darl) the feasibility of setting out now to pick up a wagon load of wood, a day's drive away, in order to earn $3; they are undecided because Mrs. Bundren may die before they get back. The discussion is interrupted by the sudden arrival of Vardaman, the youngest son (six years old), staggering under the weight of a huge fish he has just caught—a nameless species of fish, so curiously obese that it must be likened to a hog.

It is decided that Jewel and Darl will risk going for the wood after all, and they depart in the two-mule-team wagon. The doctor arrives, but because of his girth, advanced age and the steepness of the terrain, he has to be hauled up to the house on a rope. Like a hog? In any case, his thoughts reveal his awareness of the situation's classic absurdity, even beyond despair:

> *"I'll be damned if I can see why I don't quit. A man seventy years old, weighing two hundred and odd pounds, being hauled up and down a damn mountain on a rope."*

Mrs. Bundren, after refusing to see the doctor, dies while he is still there, out on the porch. Vardaman, under the impression that the doctor is responsible for her death, rushes about wildly, shouting: "The fat son of a bitch!" He then finds a stick and drives off the doctor's horse and buggy.

Having put Mrs. Bundren in the coffin, Cash bores holes in the lid; twice the auger slips through the lid and goes into her head. When the neighbors come to pay their last respects there is a good deal of terse formality attached to the event, as well as to the author's description of Mrs. Bundren's burial dress:

It was her wedding dress and it had a flare-out bottom, and they had laid her head to foot in it [the coffin] so the dress could spread out, and they had made her a veil out of a mosquito bar so the auger holes in her face wouldn't show.

Meanwhile Jewel and Darl have run the wagon into a ditch, broken a wheel and are three days getting back to the house. When the coffin is finally loaded onto the wagon, all get aboard—Anse, Cash, Darl, Vardaman, and the daughter Dewey Dell. Jewel rides alongside the wagon on one of the spotted horses he brought from Snopes; this is a cause for angry embarrassment for Anse—he, who is generally a primary source of the absurd, is for once aware of being caught in it:

> I told him not to bring that horse out of respect for his dead ma
> . . . prancing along on a durn circus animal.

It is against this backdrop, like a Hieronymus Bosch soap-opera, that they start out for the Jefferson cemetery—a pilgrimage which, for sheer visual slapstick within a framework of straightforwardness, probably has no equal. As in Malaparte's account of the first incendiary raids on Hamburg, it is almost a parody of the absurd—a parody, however, which never cracks.

From the very outset this modest caravan, on a mission of piety, is followed by buzzards, circling lower and in increasing number as the journey progresses. The bridge used to get to Jefferson is impassable because of the high waters, so they attempt to ford the river. What happens here, of course, is that the entire rig—wagon, cargo, team and all—is swept crabwise down the river, and overturned, drowning the mules and breaking Cash's leg. Despite his broken leg, Cash manages to save Jewel's spotted pony which had been knocked over during the melee and was floundering in a near-drowning panic; as he leads him out of the water, the horse kicks him in the stomach and he is unconscious for about an hour.

Naturally the coffin has thrown its moorings during the capsize and now runs free with the current, so that a downstream Mack Sennett chase is necessary to retrieve it. This is followed by an insane underwater search for Cash's hammer and saw and other small tools which were in the wagon and are now at the bottom of the raging stream.

Having lost the mules, they must get a new team, from, by a bit of ironic bad luck, Snopes—so that Anse is forced to trade his cultivator, seeder, and unbeknown to Jewel, the spotted horse. By now it is dark and they must wait until the following day before resuming the journey.

Not being able to use the bridge means that they will have to take a much more circuitous route to Jefferson. Mrs. Bundren has now been dead for five days and the buzzards become more menacing. Cash's broken leg begins to bother him, and they stop again, long enough to purchase ten cents worth of cement and pour raw concrete on the leg—shortly after which his foot turns black and he gradually sinks into a delirium. By now the stench of the coffin has become intolerable:

> Three negroes walk beside the road ahead of us; when we pass them
> their heads suddenly turn with that expression of shock and instinctive
> outrage. "Great God," one says, "what they got in that wagon?"

It is so bad, in fact that they are not allowed to stop in town, people everywhere covering their faces with handkerchiefs at the wagon's approach. Jewel, meanwhile enraged half out of his mind over the unauthorized sale of his pony, sits in a semi-catatonic state, scarcely speaking for the rest of the trip. The girl, Dewey Dell, believes she is pregnant, and at first opportunity goes into a drugstore trying to buy an abortive drug; the pharmacist says he will give it to her if she goes to bed with him; she does and he gives her some capsules filled with talcum powder. At their next stop the buzzards become so bold that they are walking around on the ground like turkeys and perching on the coffin itself when possible; Vardaman drives them about with a stick. That night they take refuge in a barn; in the night, Darl, the quiet one, sets fire to it; they have quite a bit of trouble to get the coffin out intact.

In order to avoid a law suit by the owner of the barn, Anse decides Darl should be committed at once to an insane asylum; they subdue him and turn him over to the authorities, at which point he does, of course, go raving mad.

On the eleventh day after her death, they succeed in getting Mrs. Bundren buried as planned—an anticlimax which is immediately redeemed in a Chaplin-esque manner by Anse's taking a new wife the same day, before starting the long trip back to the house.

For some years now in America there has existed a popular genre of situation comedy (as typified by Jack Benny) in which the comedian acts as his own straight man; he approaches situations in good faith and he attempts to maintain a certain amount of dignity and reasonableness under the adverse conditions which invariably arise. The humor here does not depend so much on the *failure* of dignity and reasonableness to prevail but upon the *certainty* of this failure. The audience knows something that the comedian, seemingly, does not: namely, that he is going to be confronted with lunacy and chaos; his own assumption that what is outside his room (i.e., life) can be approached in a rational manner is so far-fetched that his attitude appears either hilarious, or refreshingly naïve. This is the most primitive form of existentialist humor, and as yet the only form of it widely acceptable in America. In literature, however, or in literary appreciation, it is not unfair to assume that things have gone considerably beyond that, at least in certain fringe areas. In England they quite definitely have gone beyond that, and on a very wide front. For example, one character trait traditionally common to all young heroes in English fiction has been "heightened sensitivity"; this trait has now become "an acute sense of the absurd." David Copperfield is a prototype of the former, Lucky Jim Dixon of the latter; both are extraordinarily sensitive to the people and events around them, but the crucial difference is that David, lacking a sense of the absurd, would fail to qualify today as a cultural hero—he would not be sympathetic enough, because with all his hopeful optimism and his reverence for the powers that be, he would be considered a *dolt.* Consequently, the two terms, though antithetical in the attitudes they described in olden days, are now synonymous. When one thinks of the spate of recent protagonists in English fiction who all possess this sense of the absurd—Jimmy Porter, Sebastian Dangerfield, Charles Lumley, Billy Liar, Larry Vincent,[1] etc.—it is almost inconceivable that a sympathetic, leading character could now be presented, on a non-hack level, without it.

Another element common to them all is *candor.* This combination—awareness of the absurd and candor—gives rise to expressions of irreverence, so that these books are often mistakably dismissed as being merely "novels of social criticism," and thus "creatively impure." This interpretation—that they are, by design, novels of protest, and further, that the protest is well founded—no doubt accounts in large measure for the work's popularity, whereas, actually, the "social criticism" aspect of it is simply incidental, an understandable by-product of the combination of sensitivity and candor. The real answer is that it is an existentialist literature. That it has taken such a markedly different form in England, with so strong an emphasis on humor, is inevitable—otherwise it would merely be imitative of a school, and not, as it is, culturally integrated in a deep and inviolable way.

Discounting Burrough's *Naked Lunch*, which is not available here, and discounting the early work of Henry Miller, which, even were it not banned, would now be out of date, little use has been made of this combination of sensitivity and candor in American writing. Perhaps the nearest approach to it that received any significant cultural acceptance was *Catcher in the Rye*. This is considerably less of an achievement than *Lucky Jim*, because the hero of *Catcher in the Rye* was, after all, a *child*—and no matter how precocious, the irreverence evoked by combining sensitivity and candor, in a child, is bound to be pretty innocuous; moreover, in this particular case the irreverence was further weakened by the suggestion that the boy was about half off his rocker. The *humor*, however, was there—the existentialist humor which precedes full cognizance of "the absurd" and which theretofore had been the whole framework only in the "grotesque" (as in the Faulkner work referred to) or as fantasy (as in much of Nathaniel West's work). The significant difference, in terms of development of an existentialist literature indigenous to our own culture, is that the "grotesque" in Faulkner is not ordinarily read as humorous, because the highly personalized style tends to obscure it, and in West the very fact that it *is* fantasy (either in whole or part) limits it simply to that; it would seem that realism, at least as a guise, is a requisite to the absurd, and to whatever may stem from it—by realism is meant the *tone* at any given moment: the deadpan expression of the comedian as he climbs into the cab of a locomotive, the deadpan expression with which Faulkner informs us of Anse's "embarrassment" about some inconsequential detail while elaborately ignoring the old man's reaction to the stench of the coffin, the hazards, the auger holes, etc., or again, the grotesque routing of Croft's mountain patrol by hornets in *The Naked and the Dead*, as well as certain sequences in *A Walk on the Wild Side*—outlandish situations, in short, which are neither fanciful nor self-consciously ironic, events which are not flagrantly cynical, and acts which very often produce a reader response opposite to what is ostensibly intended, or to what ordinary literary standards indicate they could produce. The future of this literature rests with writers who retain the ability of realistic surprise, and with readers who are loose enough to unbridle their response regardless of how "unprecedented" it may seem to them at the time.

Meanwhile, rich veins of the past may continue to come to light. Certainly there remain unfathomed depths of this humor in Kafka's work, especially, perhaps, in the diaries. If one supposes that the diaries (despite anything said, or known, to the contrary—for this deception would have been a principal part of the whole concept) were written *to be read*, that their "author" was, in fact, a creation, *then* we would know how to read, for example:

> November 11. As soon as I become aware in any way that I leave abuses undisturbed which it was really intended that I should correct (for example, the extremely satisfied, but from my point of view dismal life of my married sister), I lose all sensation in my arm muscles for a moment.

And then, too, would we be well along on the hilariously unsentimental journey we have already begun.

*Note*

1. From *Look Back in Anger* (Osborn), *The Ginger Man* (Donleavy), *Hurry on Down* (Wain), *Billy Liar* (Waterhouse), and *Happy as Larry* (Hinde).

# "William Faulkner"

From *Carolina Israelite*, July–August 1962, page 5. Reprinted by permission of Richard Goldhurst, Harry Golden Literary Executor.

The test of the influence and genuine popularity of an American writer is whether a newspaper can publish his obituary and offer a literary assessment without hiring a literary expert. I have yet to meet a newspaperman who isn't passionately devoted to at least one American writer. I know toughened crime reporters who can spout T. S. Eliot from memory and financial writers who think deeply of *Moby Dick* or *Omoo* even as they study the Dow Jones report. My son, Harry, Jr., who has been a newspaperman for sixteen years, took a long bus trip to Asheville once just to be looking at the home of Thomas Wolfe.

William Faulkner was one of those writers. He commended the loyalty of a large body of working reporters. Long before he won the Nobel Prize there were newspapermen here in Charlotte who considered every book of his an event. I remarked in my book *Carl Sandburg* that American writers have a compulsion to create their own sense of place, street by street, house by house, year by year, word by word. Not Sinclair Lewis's Main Street, John O'Hara's Gibbeville or Sandburg's Rootabaga County are the grand conceptions, but William Faulkner's Yoknapatawpha County and Jefferson. Americans are not as interested in explaining their country to each other. Our distressing internal conflict now—integration—is essentially a geographic argument. It is not too extreme to say America is an idea as well as a place and perhaps this explains why we Americans take on such characteristics from our respective places.

I can remember when I first came to Charlotte and spent one hot Sunday waiting at the small downtown newsstand for the arrival of the New York papers in the afternoon. The heat was a miasma and because most of the Blue Laws were still on the books, the town was absolutely quiet. Spend such a Sunday and you can understand the true conception William Faulkner managed in his novels.

Now it is true Faulkner can be quoted as saying he would fight for Mississippi against the Federal Government. There are Southern school boys who write they wished they had died at Gettysburg just as there are Northerners who believe the South is composed of decaying mansions populated by decadent families in an incestuous triangle. William Faulkner made a great bridge between these conceptions and in a large sense Faulkner can be compared to Charles Dickens. If Faulkner loved Mississippi so Dickens loved the Victorian Age; but that love prevented neither writer from discovering the truth about both.

V. S. PRITCHETT

# "That Time and That Wilderness"

From *New Statesman*, September 28, 1962, pages 405–6.

Reprinted by permission of *New Statesman*.

Faulkner is dead, the last of the pre-freeway novelists. Victorian in tradition, Twentyish in practice, he is the only substantial American novelist since Henry James, the last to have a historical sense of the American environment, "that time and that wilderness." He got to work on the South with pick and shovel, slinging up the earth, quarrying the rock—like Adam after the Fall. He knew there had been a Fall and that it was historical. He was far from the Northern optimism of "the good trip" and its "problems": if he had written a novel about the opening up of the West it would have been about the descendants of the Donner party and the long arm of evil. He would have uncovered the covered wagon. He was as American as Huck Finn and Paul Bunyan, though his relationship with the American literature of his generation is modified by the kind of difference that separates the Anglo-Irish from the English: and by a devouring literariness that made him susceptible to Balzac, Dostoyevsky, and Joyce. The European strain is dense and strong.

Faulkner had so many skills jostling for a hand in his novels and got so much into the habit of taking to himself when he wrote, that he often achieves a massive impenetrability. So do James and Melville. It seems to be one of the American ideals—as Faulkner said of the climate: "Everything, weather, all, hangs on too long" becomes "opaque, slow, violent." The freeway generation that has followed him eschew this and the whole of Faulkner's vegetative interests. They are above all drastic in intelligence; one or two, like Saul Bellow and Bernard Malamud, are ruthless about certain American traumas. They retain the native taste for aches, pains, and problems; but these are no longer viewed with the old protective solemnity. They rip along the freeway, giving a trained, nervous glance over their shoulders before swapping lanes and moving into faster traffic. They ignore the state signs that are hung across the road, like hectic telegrams saying: "All forgiven. Home Town next seven exits." Americans exist for them but inhabited America does not. It is bypassed, felt to be somewhere else, an abstraction of some kind or, nowadays, a peculiar personal disorder like psychosomatic sore gums, a lump, a cholesterol, an alcohol problem—which stands in for things like the difficulty of deciding between Being and Becoming.

There is a good deal of the Higher Soppiness—Kerouac; the Higher Wilderness—Mailer; and the Higher Dottiness—Salinger. Rituals are sought, magic is consulted: there is a sophisticated, esoteric casting of the old New England idea that Everything equals. Everything Salinger's Zooey knows all about the syllable Om and the "Jesus prayer"; the fat lady can be Christ. The sexual tumble for some of Malamud's males is a comic contact of gooseflesh, but it is compared at least once, and with half-*croyant* ribaldry, to a crucifixion. Saul Bellow's Henderson genially returns from some Africa of the mind, with a lioness, having gone through probationary wrestling, sacred weightlifting—the heaviest old goddess in the tribe—and an allegorical spell as Daniel in the lion's den and as Nebuchadnezzar eating grass.

These novelists are very gifted and their vitality is great. They have recovered that pugnacious comic strain which made *Moby Dick* endurable before the whale swallowed the critics. They expose the skillful American realists of the North Fredrick and Butterfield kind for the pedestrians they really are; for all they all do is record the platitude that the United States has a class system, that towns have railroad tracks, so that people can be born on the wrong side of them. The tedium of the realists leads us on to hollow discussion: is there enough depth and texture to American societies to keep novelists going? Are there no American novels, but only American romances? The foreigner gazes with envy at the diversity of the American scene;

yet his American friends tell him they are dying of drought. Romance is inevitable because life is skin-deep, the spirit bleeds at once, dreams and horrors are the obvious counterparts of blandness. Your only hope is to get away from where you are or to erect a Gothic folly out of your personal nightmare.

This is not Faulkner's way. He is unique in sticking to the bypassed town where he found himself and in mixing the realities of the South with its inner torments. Faulkner's South exists in depth; for him, as Malcolm Cowley has said, the South was what New England was for Nathaniel Hawthorne. And by quarrying his way to the South, past and present, he became more than a regional writer. Dig deep enough and you come upon the basic moral experience that has fertilized the greatest American literature. The opening up of the South is not so very different as a drama from the opening up of the West. Read the opening chapters on the founding of the courthouse in *Requiem for a Nun*—the only well-built chapters in a flimsy book—and one is at the beginning of a general American tradition in history, politics, and literature. I don't mean that one learns history from Faulkner but one does learn about the interplay of life and myth and why, for example, garrulousness has been formative in American literature.

At its best, it is a sardonic garrulousness. The freeway writers like Bellow and Malamud have clipped this habit back and even Salinger, who depends on it, has adroitly lightened the load. Faulkner accepted it whole, exploited it, tried to transform it by making it richer. Like others of the generation that give the American novel its independence from England he got his tools from Europe after the 1914 war. It is he, rather than Hemingway, who most variously experimented with sentences, images, the stream of consciousness, the time-shift. He stuck to his mannerisms to the end—"evictant children," "ambulant horse"—anything that would arrest and annoy the eye. He had the self-educated writer's pleasure in language; he was always straining an ear for the note of Elizabethan Anglo-Irish which can occasionally be heard in the South.

Faulkner's experiments in style were the means of bringing his lethargic provincial stuff to life. He sought to shake us with the physical sensations of the Mississippi in flood in *The Wild Plains*. On it he put a twirling boat, a half-stunned convict and a speechless pregnant woman, forcing us to ache with the knowledge that the absurd water and the absurd victims are both dumb forces of nature. A primitive absurdity lies at the back of all his stories: this attracted French Existentialists to him. He intends to be obscure because he wants to catch what is going on dramatically in the dark places. When and how did the rape occur in *Sanctuary*? One has to pick up the facts as best one can. When Faulkner is unreadable it is in the sense that vernacular narration is: there is willful, sly, longheaded determination of the tobacco-chewers round the stove in the store to obfuscate in the interests of myth. Man is a myth-making animal. We see Faulkner in the act of collecting a people's never-ending revisions of its experience. You read Paul Bunyan for the inspired lies, you read Faulkner for the mind of a people forming its own legend.

Gide complained that Faulkner's characters had no soul or no moral conscience. They were blind impulses driven by some Balzacian theory of dominant passion. Half-true, but very American: black and white are Puritan and dramatic. Faulkner has been reproached, not always justly for importing a didactic moral consciousness in his later work. If the boy in *Intruder in the Dust* is likely to side with the accused Negro, it is above all for a physical reason: he will always remember what the smell of a Negro is after being wrapped in the old Negress's quilt in her cabin. It is also the smell of poverty.

There was a deposit of humanism in Faulkner's writing from the beginning. It is interesting here to compare his famous bear heart with Hemingway's many hunting scenes. Both writers are absorbed in the craft instinct and experience of the hunter, but in Hemingway the hunt culminates in the hunter's pride in the perfection of his own knowledge and touch. He graduates as a hunter. But in Faulkner's *The Bear*, the growing boy, his elders, and the Negro are human beings living together in their peculiar group. The boy becomes not merely a hunter but a man—a man matured among men who do not, after all, spend their whole lives hunting bears.

A concern with initiation into the knowledge of good and evil is usually present in Faulkner, whether he is pursuing the direct visions of his imagination or falling back on the folk memory of Yoknapatawpha County. In *The Reivers*, his last and posthumous novel, a boy grows up. The striking thing about this superlative book is that it is

Faulkner's only complete comedy. Elsewhere his comic genius has been rich but fragmentary. This is a story of 1905 and the arrival of the first motor car in a Southern family and of how, while his parents are away, the 11-year-old son is suborned by the chauffeur who takes him off in the car on a picaresque escapade. The farce is as deeply embedded in local life as everything else in Faulkner is. It easily surpasses Somerville and Ross or Surtees: it matches Mark Twain.

The overt moral of a wildly comic and brilliantly invented tale is that the boy must learn to bear, "like a gentleman," the pain of knowing, precociously, that sex exists and that sinful human nature steals, blackmails, cheats, goes whoring and can be inflamed to the point of murderous fright. Those who suspect Faulkner's ethical views will note that his favorite ideas of authority, necessity, blind obsession, and fate now appear in the tolerant terms of the vested rule of the old families who behave with conservative firmness and sagacity. The Fall is inevitable; the saving things in man are his sense of honor—plus his wits.

Despite all the obscurities and mystifications, Faulkner was always a master of construction and story-telling and especially of that kind of American humor that becomes funnier and faster the more it digresses. At the back of *The Reivers* is the war of the new and the old: the motor car versus the horse, the chauffeur versus the coachman. The nervy chauffeur reproaches the boy for having made a smell. The boy indignantly denies this. The chauffeur then lifts the tarpaulin at the back of the car and finds the old coachman secreted himself there, unable to resist the common sin.

From now on the tale gathers strength like the bidding at an auction. The chauffeur's secret object is to stay at a Memphis brothel—closed on Sundays—and visit his girl there. The arrival of a mud-spattered boy of 11 is upsetting to the girls. They turn to washing his clothes. Here Faulkner could have left us with an American *Maison Tellier*, but his powers have opened up. Like the finest comics, Faulkner gets his best effects from respecting the seriousness rather than the obvious humor of the situation. The innocent boy is bound to find out what a brothel is, and Faulkner arranges that the facts shall be revealed to him by another boy, the child of a visiting whore, who is already a nasty young pimp in the making. And then—this is the masterstroke—the car is swapped with a racehorse by the delinquent coachman: all parties are now caught in the vast and irresistible temptation, to sin on the grand scale and make a fortune on the racehorse. This leads to the great central scene: the long account of how this solemn riff-raff smuggle a frightened horse through the town at night, under the nose of Sabbatarian respectably, and get it, after nerve-racking struggles, into the box-car of the night train that will take it to the course.

Mere farce opens up the deplorable archives of human nature. Even the happy ending—the chauffeur's girl has been so shaken by the sight of a boy of 11 in the house that she "quits," goes straight, and marries the man—is moderately satisfying to us: not because she has reformed, but because her reformation causes more trouble and more comedy. The experts who dilate on Faulkner's unsettling neuroses will find them here, but cunningly subdued to the purposes of comedy. Great artists make asses of their solemn critics. The gargoyles grin back at the theorists who discuss Faulkner as an hysterical Gothic novelist, making melodrama out of an arrested emotional equipment.

The real danger to Faulkner's art did not come from his later spell of uplift, but his lapses into literary mysticism, as in *A Fable* where the condemned soldier in Flanders becomes a Christ-figure. In *Light in August*, his finest novel, the violent tale is direct. There is a slight muzziness in the character of the self-pitying Hightower, but the rest is clear and devastating. The time-shifts, the apparent divagations, both advance the story and broaden its foundations until it becomes formidable. Critics like Fiedler have thought the sexual affair of Christmas and the hard middle-aged woman an example of Faulkner's hysteria. This is nonsense. The affair is understood phase by phase; no addict of the Romantic Agony would have been capable of an analysis so exact. Faulkner's portraits, in this book, are as minute as Dostoyevsky's.

Faulkner's successors are not interested in destiny and place. They belong to the city and one city is like another. The only "time and wilderness" with any meaning for them is inside themselves, and picketed by their intelligence. There are the timidities, the anxious ventures of Malamud's immigrants. They did not expect much of

America except a passing hope; it passes; they pull a face. Obviously, humility and patience under more and more punishment are the best guides. The sad Jewish teacher who goes to northern California in hope, and finds dullness, who seeks Nature and gets—in this age of vital statistics—a mother-figure with breasts like a pair of pimples, two adopted children, and a helplessly irregular menstrual cycle, appears to be debunking an American dream. But in fact this book is not satire. It is a piece of ironical persuasion. He will sigh and school himself to murmur Hosanna! every time he loses a job and she gets a new pain. Salinger, Malamud, and Bellow are full of the high comedy of "Thank you for nothing," but they enjoy the nothing. They find a whisper of satisfaction in something which is not quite the syllable Om or the "Jesus Prayer" of Franny and Zooey, upon whom bits of culture are flicked like custard by some funny God off-stage, as they pass through adolescence to more adolescence. If that something has a syllable, it sounds to me like Nix.

In their second look at the things American writers have been worrying about for a generation—women, identity, the boy-man—some respectable fantasies have been deflated. There are no sleeping-bag girls, no Contessas, no Temple Drakes out to castrate the male, no Earth Mothers. It is true that in the second, showy and inferior part of *Augie March* there is a *belle dame* with a terribly chic bird of prey; but one's general impression is that women are getting a better deal: they are liked because they are so awful and tell such lies. One even has the sight of a generation of American novelists who are, at last, becoming curious about women and surprised by sex. As for the boy-man, Bellow's *Henderson the Rain King* is, on one level, a second look at that persecuted character. If one cares to interpret the mysterious book in this way, he is provided with a rich and outrageous dream-life, something far fuller than any Walter Mitty stuff. He behaves in his imaginary Africa like a hot-tempered, hypersensitive Tarzan, and is softened up by a couple of tribes who divert his energies and teach him courage. Henderson is a vast character worthy of uproarious success and ludicrous disaster; there is nothing mingy in his mind, and he has a cheerful time as he passes through the conflict between Being and Becoming. If Bellow's allegory is an attempt to supply the American male with an inner life or motive for living, then I prefer it to Hemingway's merely physical struggles with fish; and the intelligent, bullying, and resourceful eloquence of Bellow offers more than the wistful matterings of Zen.

# "William Faulkner"

From *New Statesman*, September 28, 1962, page 408. Reprinted by permission of the Estate of Allen Tate and Ellen H. Tate.

I am writing this memoir, or perhaps it had better be called an obituary, in Italy, where it is so difficult to find William Faulkner's books that I have not even tried. But at one time or another I have read them all except *Knight's Gambit* and *The Reivers*, and it is probably better, on this occasion, to rely upon one's memory than to try to read again and "reevaluate" the greater books. I am not sure of what I am about to write, but I am thinking of it as recollection and appreciation, not criticism, yet without what amounts to a profound admiration of his works (this is a kind of criticism) I should not have accepted the editor's invitation to write about William Faulkner at all. For in the 31 years of our acquaintance I saw him no more than five or six times, and but for one meeting in Rome about 10 years ago he seemed to me arrogant and ill-mannered in a way that I felt qualified to distinguish as peculiarly "Southern": in company he usually failed to reply when spoken to, or when he spoke there was something grandiose in the profusion with which he sprinkled his remarks with "Sirs" and "Ma'ms." Years ago, when I was editing a quarterly review, I had some correspondence with him; his letters were signed "Faulkner." I wrote him that English nobility followed this practice and I never heard from him again.

I suppose the main source of my annoyance with him was his affectation of not being a writer, but a farmer; this would have been pretentious even had he been a farmer. But being a "farmer," he did not "associate" with writers—with the consequence that he was usually surrounded by third-rate writers or just plain sycophants. I never heard that he was a friend of anybody who could conceivably have been his peer.

One may leave the man to posterity, but the work must be reread now, and talked about, lest Faulkner, like other writers of immense fame in their lifetime, go into a slump. However great a writer may be, the public gets increasingly tired of him; his death seems to remove the obligation to read him. But, if I had read *The Reivers*, I should be willing to say something about the work as a whole and an essay would make some of the points that I can only suggest in this "obituary" of a man I did not like, but of a writer who since the early Thirties I have thought was the greatest American novelist after Henry James: a novelist of an originality and power not equaled by his contemporaries, Hemingway and Fitzgerald.

Leaving aside the two books that I have not read, I should say that he wrote at least five masterpieces (what other American novelist wrote so many, except James?): they are *The Sound and the Fury*, *As I Lay Dying*, *Sanctuary*, *Light in August*, and *The Hamlet*. I know people of good judgment who would add to this list *The Wild Palms* and *Absalom, Absalom!*, books that contain some great writing but that in the end are not novels. Of the four first titles on my list, none appeared after 1932; the fifth in 1940. *Absalom, Absalom!* and *The Wild Palms* came out in 1936 and 1939. All Faulkner's seven great books were written in a span of about 11 or 12 years. The fine long history "The Bear" was written towards the end of this period. The later books round out the picture of Yoknapatawpha County (Lafayette County, Mississippi), but nobody would know them had the earlier books not been written. William Faulkner wrote only one bad novel, *A Fable*, his version of the Grand Inquisitor, conceived in theological ignorance and placed in a setting that he had not observed.

Observation of a scene is the phrase that will take us closer than any other to the mystery of Faulkner's genius; the three plots of *Light in August* are all in synopsis incredible, but we believe them at last, or accept them as probable, because the characters are in the first place credible. The famous violence of William Faulkner is a violence of character, not of action; there are, of course, violent scenes, yet these scenes, like the murder of Joe Christmas in *Light in August*, or the Bundren family crossing the swollen river with Addie's coffin, all add up to a powerful direct impression of life which Henry James said some 90 years ago would be the province of the novel. I am not indulging myself in paradox when I say that nothing "happens" in *The Sound and the Fury*, just as nothing happens in *Madame Bovary*: in both novels there are famous suicides. Yet, Quentin Compson's death, though it comes before the end of the book, is the last brushstroke in the portrait of the Compson family; and likewise the suicide of Emma Bovary rounds out a picture, not an action.

The European reader finds something uniquely American in Faulkner, and obviously no European could have written his books; the few European commentators that I have read seem to me to glorify William Faulkner in a provincial American (or Southern) vacuum. I believe that as his personality fades from view he will be recognized as one of the last great craftsmen of the art of fiction which Ford Maddox Ford called the Impressionist Novel. From Stendhal through Flaubert and Joyce there is a direct line to Faulkner, and it is not a mere question of influence. Faulkner's great subject, as it was Flaubert's and Proust's, is passive suffering, the victim being destroyed either by society or by dark forces within himself. Faulkner is one of the great exemplars of the international school of fiction which for more than a century has reversed the Aristotelian doctrine that tragedy is an action, not a quality.

William Faulkner's time and place made it possible for him to extend this European tradition beyond any boundaries that were visible to novelists of New England, the Middle West, or the Far West. The Greco-Trojan myth (Northerners as the upstart Greeks, Southerners as the older, more civilized Trojans) presented Faulkner, before he had written a single line, with a large semi-historical background against which even his ignorant characters, like Lena Grove or Dewey Dell Bundren, as well as the more civilized Compsons and Sartorises could be projected in more human dimensions. I had occasion some years ago to say in the *New Statesman* that had William Faulkner invented this myth, it could not have been as good as it turned out to be. (Sophocles was doubtless in a similarly advantageous position with respect to the Oedipean cycle.) Faulkner brought to bear upon the myth greater imaginative powers than any of his contemporaries possessed; but he was not unique; for it is only further evidence of his greatness that he wrote in an age when there were other Southern novelists almost as good: Robert Penn Warren, Caroline Gordon, Andrew Lytle, Stark Young, Eudora Welty, Katherine Anne Porter—and Faulkner would have included Thomas Wolfe, though I did not credit his honesty when he placed Wolfe at the top. (He never mentioned the others.)

Two secondary themes in Faulkner have obscured the critics' awareness of the great theme. These are: the white man's legacy of guilt for slavery and the rape of the land. These themes are almost obsessive, but they are not the main themes. William Faulkner was not a "segregationist." (Whether he was an "integrationist" is a different question.) But how could he not have been a segregationist when he said that he would shoot Negroes in the streets if the Federal Government interfered in Mississippi? Unless the European—or for that matter the Northern—reader understands that for Faulkner, and for thousands of other Southerners of his generation, the separatism and possible autonomy of the South came before all other "problems" he will misread Faulkner because he will not have discerned the great theme. I will repeat it in a different language: the destruction of the Old South released native forces of disorder and corruption which were accelerated by the brutal exploitation of the Carpetbaggers and an army of occupation; thus the old order of dignity and principle was replaced by upstarts and cynical materialists. Federal interference in the South had brought this about and when Faulkner said he would shoot Negroes if that were necessary to keep Federal interference at bay, his response came directly out of the Greco-Trojan myth; and yet it was the response of a man who had depicted Negroes with greater understanding and compassion than any other Southern writer of his time.

He is, I think, with Hawthorne and James, in the United States, and one of the great company in Europe that I have mentioned. "I salute thee, Mantovano." The Tennysonian-Vergillian reference is not inappropriate, for William Faulkner's rhetoric goes back to the Roman oratory of the Old South. He was a great writer. We shall not see his like again in our time.

JOHN DOS PASSOS

# "Faulkner"

From *Occasions and Protests* (Chicago: Henry Regnery, 1964), 275–77. [Written in
1962 and published in *National Review,* January 15, 1963, page 11.] Reprinted by
permission of the Estate of John Dos Passos and Lucy Dos Passos Coggin.

Faulkner's storytelling appeals to me so much, I suppose, because it is the kind of storytelling I remember as a child down in the North Neck of Virginia. Sitting in a row of men on some rickety porch after the dishes had been cleared off the supper table on a hot August night when the dry-flies shrilled, rocking and smoking or chewing tobacco a man would start talking. Usually he didn't explain who the people were he was telling about. You were supposed to know that. It would be "he" or "she" or sometimes "what's his name" did this or that. Gradually out of a web of seemingly disconnected incidents a story would evolve. Characters in situations scary or mirthful would take shape. A scene would light up as if you were there watching. Listeners would draw in their breath or laugh and slap their knees. I'd be sitting on the porch steps keeping out of sight for fear somebody would notice me and send me off to bed, never minding the mosquito bites, listening till my ears burst.

Reading Faulkner brings that lost world back to me. It's so often an eleven-year-old boy who is the listener through whose ears the outlandish scrambled tales pour into the reader's blood. Faulkner's writing has a way of pouring direct into the bloodstream like a transfusion. It was his oldtime rural storyteller's gift that enabled him somehow to keep his steaming turgid inventions—blood and thunder mixed with often false psychological subtleties out of the psychiatrist's clinic—within the margins of the tall story tellingly told. You are carried away whether you believe it or not.

At his best Faulkner's gothic caricatures of men and women, for all the claptrap of the plots, come to life as Dickens's did. Always the emotions ring true.

Storytelling is the creation of myths. A good acting myth doesn't have to be plausible but it has to impose its own reality on mankind. I defy anybody who has been reading Faulkner to look at a map of the state of Mississippi without expecting to find Yoknapatawpha County there.

Faulkner's characters impose their nightmare reality upon you because they are built out of truths, the truths of the stirrings of the flesh and blood and passion of real men observed tenderly and amusedly and frightenedly, just as Homer made his goddesses and heroes real because he built them out of traits he knew in men and women. In Faulkner what I like best is the detail, the marvelously accurate observations he built in his narrative out of the raw material of his inventions. Has there ever been a bear more real than Old Ben in *Big Wood*? His unendingly cordial study of the struggle between the bloods of various races under one man's hide is truthtelling of the highest order. So are his descriptions of the happy symbiosis that builds up under certain conditions between men of discordant races and disparate backgrounds. The Chickasaw Indians who bought the steamboat, the hound dogs, the hunting dogs, the little fyce dogs, the horses, the mules, the trees, the streams, and the swamps; and the kitchen clock (I think it was in *Soldiers' Pay*) that ticked out: life, death; life, death.

And now the great storyteller is dead. I don't imagine death came too hard to him. He had met death before many times in his storytelling. His stories are full of the knowledge of death. He did not meet death as a stranger.

# "Author Gave Life to Fictional County"

From *On Faulkner* (Jackson: University Press of Mississippi, 2003), 43–44.
[Written for the Associated Press and first published on July 7, 1962, in
newspapers throughout the United States.] Copyright © 1962 by Eudora Welty
and 2003 by the University Press of Mississippi. Reprinted by permission
of Russell & Volkening as agents for the author.

William Faulkner saw all the world in his fictional county where we can see it now—where he made it live. His work is a triumphant vision. This vision, like life itself, has its light and dark, its time and place, and love and battle, its generations of feeling, and its long reaches of what happens to people out there and inside, in heart and mind, which is so much.

Of course he wrote what was more, and will remain more, than others knew before him; he has instructed as well as moved and amazed us, a great artist.

So unmistakably born out of knowledge of his own, out of his sense and feeling (love, apprehension, outrage, compassion, pride, grief) for his own, his novels and stories were built at every step and stage out of his long passion of seeing life he knew by seeing as well as he could into it and around it.

All this required, and took, an imagination that has shone incomparably the brightest in our firmament.

What is great and puny, what is tragic and uproarious about us all in our own dogged lives everywhere, is a living life itself on any page of his. And in literature it is this that matters and always will matter.

Humanity was his subject, but he was a poet when he was born to see what he saw. Laid, nearly all of it at home in Mississippi, his work has a poet's authority by which it travels the world and puts the world to measure. Indeed, these days, it seems itself when the world does not.

We have learned lately that it sank into the bones of the Japanese as readily as into ours here. Though once you could buy his books in France, I believe, and not in New York, except with luck at second-hand, and not anywhere in Jackson, Miss.

Surely he never wrote a line except what his own eyes, ears, memory, and his poet's imagination told him what was not "true" but truth.

He went out on every limb, I believe, that he knew was there.

GEORGE GARRETT

# "The Influence of William Faulkner"

From *The Georgia Review* 18 (Winter 1964): 419–27. Copyright © 1964 by the University of Georgia. Reprinted by permission of *The Georgia Review*.

No contemporary writer can ignore the work of William Faulkner. If he is a young American writer, the chances are that he will have read and studied books by Faulkner and about Faulkner in school; and it is likely that our next wave of writers, those now in schools and colleges, will have been even more extensively and systematically exposed to his art. What effect this latter development will have remains to be seen. It is possible that it may tend to generate the inevitable rebellion of the bright student against what he is made to read and told to like. However, those who cherish the work of William Faulkner can be sure that the power and mastery of that great artist will overwhelm even the natural recalcitrance of the students and the well-meaning ineptitude of teachers.

It is difficult in many ways for a young writer to have to stand in the long shadow of a master. Dryden no doubt voiced the deep feeling of many other poets when he complained about having to follow after Shakespeare. Yet he went on working, and our young writers will go on writing novels and hoping to write better ones as long as our language lives. Whatever happens to the novel, even if, as pessimists in unison declare, it dwindles in its audience and importance to the tiny, insular world of poetry in our time, novels will go on being written, just as poems go on being written and dutifully, hopefully sent off (with return postage and self-addressed envelope) to cross the chaotic desks of magazine editors who are at best jaded and at worst indifferent. (I have been editing the poetry for *The Transatlantic Review* since it was founded in 1959 and I confess to being a little of both.) There is no stifling of the creative impulse, though that impulse may, indeed, become less and less rational as it offers fewer rewards. It is *especially* difficult to be a "southern" writer, that is, a writer born and raised in the South, at home with its traditions and history, and to follow in time after William Faulkner. One of the most exciting discoveries about Faulkner for the young southern writer is his use of the *material* of southern life and history. The South is many places and peoples, all quite different, yet there is much that is common to it all. The southern writer is very much aware that Faulkner did not invent his material. It was there to be mined and explored. The close student and the scholar of southern literature become increasingly aware of how much of that basic material was *already* a part of the literary tradition of the South before Faulkner came on the scene. Some of this will begin to show up in forthcoming studies— the extent to which Faulkner deliberately worked within and with a tradition of whose conventions he was acutely knowledgeable. Professor J. L. Blotner of Virginia, who has had the privilege of examining Faulkner's library with some care, has remarked that the number of "old southern books" is surprising. It should not be so. If it were not for the public myth he so carefully cultivated in order to preserve his precious privacy, that of being an inspired "farmer" who just happened to write books, it would surprise no one.

The southern writer is able to see Faulkner as realist. He is capable by birth and inheritance of divorcing subject and treatment and thus able to acknowledge the real genius involved in the choice of subject and the supreme mastery of technique, a dazzling virtuoso performance of more than thirty years of professional writing without ever going stale or ever repeating himself. The trouble for the southern writer begins with the old, immutable fact that most of his editors and a large proportion of the book reviewers and critics with whom he must contend are *not* southern and not versed in the southern tradition, literary or actual. Of course, it isn't their fault. They can't really be blamed for being born elsewhere. But they can and should be blamed for failing to recognize that many of the themes and subjects he used do not belong to Faulkner, who never for one moment proposed that he was inventing them, but to a time and a place, already changing fast as the world changes, but still all of a piece and close enough in time for his history to be our history. In fact the works of William Faulkner are now a part of our southern history. The sane solution for the young writer is, of course, not to avoid writing about something he knows just because Faulkner also may have written on a similar subject. But the enormous difficulty of convincing editors, publishers, and finally readers who are strangers to the South (except in the Press version, also composed and contrived by strangers and for strangers) that one's work is merely a bucket from the same deep well has forced many southern writers of recent times into the strategy of innovation for its own sake or into exile from their proper subject. Most of the old Fugitives are fugitive indeed, expatriates living in the suburban North, far, far from their real soil or their nostalgic, agrarian dream.

These same expatriate southerners have not helped the situation by insisting in public and private that William Faulkner might have been a better man and a better writer had he only moved north and surrounded himself with literary types, rather than living in Oxford and working alone. Many northern critics have suggested this as well, and it was with some astonishment that I heard Faulkner's editor, the late Saxe Commins, express the same opinion. I have heard this from a number of distinguished writers, editors, and critics, some of them southerners by birth. The most recent example in print I know of is in a piece by Allen Tate written for the *New Statesman* (28 September 1962), which Tate calls "a memoir, or perhaps it had better be an obituary . . . ." There Tate takes the occasion of an obituary to bring up the old saw, though in literary terms, of William Faulkner wasting away in the benighted wilderness:

> I suppose my main source of annoyance with him was his affectation of not being a writer, but a farmer; this would have been pretentious even if he had been a farmer. But being a "farmer," he did not "associate" with writers or just plain sycophants. I never heard that he was a friend of anybody who could conceivably have been his peer.

Friendship, "belonging," "togetherness," seem important to Tate here. One need not be so cynical or unkind as to ask whom Tate would name as Faulkner's peers. Still, this view is important because Faulkner, indeed *belonging* by choice to a time and a place and a literary tradition, did not need the additional stimulus of being deeply involved in "the literary life." It is just as well. The work might not have been written at all if he had allowed himself to be surrounded by literary friends and enemies and cliques, all chattering brightly over the edges of martini glasses about the latest news from Olympus, the latest quotations from what Frost always called "the literary stockmarket," and the latest gossip and odds on who will win what prizes year after next when the judges and committees change. The combined novels of all the Fugitives add up to less work than Faulkner's, which in itself stands as an example of dedication and professionalism for any young writer and, as well, an estimate of the price that must be paid in the coinage of misunderstanding by one's own countrymen, by long neglect, and by the indifference of the reading public.

Faulkner made a definite and significant choice at a certain point early in his career. When his third, and most ambitious book at that stage, *Sartoris*, was rejected by everybody and finally accepted by Harcourt Brace with some humiliating provisos and stipulations, he suddenly realized that "the literary world" was a world well lost. He rejoiced in his new freedom and set about the writing of *The Sound and the Fury, Sanctuary*, and *As I Lay Dying* in rapid order. Of this decision he has written: "I seemed to shut a door between me and all publishers' addresses and book lists. I said to myself, Now I can write."

Most of the young writers I know have been *inspired* by William Faulkner. All have been influenced one way or another. There are clear and present dangers in the process of influence. There is something marvelously hypnotic about the style and method; though, contrary to the opinion of most critics, there never was *a* style, but many and all designed to fit a subject. Perhaps even more than with the single style of Hemingway, Faulkner's stylistic virtuosity has a way of so overpowering the young and highly receptive talent that the young writer can shake off this specific influence only with effort and difficulty. There are a few writers who have on occasion deliberately, and

not without some success, cultivated this process rather than resist-
ing it. I would cite Shelby Foote's *Jordan County*, William Styron's
*Lie Down in Darkness*, and William Humphrey's *Home from the Hill*.
Humphrey has stated in talks and interviews that he subscribes to the
notion of Robert Louis Stevenson, that of a deliberate, conscious imitation in detail of the methods of a master whose work one admires.
Styron has managed to outgrow the initial effect of this influence, im-
proving through to other novels and gradually finding his own way
and his own voice. It is significant, however, that Styron's most successful novel to date, *Set This House on Fire*, is only briefly and partially set in the South. Calder Willingham has been called a satirist of
the Faulkner style. This may indeed be so, but it is difficult to establish
and, if so, pointless except as a typical example of a young southern
writer living with and wrestling with the problem.

In my first novel, *The Finished Man*, I tried something else, a fancy
trick for which I got my knuckles rapped and probably deserved to.
Only once in the book did I attempt to use something reminiscent
of Faulkner's style, a vague echo, for a particular purpose. One character was telling another of the most crucial event in his life. I tried,
in a somewhat different vocabulary, to imitate some of the sweeps
and pauses of the Faulknerian rhythm, hoping to suggest to the ideal,
alert reader that my character was not really telling the truth, that he
had already over the years made something "literary" out of the event.
(My character was decently educated and would very likely have read
some Faulkner, though I never explicitly said so.) It was intended to
be a kind of allusion, not for the purpose of satire or parody, but as a
part of the preparation for revelations to come. It did not work. One
reviewer after another quoted this particular passage, a very brief one
in a longish book, as typical of the book and as an example of how
much I had been "influenced" by Faulkner. I had and have been much
influenced. But not in that particular passage. And not in that particular way.

The influence of technique, of course, has not been confined to
southern writers. A great many American writers, dealing with other
regions and sometimes radically different subjects, show the signs of
a careful study of Faulkner's narrative techniques. Wright Morris, for
example, is clearly indebted to Faulkner in a number of his novels;

this in spite of the fact that in his critical writings he has not been altogether fair to his model, accusing Faulkner of being the victim of a vague nostalgia and further arguing that the only really soundly created characters in Faulkner's work are his Negro characters. The latter, Morris insists, is the result of the fact that the Negro is inherently superior to the southern white and not a result of Faulkner's deliberate characterization in the context of a given story. In other words, Morris sees this as *unintentional*. These points deserve some scrutiny, if only because Wright Morris is a very "literary" writer, much involved, *engaged* in the literary scene, and therefore these opinions are apt to be as much shared as they are original. There are, in fact, three myths of current literary criticism at work behind Morris's statements: the myth of Faulkner as the "unintentional," spontaneous writer, a misunderstanding, deriving from that rather incredible and far-reaching assumption, about "the message" of his work, and coming from both these misconceptions, a conclusion that characterization in Faulkner's books was overcome by a propensity toward symbolic statement. The first of these myths, what might facetiously be called "the unintentional fallacy," is partly attributable to the mystery of Faulkner himself deliberately cultivated in order to protect his privacy. But now, with many of his manuscripts and papers available for study at Virginia and Texas, this has been shown to be sheer nonsense. If anything Faulkner was a finicky, compulsive reviser of his work. Another factor which gives the lie to the unintentional theory, and one that has not been seriously considered in its relationship to his whole body of work, is Faulkner's considerable experience and success as a screenwriter. A chapter in J. B. Meriwether's fact-filled *The Literary Career of William Faulkner*, with careful reference to other little known studies of Faulkner's Hollywood work, indicates that he worked on films over a considerable period of his career. He has an impressive list of credits, and when one realizes that until quite recently credits were not given as a matter of course or right, it is probable that he worked on a good many more. It is also likely that we shall never have the whole story. The point is relevant to this extent: screenwriting, though it may not be art in itself, is terribly exacting work. All effects are and must be calculated. As one who has done a stint in Hollywood, I am amazed at the variety of success of William

Faulkner's work there. Most "serious" writers cannot stand the strain. Judging by his interviews, I believe he was able to do the job well because he never took *it* seriously, always realizing that a multiple form, involving so many disparate hands, could never be controlled by the writer. He was careful never to become deeply involved in the filming of any of his own books, thus allowing himself a proper distance. If the screenplay is highly calculated in all its effects and if Faulkner was a good screenwriter, it follows inevitably that in his serious work he was at least capable of control. It is high time that we give an artist the basic credit he deserves. He knew what he was doing.

Brief mention should be made, even at the expense of digression, of the fact that we need someone to study with care and dedication the extent of the influence of the film on Faulkner's writing. Visiting at the University of Virginia recently, John Dos Passos admitted the film, even certain precise films, as a major influence in his own documentary and chronicle method. It is possible that Faulkner, who was a good deal more involved with the industry of making movies, was also influenced. I see this influence in two ways. First a kind of anti-cinematic method of narration in the novels, as if to dare adaptation. He has created the kind of books that break the heart of the hack adaptor. They are not easily converted to the medium. They must be translated like poems in another language. Which may be the reason why the successful adaptations of his novels have been so few and far between. Ironically, he showed the way, *how* it can be down, by his own free-wheeling film adaptation of Hemingway's *To Have and To Have Not*. At first glance it shares little more than the title. Yet the whole *milieu* of this film is the *milieu*, the world of Hemingway. Bogart is the perfect Hemingway hero. (Perhaps there is even a bit of literary criticism subtly at work there. As if Faulkner were saying: "This is what it *really* adds up to.") In any case *To Have and To Have Not* is a far better film than any of the more "accurate" adaptations of Hemingway's work, except, perhaps the first version of *A Farewell to Arms*. The second way in which I believe the film form influenced Faulkner is more positive. This would take some doing to *prove*, a patient Ph.D. dissertation. I think it can be shown that the methods of transition—cuts, dissolves, and fades—are at work in his prose fiction, as well as camera-like angles—pans, high shots, close shots, long shots, etc., montage effects, and finally even the curious continual present time of the framed celluloid world. Of all our novelists, William Faulkner has been the most successful as a screenwriter, a fact that is not without honor and one which certainly cannot be safely ignored by the critics.

Back to the fallacies of Wright Morris (and others).

The problem of "message" and character. Morris's notion is old and new. *The Art of Faulkner's Novels* by Peter Swiggart is entirely based on this idea. Swiggart states it explicitly at the outset. "Faulkner's narrative achievements may be explained in terms of his ability to express abstract themes by means of stylized characters without detracting from the dramatic force, and the apparent realism, of his narrative situations. Arbitrary stylization is compensated for in his work by the creation of characters who have explicit symbolic functions, yet live in the reader's imagination as if they were real people." Reduced of its excess of jargon and critical terminology, what this adds up to is that Faulkner *fools* the reader. He was more interested in saying something than in character, that his people are really two-dimensional. If this is so, it is a serious charge; for it means Faulkner failed in his primary intention. Talking to a writing class at the University of Virginia, Faulkner, who was always interested in young writers (recall that his Nobel Prize speech was in part addressed to "the young men and women already dedicated to the same anguish and travail"), said this about message: "A message is one of his [the writer's] tools, just like the rhetoric, just like the punctuation . . . . You write a story to tell about people, man in his constant struggle with his own heart, with the hearts of others, or with his environment." Another time he told the students: "I'm not expressing my own ideas in the stories I tell. I'm telling about people, and these people express ideas which sometimes are mine, sometimes not." He went on to say in his fiction he was neither satirizing his own country, nor trying to correct it, though he might do both publicly as a private citizen. He was writing about people. Too many critics and some writers (who ought to know better) have tended to blame Faulkner for the opinions, prejudices, and defects in his characters. In one sense this is a tribute to his mastery, but it has created problems. James Baldwin, with both error and ignorance, has assumed Faulkner to be a racist and denounced him for it. Norman Mailer in his incredible example of exhibitionism, *Advertisements for Myself*, reveals the same bias and ignorance. Both these writers have clearly been influenced technically. There are many recent books which show the signs of technical influence. Edmund Keeley's *The Libation* takes its intricate time scheme, along with certain other details, directly from Faulkner. The very new book *The One Hundred Dollar Misunderstanding* is a student exercise in the Faulkner technique of alternative viewpoints.

There is another kind of influence which, paradoxically, while seeming negative is more positive. It is perhaps best illustrated by the beautiful statement of another kind of fiction presented in Glenway Wescott's *Images of Truth*. Wescott, along with others, is for a return to the fabric and pace of narration, the avoidance of technical fiddling and foolery for its own sake, and, as far as possible, the divorce of the novel from the deliberate cultivations of the effects and devices of modern poetry. Faulkner began as a poet, was much influenced by the directions of modern poetry in his prose; and it is at once a tribute and a criticism that no two of his novels employ the same narrative method. He blazed his trails, broke ground, opened up new country for the American novelist. But it does not follow that the novelists now writing should do the same thing or try to duplicate his pioneering. His achievement is a fact. That may be what the subtle and gifted Mr. Westcott meant when he told students at the University of Virginia (in reply to a direct question about Faulkner) that the works of Faulkner were for him like the Blue Ridge Mountains in the distance, beautiful to look at, but he did not intend to climb them.

From his earliest critical writings while still a student at the University of Mississippi, William Faulkner showed a great desire to be a part of the creations of the worthy *American* traditions of writing. He saw himself as a pioneer, not the first, for he honored Twain, Dreiser, and above all Sherwood Anderson, but among them. He left behind a large, varied body of work and the record of a long professional career. He preserved much of his past. He opened new vistas for writers to follow. It is hard to guess what his influence will be in the future. It is as certain as the changing weather that his reputation will go up and down. And it looks as if it will be a long time before a great many myths and misconceptions about the man and his work are dispelled.

There are good men trying to get at the truth, for example the dedicated scholar Meriwether at Chapel Hill and, as well, Carvel Collins of M.I.T. But the articles based on other articles and the books based on other books, most of them just plain bad, proliferate like Error. No doubt they will always be with us like the poor.

For myself, and for many of the young writers I know, he stands as a master, an *example* from whom we can always learn. There is no sense of competition. Art is not a horserace. Nor is there any particular need for technical thievery. We will borrow when we need to, just as he did, but we will strive not to be copy cats, instead to find our own voices. Just as he did. Most of all he is a model for behavior as novelist. He kept going, kept writing in spite of indifference and hostility, praise and blame for the wrong reasons. And through it all he preserved his sanity, his humor, his courage, and his integrity. When Homer began the *Odyssey* with Telemachus, the untried son, he was giving us the point of view from which to regard the fabulous adventures to follow. Besides the story of the hero's homeward journey Homer tells the story of the education of a young man (one of Faulkner's favorite subjects), not so that Telemachus could make the same journey, but so that he could profit by the example and one day become a man himself. We have in the long and full career of Faulkner, a heroic example against which to measure our woes and joys. If there is any meaning in human history or the life of a great man, then some of us, with luck and perseverance, will be better writers than we deserve to be because he has gone before. All of us are given a literature in our language that is better than it deserves to be because of his selfless dedication to the craft and art of fiction.

# "Faulkner: Past and Future"

It was in the Spring of 1929 that John Gould Fletcher, on a visit
to Oxford University, where I was a student, gave me a copy of
*Soldiers' Pay*. I had been out of the South for a long time—in a
sense, in flight from the South—and at least half of me was oriented
toward Greenwich Village and the Left Bank and not toward the
Cumberland Valley in Tennessee; but at the same time I was, I suppose, homesick, and was making my first serious attempt at fiction,
fiction with a setting in the part of the South where I had grown up.
As a novel, *Soldiers' Pay* is no better than it should be, but it made a
profound and undefinable impression on me. Then came, in the order of my reading, *The Sound and the Fury, As I Lay Dying, Sanctuary*, and *These Thirteen*.

What happened to me was what happened to almost all the book-
reading Southerners I knew. They found dramatized in Faulkner's
work some truth about the South and their own Southernness that
had been lying speechless in their experience. Even landscapes and
objects took on a new depth of meaning, and the human face, stance,
and gesture took on a new dignity.

If you, in spite of your own sometimes self-conscious and willed
Southernness, had been alienated by the official Southern pieties, ali-
bis, and daydreams, the novels of Faulkner told you that there was,
if you looked a second time, an intense, tormented, and brutal, but
dignified and sometimes noble, reality beyond whatever façade cer-

tain people tried to hypnotize you into seeing. With this fiction there was not only the thrill of encountering strong literature. There was the thrill of seeing how a life that you yourself observed and were part of might move into the dimension of art. There was, most personally, the thrill of discovering your own relation to time and place, to life as you were destined to live it.

Even the images of degradation and violence—by which Southern pride, as officially exemplified by the DAR and the Chamber of Commerce, was so often shocked—seemed added certification of the reality of the novels: a perverse and perhaps self-indulgent delight, which you yourself recognized, in the dark complications of Southern life, a reflexive response to an unidentified tension and a smoldering rage beneath the surface of Southern life. What, in other words, the fiction of Faulkner gave was a release into life, into the sense of a grand and disturbing meaningfulness beneath the crust of life, into a moral reality beneath the crust of history.

I am offering this local and personal testimony, because I want to indicate that the first, powerful impact of Faulkner's work was by an immediate intuition, not by the exegesis of critics. The great images—which the novels contain, and are—spoke in their own always enigmatic and often ambiguous terms, by an awakening of awareness, by a kind of life-shock, long before the exegeses were written.

This is not to disparage the work of criticism. It is, rather, to do it proper honor by saying that it refers, and fulfills, a fundamental relation between life and art. It re-orders, refines, reinterprets, and corrects the burden of the original institutions; it may even make new institutions possible. Criticism may not only make more available the life-meaning of art—that is, may make clearer how the art it deals with may be read as significant for life. It may also make more available the art-meaning of life. And I may add that it is in this perspective that the non-Southern, even non-American, critics have done their greatest service, for, not knowing Southern life firsthand, they have sometimes been freer to regard the fictions as a refraction in art of a special way of life and not as a mere documentation of that way of life.

Let us look back to the place and time when Faulkner began to write.

In a profound way, Faulkner resembles Robert Frost, and his relation to the South resembles that of Robert Frost to New England.
Both men seem so deeply demanded by their moment in history, at
the very end of their respective cultures, that, forgetting the matter of
genius, one is tempted to say that the moment is the man, and the man
a role created by the moment. Both Faulkner and Frost were firmly
and intransigently rooted in old America, the America which was liq-
uidated by the First World War, and both were even more firmly and
intransigently rooted in a particular locality and in the history of the
locality. Both made a characteristic drama out of the locality and the
history, and both—most importantly of all—created a role, a *persona*,
a mask that defined a relation to the locality and the world beyond,
and the mask gave the voice. Both, that is, knowing the shape and feel
of life in a particular place and time, felt the story of man-in-nature
and of man-in-community, and could, therefore, take the particular
locality as a vantage point from which to criticize modernity for its
defective view of man-in-nature and man-in-community. Last of all,
in a paradoxical way, the appeal that both Faulkner and Frost have for
the world of modernity stems from the fact that they represent something strange and lost—something that the modern world is deeply
ambivalent about and therefore cannot quite ignore, no matter how
much it would like to ignore it.

To return specifically to Faulkner: he was of the generation of
World War I; but except for a brief period as a Royal Air Force ca-
det pilot in Canada, he missed the war, and this fact, if we may judge
from his fiction may have marked him, in its own way, more deci-
sively than even combat could have done. He missed participating in
the great communal effort that made the new United States. It is now
hard for us to realize that in 1917, despite the adventure of 1898, the
shadow of the events of 1861–65 was real, and there was concern that
the South might not feel committed to the national effort; and if, in
a sense, Belleau Wood and the Argonne finished the work of Appo-
mattox, and confirmed the new United States, Faulkner had no hand
in that work. It may also be significant that, in the general context of
things, Faulkner's effort to participate in the war was in the Royal Air
Force and not in that of the United States. In any case, these things,
the fact that he enlisted in Canada and that he missed combat, may

have emphasized his sense of "outsideness" vis-à-vis the new nation and its new boom—the sense of outsideness that must have been one of the factors that drove him to create a whole social order and a history to account for his outsideness; and on this matter of outsideness, we must bear firmly in mind that, though he knew, hated, and wrote of it, he was especially outside of the New South—the South that so desperately aspired to be like Kansas City or Cleveland, to be, in simple terms, rich.

Faulkner did not see the massive and benumbing violence of trench warfare, nor did he even see the human price exacted for the aristocratic individualism of the air. So some dreams remained intact. And some deep personal bias toward violence, some admiration of the crazy personal gesture (like that of the Bayard in *Sartoris* who gets himself killed going after anchovies on a dare from a captured Yankee officer), and an idealized version of the South's old war, could persist untarnished and uncriticized by grisly actuality. Untarnished and un-criticized, that is, until the logic of his imagination had done its work. It is hard to believe that a man as subtly aware as Faulkner of the depth of the human soul could have been unconscious of the possibilities in himself. And it is harder to believe that, in the complex chemistry of personality and of artistic creation, Percy Grimm, of *Light in August*, who has missed World War I and who lives in a dream of sadistic violence masked by military rigor, and Hightower, who, with his romantic dream of Civil War, counterpoints him in that novel, are not projections—and purgations—of potentials in Faulkner himself.

The South which Faulkner had grown up in—particularly the rural South—was cut-off, inward-turning, backward-looking. It was a culture frozen in its virtues and vices, and even for the generation that grew up after World War I, that South offered an image of massive immobility in all ways, an image, if one was romantic, of the unchangeableness of the human condition, beautiful, sad, painful, tragic—sunlight slanting over a mellow autumn field, a field more precious for the fact that its yield had been meager.

Even if one had read enough history to know that things *do* change, that even the romantic image in the head was the result of prior changes, that the image of an elegiac autumn implied the prior image of a summer of violent energies, the image still persisted, as though the process of history had led to this stubbornly, and preciously, held vision of non-history.

Strangely, this elegiac vision in which energy was sublimated into poetry was coupled with another vision, a sort of antithetical vision, in which violence irrationally erupted through the autumn serenity to create the characteristic "Southern" drama. And in another way the vision of the South was paradoxical. The South, with its immobility, seemed the true challenge to youthful energy that always demands change, and at the same time it was, as I have indicated, the place where history *had* been, had already fulfilled itself, had died—and could be contemplated.

But this vision of non-history is only half the matter. The First World War had brought America into a shocking cultural collision with Europe. For the South, withdrawn and somnolent, came into collision not only with Europe but with the North and the new order there. It is true that in some ways the effects of World War I seemed more obvious in the North; for instance, the great Northern industrial and financial establishment was now out of debt and dominant in the world, with all the consequences which this entailed. But such changes in the North were changes, not so much of kind, as of degree. In the South, on the other hand, the changes, even if often concealed, were often more radical and dramatic; there were profound tensions, deep inner divisions of loyalties, new ambitions set against old pieties, new opportunities, new despairs, new moral problems, or rather, old problems which had never been articulated and confronted—all the things that stir a man, or a society, to utterance. The South, then, offered the classic situation of a world stung and stirred, by cultural shock, to create an art, in order to objectify and grasp the nature of its own inner drama.

The very style of this new utterance in the South is instructive. There was, of course, a strain of realism in the South, best exemplified in that period by Ellen Glasgow and T. S. Stribling, but this strain was not dominant. A variant of symbolism was often characteristic, as might be expected from the nearly irreconcilable tensions and the deep inwardness of the drama with which it dealt. Furthermore, as a fact to be associated with the tendency toward symbolism, Southern

writing was often radical in method—more radical by and large, than the writing in other parts of the country. Its radicalism often had a European orientation, its ancestors in Dostoyevsky, Conrad, Baudelaire, Proust, Joyce, and Yeats; and the Americans it found most compelling were usually those with a European bias—James, Eliot, Pound, Hart Crane. If in the moment of cultural shock Southern writers were impelled to explore the traditional basis of their world, the language and techniques which many of them used for that exploration were antitraditional. This fact in itself implies the very spiritual tensions in the work; for a language and a technique are not mere instruments, they are gauges of attitude, instruments of evaluation and modes of discovery, and even against a man's will may modify what he makes of his own world. At the same time, as another point of tension, in contrast to the sophistication of technique, the folk tradition, especially folk humor, was very much alive for many Southern writers. We must recall, as the most obvious example, that Faulkner is a great humorist, in the line of Mark Twain, as well as a great technical virtuoso.

As a technician, Faulkner, except for his peers, Melville and James, is the most profound experimenter in the novel that America has produced. But the experiments were developed out of—that is, were not merely applied to—an anguishing research into the southern past and the continuing implications of that past. We may remark, for instance, that the period when Faulkner developed his experiments is the period when his fundamental insights were achieved, when he pierced the crust of his traditional material, when he most deeply dramatized the key moral issues of Southern life. In that strange interfusion which seems to be characteristic of such a situation of cultural shock, the complexity of issues demanded the technique, but at the same time, the issues would not have been available, been visible in fact, without the technique. The cultural shock and the technical development go hand in hand.

The great period of Faulkner's achievement—from *The Sound and the Fury* to *The Hamlet*—overlaps, too, with the Depression and the time of the premonitory shadows of World War II, with another time, that is, of deep cultural shock. The tension and changes in this time were acute. This is not to say that Faulkner specifically took the Depression as a subject, but it is to say that the Depression accentuated the issues of the time and change which Faulkner had already located as seminal for him. The sense of the unchangeableness of the human condition which had characterized the life of the rural South even after World War I, was now, suddenly, with the Depression, changed. Conversation turned to the question of what could be done to "change" things, even if for some people the desired change was, paradoxically enough, to change things back to their old unchangeableness; to escape, to phrase it another way, from *history-as-lived* back to *history-as-contemplated*; from *history-as-action* to *history-as-ritual*. But even to change back to unchangeableness would be a kind of change. There was, then, no way to avoid the notion of change; you had to take a bite, willy-nilly, of the apple from the mysterious tree that had sprung up in the Confederate garden.

We can, in fact, think of the poles of Faulkner's work as *history-as-action* and *history-as-ritual*. We may even see this polarity as related to another which he was so fond of—and so indefinite in the formulation of—the polarity of fact and truth. We may see it, too, in the drama of his outraged Platonism—outraged by the world and the flesh.

Faulkner began writing, of course, in the full tide of the Coolidge Boom, but the crash had long since come—in October 1929—by the time *l'affaire Faulkner* was presented to general attention with the publication, in 1931, of *Sanctuary*. Certainly, the assumptions and tone of Faulkner's work would have seemed irrelevant in the context of the Boom; in the context of the Depression they often seemed, not irrelevant, but inimical.

In the great objective world, in a context of human suffering, issues of the most profound social, political, and moral importance were being fought out, and it was only natural that practical men, if they happened to have read or have heard of Faulkner, should regard his work as merely a pathological vision happily distant from serious concerns—unless, of course, it could be used as evidence of the need for an enlarged PWA program or free shoes in that barefoot world. It was, as I have said, only natural that practical men, if they read Faulkner at all, should have read him in this spirit, and the fact is not significant.

What is, however, significant—and significant in a way far transcending the fate of the work of Faulkner—is that, by and large, the world of "impractical" men, of intellectuals, betrayed its trust by trying to be "practical," resigned its function of criticizing and interpreting the demands of the practical world, and often became a comic parody—comic because dealing with the shadow, not the substance of power and action—of the world of practicality. What could not be converted in a mechanical, schematic, and immediate way into an accepted formula for social action was interpreted as "reactionary," "decadent," "gothic," "fascist," or merely "Southern."

All these elements were, in fact, in Faulkner's work. The work was certainly Southern life, and in Faulkner's work, which, taken in isolation, might suggest the word *fascist*, and all the rest. For instance, the delusions of a Gail Hightower might provide the compost for breeding fascism, and there was, thirty-odd years ago, as now, many a Percy Grimm in the South, a type not too unlike a certain kind of fascist bully-boy. But the mere presence, in isolation, is not what is important. What is important is the context, the dialectic, in which such elements appear. We have only to look at the role of Hightower in *Light in August*, or to remember that Faulkner prided himself on Percy Grimm as his invention of a Nazi Stormtrooper. Or we may set the distortions some critics made of the role of Negro characters in Faulkner's work over against the role Negroes actually play in the work. The fact that meaning is always a matter of relation should be clear to anyone—though it was not clear to certain well-intentioned men who had sacrificed their intelligence in the cause of what they regarded as virtue.

This is not to say that Faulkner was the victim of a conspiracy among card-carrying, or even fellow-traveling, book reviewers. A climate can be more lethal than a conspiracy, and the climate was that of para-Marxist neo-naturalism, with the doctrine of art-as-illustration—debates concerning which we can find embalmed, for example, in the proceedings of the American Writers' Congress. Since such "leftism" had become intellectually chic, the new attitudes were assimilated with no pain and little reflection by college professors, ladies' clubs, news-minded literary editors, and book reviewers who a few short years before might have attacked Faulkner merely because he was dirty and not very optimistic. In the new context, the com-

bination of tragic intensity, ribald and rambunctious comedy, violence and pathology, Negro field hands and Mississippi aristocrats,
old-fashioned rhetoric and new-fangled time shifts, symbolism and
obscurity, amounted to outrage—and probably to fascism.

Even if *Sartoris, The Sound and the Fury*, and *As I Lay Dying* were
commercial failures, a certain number of reviewers had recognized
talent but as the new decade took shape, the talent, even when recognized, was often recognized more grudgingly—or even with the
sense that the presence of talent compounded the original outrage.
This clearly was not a literature in tune with the New Deal, the new
post office art, the new social conscience, the new Moscow trials, or
the new anything. It was, simply, new: that is, created. And in some
circles, at all times, for a thing to be truly created, is to be outrageous.[1]

The literary criticism of the Depression slipped without any grind-
ing of gears into that of the War period. The literary criticism of the
war period, stimulated by the War in Spain, antedated Pearl Harbor
by several years. The atmosphere of war simply added a new element,
and a new justification, to the attitudes of the Depression, and added
to the list of writers to be taken by men of good will as irrelevant, or
inimical, to social progress. As the shadow of war grew, critics more
and more found reprehensible all literary work that emphasized lags
between our professions of national faith and our performance. In
fact, it sometimes seemed that, with the pressure of events, the rise
of patriotism, and the exigencies of propaganda, it was less important
to clean up our messes than to sweep them under the rug. If America
was the temple, as well as the arsenal, of democracy, it should be presented, for the sake of a higher truth and by a higher law, in the most
effective way possible, with *son et lumière*—appropriate music and
strategically placed floodlights for tourists, who were to be admitted
to the spectacle only after the vulgar, factual glare of day had been
mercifully withdrawn.

In a way somewhat unfair to what he actually said, Archibald MacLeish's essay "The Irresponsibles" was generally taken as the prime
statement of this attitude. But MacLeish did see and deplore a split
between literature and what he regarded as political responsibility—
an attitude which he put more precisely in another essay "Post-War
Writers and Pre-War Readers"[2] where he specifically condemned

Barbusse, Ford, Hemingway, Dos Passos, Remarque, and Aldington because "what they wrote, however noble it may have been as literature, however true to them as a summary of their personal experience, was disastrous as education for a generation which would be obliged to face the threat of fascism in its adult years."[3] Faulkner, of course, became—or rather, long before, had become—the most obvious target for this attitude; and the notion that he was a liability for which American patriots should apologize, persisted even in the editorial in which the *New York Times* commented on the Nobel Prize:

> His [Faulkner's] field of vision is concentrated on a society that is too often vicious, depraved, decadent, corrupt. Americans must fervently hope that the award by a Swedish jury and the enormous vogue of Faulkner's works in Latin America and on the European Continent, especially in France, does not mean that foreigners admire him because he gives them the picture of American life they believe to be typical and true. There has been too much of that feeling lately, again especially in France. Incest and rape may be common pastimes in Faulkner's "Jefferson, Miss." but they are not elsewhere in the United States.

To return to the time of the coming of World War II, the notion that Faulkner's complicated techniques were somehow associated with reprehensible content anticipated a line of criticism brought to bear on Pound's poetry after his capture and imprisonment. Back in 1940, Percy Boynton had commented on such a connection in Faulkner's work by affirming that "the technique is simple and the content more lucid in those tales which have the greater normality," and becomes "more intricate and elusive in the tales of abnormality," and that "technique becomes a compensation for content as content sinks in the social scale." By this line of reasoning the prose of the famous corn cob scene would, of course, make that of *Finnegan's Wake* look like a selection from *The Bobbsey Twins*.[4]

Faulkner's trouble with the patriots was compounded by two other factors. First, he had no truck with any obvious programs for social salvation. Steinbeck and Caldwell, though they both showed abuses and degradation in American life, showed them with a diagnosis and the hint of a quick cure that was fashionable in the reviewing trade. Second, Faulkner was Southern. Of course, Wolfe was Southern, too; but nobody ever took him for a fascist; he showed none of the dark ambivalences of Quentin Compson, off at Harvard, telling the story of Sutpen to the innocent Canadian. Furthermore, Wolfe hymned America in terms reminiscent of, it was said, Whitman.

A little later, with the War well started, *The Valley of Decision*, by Marcia Davenport, was widely hailed as a major contribution to literature and to the war effort. A little later still, *Strange Fruit*, by Lillian Smith, in the moment of a new conscience on the race question stimulated by the need for black factory hands and black troops and by A. Philip Randolph's March-on-Washington movement, was received with hosannahs by a chorus of critics led by Eleanor Roosevelt. By this time Faulkner's most recent book, *Go Down, Moses*, which also had something to do with conscience and the race question, was forgotten, and by 1945, all seventeen of his books were out of print.

The great watershed for Faulkner's reputation in the United States is usually, and quite correctly, taken to be the publication of *The Portable Faulkner* in 1946. Several factors contributed to the effect of the *Portable*. First, Cowley's Introduction,[5] developing but substantially modifying a line of interpretation originally suggested, in 1939, by George Marion O'Donnell,[6] persuasively insisted on the significant coherence of Faulkner's work taken as a whole. Second, the selection itself was made with taste and cunning to support the thesis. Third, the fact that the reputation of Cowley himself as associated with the "left wing," as critic and as editor of the *New Republic* (in which *The Sound and the Fury* had been reviewed, though not by Cowley, under the head "Signifying Nothing"), gave certain piquancy, and in some circles, an air of authority and respectability to his estimate of Faulkner. Fourth, the time was ripe.

By 1946, the climate had changed—if not for the better, at least for a difference. With Hitler dead in his bunker and the Duce hung by his heels at the filling station in Milan, and with the marriage of American liberalism and Joseph Stalin running on the rocks, a new kind of idiocy became fashionable and raced forward to fulfillment in Joe McCarthy; and Faulkner no longer served the old function of scapegoat of all work. He had survived—endured, in fact—and was part of the landscape, like a hill or tree.

I do not know what force the college classrooms of the country exert in making or breaking literary reputations, but in the period of late thirties and early forties, when professors of American literature and of the then new-fangled American Studies were often inclined to speak of Steinbeck's *In Dubious Battle* and of Howard Fast's *Citizen Tom Paine* in the tones of hushed reverence once reserved for the works of Sophocles, Faulkner had received short shrift. After the War, with the horde of returning GI's, the process backfired. As one GI put it to me, "I been robbed!" He reported that in the good university where he had pernoctated before the call to arms, his class in American literature had dedicated six weeks to *The Grapes of Wrath* and thirty minutes to Faulkner, thirty minutes being long enough to allow the professor to document from "A Rose for Emily," the only work investigated, that Faulkner was a cryptofascist. Such young men immersed themselves in the work of Faulkner with ferocious attention. As far as I could determine, they had little of that kind of romantic disillusion that was reputed to have been common after World War I. They were motivated, rather, by a disgust for simple, schematic, two-dimensional views of the worlds. Many of them had had, first-hand, a shocking acquaintance with the depths and paradoxes of experience, and now literary renderings that did not honor their experience were not for them. Furthermore, as a corollary, they, having been caught in the great dehumanizing machine of war, were forced to reflect on their own relation to the modern world, not in terms of political and social arrangements, but in terms of identity itself. That is, they found in the works of Faulkner and in the method of his works something that corresponded to, and validated, their own experience.

Returning GI's did not, however, exclusively constitute the new and expanding readership of Faulkner, though their view of the world may have had something in common with that of some nonmilitary citizens of the United States, or with that of the Japanese, French, and Italians, military and nonmilitary, who took his fiction to their hearts. It can, perhaps, be plausibly argued that Faulkner is one of the few contemporary fiction writers—perhaps the only American—whose work is to any considerable degree concerned with the central issues of our time, who really picks at the scab of our time, in the way that, in varying degrees of intensity and scale, Melville, Dostoyevsky, Kafka, Conrad, Proust, Eliot, Yeats, and Camus, also do.

In thinking of such a question, we must remember that being topical and being central are two very different things. In the 1930s—as now—there were battalions of writers in the United States who programmatically tried to will themselves into tune with the Zeitgeist. The trouble was that, almost to a man, they confused the Zeitgeist with current newspaper headlines and lead reviews in the Sunday book sections. The Zeitgeist may speak through the headlines, just as it may speak through a new metric or a theory of corporate structure; but we cannot therefore assume that the headlines *are* the Zeitgeist. Rather, some writer who most obviously seems to be in tune with the Zeitgeist may be merely caught in a superficial eddy of history, which often, as Melville, in "The Conflict of Convictions," puts it, "spins against the way it drives." By the same token, the writer who seems alienated and withdrawn may appear, in the light of history, as central. For instance, at the moment when Milton, blind, defeated and obscure, was composing *Paradise Lost*, would anybody have thought him central?

Perhaps what the returning GI's found in Faulkner is what had drawn other readers, too. Perhaps the blind, blank, dehumanized and dehumanizing, depersonalized and depersonalizing modern war is the appropriate metaphor for our age—or for one aspect of our age—and paraphrasing Clausewitz, we may say that war is merely an extension of our kind of peace. In that case, we are all GI's, and any reader may come, in mufti, to Faulkner's work with the same built-in questions as the GI of 1946, seeking the same revelatory images of experience. Perhaps the images of violence, in which Faulkner's work abounds, are, to adapt a famous remark by Poe, not of the South but of the soul; and perhaps their Southernness has such a deep appeal because this order of violence, with the teasing charm of antiquity, is associated with the assertion of, or the quest for, selfhood, the discovery of a role, or the declaration of a value, in the context of anonymous violence or blankness. Perhaps all the images in Faulkner's work of the mystic marriage of the hunter and the hunted have a meaning more metaphysical than anthropological; and all the images of isolation, self-imposed by a wrong relation to nature or to history, or visited blindly on the individual, are to be taken as images of the doom that we all, increasingly in our time, must struggle against; and the images of Southern alienation are only images of Everyman facing one of the possibilities in his world. Perhaps we see in the agonies, longings, and nobilities of the unimportant people like Charlotte Rittenmeyer or the convict of *Wild Palms*, like Joe Christmas, like Ruby of *Sanctuary*, like Dilsey, or even like the idiot Snopes, some image of the meaningfulness of the individual effort and experience over against the machine of the world.

It is not only the implications of the objective dramatization in Faulkner's work—character and situation—which have attracted readers. The sense of the work's being a subjective dramatization has been there too—the sense that the world created so powerfully represents a projection of an inner experience of the author somehow not too different from one the reader might know all to well. Faulkner has a remarkable ear for speech—either in dialogue or in the long narrative monologue, like that of Jason, for instance, or that of Ratliff in "Spotted Horses," the early version of the horse auction scene of *The Hamlet*. But generally Faulkner's narratives are sustained not by such reported, or ventriloquist, voices, but by a single dominant voice[7]— the highly personal style which, for better or worse, seems to be the index of the subjective drama, and which guarantees to the reader that the story is truly alive in the deepest way. As Albert Thibaudet says of Proust, the tide of his sentences carries with it as it advances the creative élan that gives it life; or as Monique Nathan puts it in her book about Faulkner, there is something "almost liturgical" in the function of his style. And we might add that, to take the Aristotelian terms, a novel of Faulkner combines the drama (or narrative) and the dithyramb, the latter being the personal medium in which the impersonal renderings of experience are sustained.

The mask-like, taciturn and withdrawn quality of Faulkner the man, and the impersonality of his fiction, compared, for example, with that of Wolfe, Hemingway, or Fitzgerald, seems, paradoxically, to attest to a deep, secret involvement, to the possibility of a revelation which the reader might wrest from the Delphic darkness. Malraux has hinted at this inner involvement, surmising that Faulkner would often imagine his scenes before imagining his characters, and that a work would not be for him "une histoire" the development of which would determine situation, but quite the contrary, springing from the encounter of faceless characters unknown to him, shrouded figures charged with possibility. If I read Malraux right, he is implying that the germ of work might lie in such an archetypal scene—a flash—in which all else, story and character, would be hidden; the scene being a living, intimate metaphor direct from the author's depth. There is some support for Malraux's surmise in the fact that *The Sound and the Fury*, according to Faulkner's testimony, developed from the vision of a little girl's muddy drawers, and *Light in August* from the vision of "a young woman, pregnant, walking along a strange road." The relation of the author to such a vision is directly personal, springing unbidden, as I have said, from the depth; the vision like a poultice, draws the characters and the action out of him. To put it another way, the vision, in the first place, is only the projection of, and focus for, that subjective drama which, though distorted beyond all recognition, may become the story, the objective drama that will carry the mystic burden of the secret involvement from which it springs.

It would be misleading to imply that there is now a massive unanimity of praise for Faulkner's work. Over the years various kinds of attack have been mounted against it, but the most important line of adverse criticism now with us is that Faulkner is basically confused in thought and unclear in style. The best advertised exponents of this view appeared a number of years ago, one being Clifton Fadiman, in his review of *Absalom, Absalom!* In the *New Yorker* in 1936, and the other being Alfred Kazin, whose *On Native Ground* appeared in 1942. Though Kazin recognized Faulkner's powers of invention, and stylistic and technical resourcefulness, he complained that Faulkner has "no primary and design-like conception of the South, that his admiration and acceptance and disgust operated together in his mind"; that "as a participant in the communal myth of the South's tradition and decline, Faulkner was curiously dull, furiously commonplace, and often meaningless, suggesting some ambiguous irresponsibility and exasperated sullenness of mind, some different atrophy or indifference"; that his work does not "spring from a conscious and procreative criticism of society"; that there is a "gap between the deliberation of his effects, the intensity of his every conception, and the besetting and depressing looseness, the almost sick passivity, of his basic meaning and purpose"; and that his complicated technique "seems to spring from an obscure and profligate confusion, a manifest absence of purpose, rather than from an elaborate but coherent aim."

In all fairness it should be said that in later years Kazin's attitude has mellowed greatly, a change of which I first became aware at a round table on Faulkner at Columbia University, provoked by the award of the Nobel Prize, where Kazin eloquently defended Faulkner's work against the old charge of being primarily a neurotic manifestation. Even so, though more willing, with the years, to recognize the importance of Faulkner's work and to be more lavish of compliments, Kazin is still distressed by what he terms Faulkner's "attempt to will his powerful material into a kind of harmony that it does not really possess." This remark appears in an excellent essay on *Light in August*, which Kazin is willing to call "great" (the essay appearing as a book entitled *Twelve Original Essays on Great American Novels*), but which he says is "somewhat more furious in expression than meaningful in content." This essay does offer a brilliant and important treatment of Joe Christmas as the "incarnation of 'man,'"—but at the same time finds him "compelling rather than believable." So, here reappears, though in a more sympathetic and guarded form, the same objection that had appeared in *On Native Ground*: the objection that there is a gap between the talent ("compelling") and the meaning ("believable"), that the polarities and contradictions of the material have not been "really" put into "harmony."

There is no clear and objective way to settle this question, any more than there is to settle the similar question raised by E. M. Forster's charge, in *Abinger Harvest*, that Conrad "is misty in the middle as well as at the edges, that the secret casket contains a vapor rather than a jewel." In such cases, we usually come to a matter of temperament, training, and cast of mind. What many readers prize in Faulkner's work is often the fact of the polarities, contradictions, and inharmonious elements which they would take to be "really" inherent in life deeply regarded and which offer the creative spirit its most fruitful challenge—though the challenge is to a battle that can never be finally won. Kazin, however, would still seem to imply that the process of creation is much more deductive, that it should spring from an "elaborate but coherent aim," that good work should "spring from a conscious and procreative criticism of society . . . from some absolute knowledge."

Clearly, "absolute knowledge" is not what Faulkner's work springs from or pretends to achieve. It springs from, shall we say, a need—not a program or even an intention or criticism of society—to struggle with the painful incoherences and paradoxes of life, and with the contradictory and often unworthy impulses and feelings in the self, in order to achieve meaning; but to struggle, in the awareness that meaning, if achieved, will always rest in perilous balance, and that the great undergirding and overachieving meaning of life is in the act of trying to create meaning through struggle. To a mind that is basically schematic, deductive, and rationalistic, with an appetite for "absolute knowledge," such a writer as Faulkner is bound to generate difficulties and severe discontents. But the service which a critic with such a cast of mind may do is important; he may set bounds to enthusiasms, may drive readers to define what kinds (if any) of resolution and unity have actually been achieved, may drive readers to try to determine how much of what they admire is actually there in a given work and how much is a projection of their own needs and prejudices.

But a critic, like a writer, must finally take the risk of his own for-mulations—this, despite the favorite delusion of all critics, who are after all human beings, that their formulations are somehow exempt from the vicissitudes of life which the novel or poem must endure. As a matter of fact, the moment a critic sets pen to paper, or finger to keyboard, the novel or poem itself becomes the silent and sleepless critic of the critic, and it is just possible that the split which Kazin sees between talent and achievement in Faulkner, between furious expression and meaningless content, indicates not so much a split in the thing criticized as in the critic—a split in the critic himself, between a mind, with the laudable appetite for "absolute knowledge," and an artistic sensibility which allows for the sincere but troubling appreciation of "talent," "technique," and "effects," and for isolated instances of pathos and drama.

I have referred to Kazin because he puts the argument against

Faulkner more fully and effectively than any other critic. But the argument is an old one. It had appeared, troublingly, in Cowley's early reviews. It had appeared in Wyndham Lewis's savage and funny essay, "The Moralist with a Corn-Cob," in his *Men Without Art* (1934). There Lewis has good sport at the expense of Faulkner's style, but finds little beyond the façade of "ill-selected words." The characters, he says, "are heavily energized as the most energetic could wish," but they are "energized and worked-up to no purpose—all 'signifying nothing,'" and the "destiny" or "doom" behind Faulkner's fiction is merely a fraudulent device for operating the puppets. Sean O'Faolain, more than twenty years later, takes the same line—the style is inflated and inaccurate, is fustian, not the "artist's meaningful language" but the "demagogue's careless, rhetorical and often meaningless language," and all of this is an index to an "inward failure to focus clearly," to a lack of intelligence, to an inner "daemon" rather than a proper subject, to "ideals that he can vaguely feel but never express."

Somewhat more recently as an example of a somewhat different line of criticism, we may take an essay by Walter J. Slatoff, "The Edge of Order: The Pattern of Faulkner's Rhetoric," which maintains that Faulkner's "temperamental response rather than any theories of ideas and particular torments" are what the author "trusts to produce order in his art"—that the art represents an overabundance of oxymorons, contradictions, oppositions, polarities, which remained unresolved, that, in treating Isaac McCaslin, Faulkner has made "the choice which he can rarely resist, and which . . . seriously limits his stature, the choice not to choose." I have said that this line of criticisms, which in various forms not infrequently appears, is different from that of Lewis, Kazin, and O'Faolain: but it is different only in approach, for in the end it amounts to much the same thing, turgidity of style and inner meaninglessness, as temperament or obsession or daemon takes over the role of ideas, ideals, brains, intelligence, or "absolute knowledge."

I must refer to one more variant, and an important one, of the criticism that Faulkner's work lacks intelligence and meaning. This is the view that he has not been able to understand the nature of our age and therefore is not relevant for us who live in it. Faulkner, according to Norman Podhoretz, who best exemplifies this line of attack, has entirely missed the Enlightenment, with its "qualities of reasonableness, moderation, compromise, tolerance, sober choice—in short, the anti-apocalyptic style of life brought into the modern world by the middle class." Faulkner "doesn't even hate" the middle class "accurately," his Jason being as much a creature of compulsion as Quentin, without "sober choice," etc. Having missed the Enlightenment and not understanding the middle class, Faulkner really lacks a sense of history, and therefore cannot record the real shock of change in modernity. For instance, what has the "Glory celebrated in Yoknapatawpha got to do with the Korean War . . . a war uninspiring, nay meaningless, to the Yoknapatawpha mind, and thrilling only to children of the Enlightenment who understand its moral sublimity?" Faulkner has, in *A Fable* (and we are given to understand in his other works too) taken refuge in "Larger Considerations" and an apocalyptic view of life and literary style, because he fails to understand the real issues and values of modernity, including the sublimity of the Korean War.

Podhoretz's essay was prompted by *A Fable*, and I must say I agree with him that this novel is, finally, a colossal failure and a colossal bore, and that it is as confused in conception as in execution. What I do not agree with is that it represents merely an extension of Faulkner's work. It may well be true—and I assume that it is true—that Faulkner intended *A Fable* to be an extension, and a generalization of the *meaning*, of his previous work, and to serve as a basis of exegesis for his work. And it is true that themes and ideas do come over from the past. But there is a difference, and a crucial one, between *A Fable* and the other work (with the exception of *Intruder in the Dust*, of which I shall speak later). *A Fable* is abstractly conceived; it is an idea deductively worked out—and at critical moments, blurred out. By the very absoluteness of the failure, however, *A Fable* indicates, not so much the limit of, as the nature of, Faulkner's success. Faulkner, like Antaeus, could fight only with his feet on the ground—on home ground; he had to work toward meaning through the complexity and specificity of a literal world in which he knew his way about, as a man knows his way about his own house without thinking how he gets from one room to another; only in that world could he find the seminal images that would focus his deepest feelings into vision. And this process implies something about the kind of meaning, and kind of glory, he would assume possible in life; and remembering Podhoretz's remark that "lack of ideas is no virtue in a novelist," we may say that, be that as it may, an idea any novelist has that does not come with some tang of experience, some earth yet clinging to the roots, or at least one drop of blood dripping from it, has no virtue for a novelist. Ideas without the mark of their experiential origin can only, to use Eliot's word, "violate" the consciousness of Faulkner.

Podhoretz ends his essay by wondering "whether the time will ever come again when a writer will be able to dismiss politics in favor of the Large Considerations without sounding like a chill echo from a dead world." Again I must register agreement with the critic, not with his generalization but with the implication that Faulkner is an a-political writer. It is really strange that in his vast panorama of society in a state where politics is the blood, bone, sinew, and passion of life, and the most popular sport, Faulkner has almost entirely omitted, not only a treatment of the subject, but references to it. It is easy to be contemptuous of politics anywhere, and especially easy in Jackson, Mississippi, but it is not easy to close one's eyes to the cosmic comedy enacted in that State House; and it is not easy to understand how Faulkner, with his genius for the absurd, even the tearfully absurd, could have rejected this subject. Unless, as may well have been the case, contempt overcame the comic sense. Furthermore, in *A Fable* and *Intruder in the Dust*, novels that do impinge on political realties, Faulkner seems to have little grasp of them. In *A Fable* the failure is at root one of tone—we don't know how we are to take his fable in relation to the "realities." In *Intruder in the Dust*, Faulkner, like many other Southerners, black and white, including the present writer at one time in his life, may have been beguiled by the hope that the South, on its own responsibility, might learn to deal with the Negro in justice and humanity. The fact was that such a hope, in the face of the political realities (as a reflex, perhaps, from economic and certain other realities), and with the lack of courageous and clear-headed leadership, was a fond delusion. On this point, Faulkner was as much out of touch with the political nature of his own world as Camus was with the *colons* of Algeria when he tried to address them.

More significant than that hope was, however, the idea, expressed by Gavin Stevens, of a cultural homogeneity of Negro Southerners and white Southerners that would prevail against the rest of society. The whole idea is foggy in the extreme, and is foggily expressed, but, as I read it, it implies that the shared experience of the races in the South, for all the bitterness and tension, has created a basis for reconciliation. Some Negroes, in fact, have held this view—or hope—and many whites. But this bond, whatever its force or meaning, which is referred to by Gavin Stevens, came from a rural, individualistic society, or from a town life which still carried its values over from such a society. What Gavin Stevens (and Faulkner, and many other Southerners, white and black) did not do was to take a look at the Negro slums in the great Northern cities, and see there the shape of the future in the South as the mechanization of farming, and other factors, drove, and drew, the Negro from the land, and, in fact, subtly but deeply changed the nature of the whites who remained on the land. Furthermore, a "homogeneity" would, in the world of practical affairs, come too late to have any effect—certainly too late to seal off Mississippi from Freedom Riders, workers for CORE, SNCC, and SCLC, to prevent the founding of the Freedom Democratic Party, or to halt U.S. marshals at the border.

Gavin Stevens was talking some twenty years ago, and had not had the benefit of instruction from this morning's newspaper. It is easy for us, with the newspaper in hand and with the grass green, to say that we heard that grass growing. We can see things that Gavin could not, or would not, see, and among those things is one that has a certain comedy about it. In the South, even in small Mississippi towns like Philadelphia, McComb, Canton, Grenada, Greenwood, and Oxford, it will probably be the middle-class business men, the group for whom Faulkner cherished no particular fondness, and who, in Oxford, were not particularly enthusiastic about closing their stores and offices for his funeral, who, not from moral virtue or any theory of homogeneity, but from stark self-interest, once the message gets through to them that "nigger-trouble" is bad for business, will take the lead in working out some sort of reasonably decent racial settlement.

Faulkner was a-political, and he was, as Podhoretz puts it, "out of touch with contemporary experience"—if by contemporary experience we mean experience at the level Podhoretz specifies. But this leaves us with some troubling questions. For one, if Faulkner, because

he is a-political, is not relevant for us, why do we still read such a-political works as *Moby Dick, The Scarlet Letter, Madame Bovary, A la
récherche du temps perdu*, and *The Portrait of a Lady*—or an outright
or anti-political work like Shakespeare's *Troilus and Cressida*?[8] Or
do we read them merely from academic interest, plus the incidental
pleasure of being able to say that they are not "relevant"? There is
indeed a problem of relevance, of what makes a work of literature
specially valuable for one age and not for another. Works are not arranged in a great museum in a Platonic outer space drenched evenly
by the chill white light of Eternity, bearing placards to indicate category and value. They do have a relation to the continuing life process,
a relation of enormous complexity, certainly of greater complexity
than I hinted at in the essay now under discussion. In fact, the whole
argument for "relevance" as put in this essay has, as Podhoretz says
of the work of Hemingway, Faulkner, and Dos Passos, taken on "that
slightly stilted archaic look" of an old photograph—and the archaic
look, in this case, is that of the 1930s, when it was fashionable to assert a wide assortment of writers, including Flaubert, Proust, Frost,
and T. S. Eliot[9] were not "relevant." But those writers have, somehow,
survived, and we even have the comic fact that Faulkner, who in those
days was often rejected as the most irrelevant of all, was passionately
read in places as different as Tokyo and Paris for the simple reason
that he was taken to have something to say to the modern soul. The
fact is that man, though a political animal, is many other kinds of animal, too. He is, even, a human animal.

I do not accept the basic thrust of the argument of Lewis, Kazin,
O'Faolain, Podhoretz *et al.*, but I do think that these critics point to
what might be called the defects of Faulkner's virtues, and I think that
their views help to locate and limit some of the critical problems appropriate to Faulkner's work; for always when a reputation is resur-
rected from the dead—and some twenty years ago, in America at least,
Faulkner seemed to be consigned to the shades—there tends to be,
among the faithful as well as the newly redeemed, especially among
the latter, the notion that the final revelation is at hand. Now, not
only in the South but elsewhere, there is, clearly, the atmosphere of a
cult about Faulkner, as there was about Eliot in the dark days of the
Marxist dispensation, or about Pound in the period of rehabilitation.

Something of this tone appears in a letter by Russell Roth in

*Faulkner Studies:*[10] "I have the feeling that many critics—most of them, in fact—would prefer not to see that what he [Faulkner] has been driving at . . . what Faulkner says—is saying—cuts the feet out from under us; it flatly denies, or contradicts, or takes issue with most of our fundamental and most dearly cherished assumptions regarding our relation as individuals, to the world." There is, of course, always—no matter how often we may deny it—some issue of the kind and degree of "belief" in relation to any work of literature. True, there is more than one spirit and one way in which such an issue may be resolved—or it may be argued, with some plausibility, that such an issue can never be finally resolved, that in one way or another we must believe in a work or reject it. And certainly all really new work of literature comes into the world with the promise of a new view of man and the world, with, in short, a new doctrine, stated or implicit. The new work, even though it may seem to be merely a new style succeeds only because of the promise, usually secret, of some kind of redemption.

There is indeed a value, though not necessarily the final or overriding value, in such a promise; certainly there is a value in the fact—or in what I take to be the fact—that the issues implicit in Faulkner's work are deeply central to our time. But a cult does more than recognize such situations and values. A cult really denies the complexities of such a situation. It equates, quite simply, the doctrine with the value of the work, or if sophisticated, finds the values of style, for example, an implicit affirmation of doctrine, the emphasis here not being on the inner coherence of the work but on the doctrine which the style, and other technical elements, may be said to affirm. In other words, the present cult tends to repeat, in reverse, the old error of the 1930s, to make doctrine equal value.

The long period of exegesis in Faulkner criticism has contributed to the atmosphere of a cult. Exegesis delivers meaning from the cloudiness of text, and there is only one step from this fact to the conviction that the cloudiness was an aura of mana, a sacred cloudiness, and that those who have penetrated it are saved and set apart. And it is well to recall that the snobbery of the cult merges with the snobbery of the academy, and the process of exegesis has contributed to the sense that only by the application of academic method and in the exfoliation of theses can the truth be found, be packaged, and be delivered for consumption. The very classrooms—sometimes the very same professors—which once granted a grudging half-hour to document Faulkner's social irrelevance or perhaps his fascism, have now set about the canonization.

By and large, the cultism and the academic snobbery were accidental, merely an unfortunate by-product of a necessary endeavor. For the exegesis was necessary. Only by exegesis—such attempts at general schemes as those pioneering essays by O'Donnell and Cowley or such attempts at exploring the logic of method and style as the essays by Aiken and Beck, or the later studies of individual books—could the charge be rebutted that the work of Faulkner was, at center, pernicious or meaningless, and that the complications of method and style were no more than incompetence or self-indulgence.

But the period of exegesis seems to be drawing to a close. I do not mean that new exegeses will not appear. They should appear, if we are not to see criticism puddle and harden into an orthodoxy. But other kinds of interest are beginning to be felt, and will, no doubt, be felt more urgently. For instance, though much has been written about Faulkner and the South, much is repetitious, and there is clearly need for further thinking about the writer and his world. Related to this but not to be identified with it, are the questions of Faulkner's own psychology—his own stance of temperament. Both of these lines of interest are primarily genetic, they have to do with the question of how the work came to exist; but if this kind of criticism is pursued with imagination and tact, it can lead to a new awareness of the work itself, with a fuller understanding of the work as that unity of an art-object and a life-manifestation.

The most immediate need, however, is a criticism that will undertake to discriminate values and methods among the individual items of the canon. Faulkner was a fecund, various, and restless artist, and he paid a price for his peculiar qualities; some of the work is so uneven and unsure, so blurred or pretentious, that it provides apt texts for the most virulent of his detractors. We need a criticism that will do something by way of sorting out the various strands and manifestations of Faulkner's work, and by way of evaluating them. Furthermore, an overall definition and evaluation of the achievement has not been seriously attempted.

Undoubtedly, as in the natural history of all literary reputations,

Faulkner's work will enter a period of eclipse. Though man is, not merely a "political" animal, but a "human" one too, emphases do indeed shift, with the shift of time, from one aspect of his humanity to another, and his tastes and needs change; what appeals to some of us now will not appeal to another generation. But it is the obligation of criticism not merely to assert the taste and needs of one age, but to try to discriminate what values, if any, in a work may survive merely accidental factors of taste and need. Criticism is, in part, committed to the task of trying to build a bridge to the future. It is a hopeless task, certainly, it is, even, superfluous. A work itself is the only bridge possible, and that bridge may even lead the critic over into the future, where posterity may gather around to regard him, perhaps, as something as strange as the dodo or as blind as a fish drawn up from a stream in a cave.

*Notes*

1. For the record, and for their honor, it must be pointed out that some of the critics most firmly grounded in, and best informed about, Marxism did not fall into the trap. For instance, that brilliant and seminal critic, Kenneth Burke, the whole thrust of whose work was counter to such bigotry, and who, in 1939, after war had begun, remarked in a letter to the present writer that one could still learn more about men "from tropes than from tropisms." And there is Malcolm Cowley, the differences in whose background and philosophical and political assumptions did not prevent the long struggle of imagination which led to his editing of *The Portable Faulkner*.

Some documentation of this struggle is to be found in the series of reviews (*Pylon, Absalom, Absalom!, The Wild Palms, The Hamlet, Go Down, Moses* which Cowley did in the *New Republic*). Cowley's main objection is repeated several times—that there is some sort of split in Faulkner, "a lack of proportion between stimulus and response," as he says of *Pylon*, and in other terms about *Absalom, Absalom!*, which, he says, falls "short of the powerful mood it might have achieved." In fact, even as late as 1940, in reviewing *The Hamlet*, Cowley says that "one admires the author while feeling that most of his books are Gothic ruins, impressive only by moonlight." By 1942, however, in reviewing *Go Down, Moses*, he can say that "there is no other American writer who has been so consistently misinterpreted by his critics, including myself." Then after an attack on the views of Maxwell Geismar and Granville Hicks, he says Faulkner is "after Hemingway and perhaps Dos Passos, the most considerable novelist of this generation."

2. *New Republic*, June 10, 1940.

3. There was a kind of comic justice in the fact that MacLeish was occasionally tarred with his own brush. Oscar Cargill, in a book called *Intellectual America: Ideas on the March* (1941), did not forgive him, despite "The Irresponsibles," and pilloried him among those he calls the "decadents"—a group including Eliot, Hart Crane, and Pound. Cargill admitted that it was "hard to find four other poets with equal importance," but went on to say that, "Like Naturalism, Decadence has exerted an enfeebling influence on American character . . ." "The fall of France," he adds elsewhere, "was brought about in part (as Mr. MacLeish must realize) by decadent intellectualism."

This book, *Intellectual America*, is undoubtedly one of the curiosities of our (or any) literature. It also has a less morbid value as a reference book, in that it encyclopedically commemorates, in a naked and simple form, all the clichés of thought and expression of a decade. Mr. Cargill desperately wanted literature to serve the good of mankind but having not the foggiest notion of what literature is, he couldn't easily figure out what good it might serve—not any good from the "Naturalists," nor the "Decadents," nor the "Primitivists," nor the "Intelligentsia" (with a sub-head for "Modern Cynicism") nor the "Freudians." Among those Polonian (and Procrustean) categories Faulkner is crammed among the "Primitivists."

4. In a section from *Love and Death in the American Novel*, by Leslie Fielder, he uses the same kind of argument about style in passages where Faulkner writes of characters of mixed Negro and white blood.

5. P. 34.

6. P. 23.

7. The transfer of the horse auction scene from Ratliff to the "voice" in the novel affords a beautiful case history of this point.

8. A case might be made out that the politics of Shakespeare's History plays and Roman plays is really nothing more than a façade, and that they, too, are basically anti-political.

9. The game was carried so far that even a writer as definitely concerned with history and politics as Conrad, was said to be irrelevant; for instance, David Daiches, in *The Novel in the Modern World* said that Conrad was irrelevant because he was concerned only in the conflict of man against geography.

10. Summer 1952.

THOMAS MERTON

# "The Sounds are Furious"

From *The Critic* 25 (April–May 1967): 76–80. Copyright © by Thomas Merton.

Reprinted by permission of Anne H. McCormick for the Merton Literary Trust.

Thirty years ago, when Faulkner was at the height of his powers, the critics were doing their best to write him off as a failure. Even the few who, like Conrad Aiken, numbered themselves among his "passionate admirers" had serious reservations about Faulkner's style. In 1936, Clifton Fadiman reviewed *Absalom, Absalom!* in the *New Yorker* and decided that it represented "the final blowup of what was once a remarkable, if minor talent." However, Faulkner went on to publish the *Unvanquished* in 1938, *The Wild Palms* in 1939, *The Hamlet* in 1940 and *Go Down, Moses* in 1942. And at least two of these are admitted to be among his most important books. Nevertheless, by 1945 all seventeen of his early books were out of print. A period of silence, followed by *Intruder in the Dust* (1948) and the award of the 1950 Nobel Prize, reminded everyone that Faulkner was still around, but even then the critics tended to boycott him. He was dismissed as an irrelevant oddity, a pessimist, a sensationalist, a poseur, a mere "Southern writer." Above all, he was out of touch with the times. He did not come up with the acceptable slogans. He wrote of the South but what he wrote was trifling because it was myth rather than sociology. Those who grudgingly recognized that he had talent, felt that this only made matters worse: His talent was being wasted in lamentable eccentricities. When he was awarded the Nobel Prize, the *New York Times* scolded him in terms which, though far milder, remind one a little of the Soviet objections to Pasternak receiving the award. It was felt that perhaps Faulkner was too well liked in Europe because he presented a disgusting image of the United States.

Of course this picture must not be oversimplified. Malcolm Cowley, who had at first treated him rather roughly, edited *The Portable Faulkner* in 1946 and to this Faulkner himself contributed some original material that was not without importance (the so-called "Compson Appendix"). This *Portable*, as Robert Penn Warren shows, marked the "great watershed for Faulkner's reputation in the United States."

Faulkner's "pessimism" and the dark mythology which depressed the social-minded critics in the days of the New Deal nevertheless seemed to have something to say to men returning from World War II. They found in it a validation of their own experience of a world that Camus and so many others were describing as absurd. Again, in Robert Penn Warren's terms, Faulkner was proving to be "one of the few contemporary fiction writers—perhaps the only American— . . . who really picks at the scabs of our time in the way that Dostoyevsky, Kafka, Conrad, Proust and . . . Camus also do."

If Faulkner has been read with understanding and appreciation for this reason, it has been mostly in Europe. America still does not like scab-picking, especially when the scabs happen to be on our own hide. True, the Faulkner mythology has been much more widely accepted among us, and John L. Longley's study *The Tragic Mask* has taught us that we had a Sophocles in Mississippi and did not realize it. The mythical treatment of the wilderness-paradise theme in "The Bear" has also brought out the full positive scope of Faulkner's imaginative and quasi-religious vision of the South as a desecrated sanctuary. But myth itself is considered trivial in the minds of many American critics.

Faulkner was an outrageously and deliberately demanding writer. His tortuously involved time sequences, his interminable sentences, his multiplication of characters with the same name in the same book had one purpose above all: to ensure that the reader either became involved in the book or else dropped it altogether. Yet it is obvious, too, that Faulkner's style was often self-defeating. If it involved the reader enough to make him go back over a thirty-line sentence to puzzle out its meaning, and if after that the reader found the thirty-line sentence did not matter anyway, he would be likely to regret his involvement and throw the book aside. Faulkner's long sentences are perhaps meant more to obsess than to enlighten. But in any event, involvement in Faulkner means something more than paying close attention to a story; it means entering into the power of his mythical obsessions. In the words of the French critic, Claude Edmonde Magny, it means allowing Faulkner to cast his spells over you; for in her opinion, Faulkner works like a pre-historic Shaman who enmeshes the reader in numinous symbols and entrances him with sacred horror. To quote Conrad, the reader gets the "feeling of being captured by the incredible which is the very essence of dreams."

Unfortunately, there is a certain type of mind which fears and avoids this kind of witchery. The thing is dangerous. Too much is let loose. The spells are too awful. And there are various ways of defending oneself against them. The obvious refusal of assent is typified by easy ridicule which Fadiman poured on Sutpen in *Absalom*. "He's the fellow you're supposed to shudder at, and if you understand Mr. Faulkner you'll shudder."

The only really serious Faulkner criticism is that which assents to the myth firmly enough to be captured by the incredible and then judges it from within: is it authentic, or phony? In between these two poles of mere ridicule and serious involvement, is what one might call the standard American objection to Faulkner: the repudiation of an apocalyptic mystique of the absurd, which is Faulkner's way of celebrating the American destiny.

A typical example of this repudiation is found in Norman Podhoretz's criticism of *A Fable*—one of Faulkner's major failures. It would be well to detail the criticisms here.

To begin with, there is so much wrong with *A Fable* itself that it can easily be demolished. Writing not of the familiar South but of unfamiliar Europe and World War I, Faulkner tried to create a religious myth and succeeded only in concocting a pious allegory which has intentional Christian elements but which is without any of the usual tragic and metaphysical Faulknerian power. It does not really convince on any level. V. S. Pritchett called it a game of "rhetorical poker with the marked cards of myth and symbol." Of this equivocation Podhoretz says: It "is just another one of those proofs that an artist must either accept the religious view of the universe as literal truth or leave its myths alone." One might want to argue a little about the word "literal" here—because there is a definitely "religious view of the universe" behind a book like *Light in August,* though it is not something that is spelled out in penny catechisms. As Sartre said very rightly, writing on *The Sound and the Fury,* "a fictional technique always relates back to the novelist's metaphysics. The critic's task is to define the latter before evaluating the former." But critics like Podhoretz are not interested in metaphysics, whether Faulkner's or anybody else's. And the emptiness of *A Fable* gave Podhoretz an excuse for dismissing Faulkner's metaphysics instead of trying to define it. From the failure of *A Fable* Podhoretz goes on, as such critics often do, to generalize about Faulkner's work as a whole. The faults of this book are extended to all the others, and we learn that "Faulkner has *always* taken refuge from historical change in a vague sense of doom."

This is getting close to the heart of the matter, because in fact the great question in Faulkner—or one of the great questions—centers around his sense of time and of history. We cannot go into that here, but it is enough to say that Faulknerian time is a monstrous non-progression dominated by the past event which casts a kind of implacable shadow over the present and paralyzes all action toward a definite future. "The unspeakable present, leaking at every seam" (says Sartre of Faulkner) lets in the monstrous obsessions of past evil. Man rides in the back of a convertible looking backward, and the swirl of objects going past him comes into focus, becomes "real," only as it falls behind. And even then, the whole thing is "sound and fury, signifying nothing." The "not-yet" of the future is already overshadowed by the idiocies and brutalities of an implacable past.

The universe of Faulkner's early work thus becomes a closed universe of cyclic and tragic involvement in fate, rather than a universe of hope in an eschatological redemption. Still less does he place any hope in historical development, evolutionary progress. Yet it is perhaps too easy to accuse Faulkner (as Sartre did, also on historical and political grounds) of being enmeshed in pure despair from which he attempts to escape "by mysticism." The great religious reality in Faulkner may not be the Incarnation or the Redemption, but it is certainly something close to the Fall; and where the Fall is fully realized, the doors are silently open to eschatology if not to history.

The great question in Faulkner is this: Does he ever get beyond the sense of *doom* and arrive at the awareness of *judgment*? In my opinion he does. And furthermore, *A Fable* with all its faults represents a position of conscious and positive affirmation instead of his early despair. Both "The Bear" and *Requiem for a Nun* are mediations on Judgment in history. But that is another very good reason for Faulkner to be unpopular with writers like Podhoretz for whom eschatology has no meaning whatever. For Podhoretz, Faulkner is simply apocalyptic and this is bad manners. The middle class, says Podhoretz, has brought into the world an "anti-apocalyptic style of life"—a style of life, which, presumably, occupies itself with sociological changes which are all sweetness and light, guided by scientific ideas and led gently to a golden future by the peaceful hand of history.

The trouble with Faulkner, Podhoretz contends, is that the Enlightenment has passed him by. "As far as Yoknapatawpha is concerned, the Enlightenment might just as well have never been." This is one of the most comical remarks in all Faulkner criticism. Not only is it a prize understatement, but it serenely ignores the fact that it is precisely in the midst of the "enlightened" middle-class world that we have not only Yoknapatawpha but Auschwitz, Hiroshima, the Vietnam War, Watts, South Africa and a whole litany of some of the choicest atrocities in human history. On the basis of this diagnosis, Podhoretz goes on to deplore the fact that Faulkner is "out of touch with contemporary experience," and that though these are admittedly "difficult times," Faulkner's attempt at giving them a tragic and quasi-religious interpretation is "a typical literary symbol of a failure of nerve." Remember that at that time the *Partisan Review* was studying this "failure of nerve" in religiously inclined intellectuals. Finally, Podhoretz caps it all by saying that Faulkner shows "an unwillingness or an inability either to love or hate the world of the twentieth century enough to understand it." Proof? Well, for one thing, Faulkner did not appreciate "the moral sublimity [*sic*] of the Korean War."

This curious, artificially lucid, one-dimensional view of life in which there is no place for madness or tragedy, will obviously fail to comprehend a Faulkner. It will accuse Faulkner of renouncing history and embracing tragedy instead. But there is also such a thing as the refusal to see any tragic possibilities in history, the exclusion of madness and cataclysm from life in favor of a pure rationale of historic development. Do not such suppressions make tragedy all the more terrible and unavoidable? Faulkner's point was that they do. The tiny ripples on the reasonable surface of history are perhaps indications of sea-monsters below. As Michel Foucault has pointed out, the refusal of madness creates a *demand* for madness. Far from getting on as if the Enlightenment had never been, Yoknapatawpha was made necessary by the Enlightenment—and was necessary to it. Faulkner saw that the reason, justice and humanity of the Enlightenment and the lunacy, injustice and inhumanity of the South were in reality two aspects of the same thing. How many rapes, murders, lynchings occur in the little city called, so ironically, "Jefferson"? When we look a little closer at the "demonic" Sutpen, we find that he evaluates his own motives in the language of the Enlightenment. He is convinced that "the ingredients of morality are like the ingredients of a pie or cake and once you measure them and balance them and mix them and put them into the oven it is all finished and nothing but pie or cake can come out." The tragic irony which Faulkner—like Freud—finds in this "enlightened" rationalistic view of life is that human reality is not quite so simple: You put in what seem to you to be reasonable and good ingredients and the result is far from what you expected. Translated into the context not of pies and ovens but of computers and nuclear weapons, the supposedly "rational" aims of contemporary Sutpens, of which there are always plenty, begin to seem a bit frightening. In other words, the Enlightenment has not passed these people by—they are fully aware of it and they appropriate its formulas to justify their own obsessions. Instead of imposing restraint on their unreason, the reasons of the Enlightenment provide them with unique excuses for doing whatever they like, as long as it can be made to sound "scientific." Sutpen, says Hyatt Waggoner, is "the post-Machiavellian man consciously living by power knowledge alone, refusing to acknowledge the validity of principles he cannot or will not live by and granting reality to nothing that cannot be known by abstract rational clarity. He lives by calculated expediency." Sutpen is as much a creature of the Enlightenment as any other positivist, and his tragedy is not that he does not reason but he does not *love*.

The points that Podhoretz makes are not unreasonable in their own limited context. The trouble is that Faulkner is not there, he is somewhere else. We find such arguments repeated over and over in literary criticism: The reasoning mind cannot understand the mad mythical shoutings of William Blake. Socrates cannot abide to see tragedies and goes only when a play of Euripides is on, but only because Euripides is his friend. The Apollonian mind recoils from Dionysian dread and from the awful possibility of manic seizure. But the Faulkners of this world are not to be judged in Apollonian terms although, incidentally, Faulkner has a plainly classic side to him, and it comes out in his stoic ethic—the cult of the "old verities and truths of the heart" which he proclaimed on receiving the Nobel Prize. Podhoretz will not accept this either. "It falls on the ears with a sound dangerously like irrelevant cant." But why? Because the metaphysical basis is ignored and dismissed as irrelevant. In point of fact, the verities of the heart which Faulkner praises turn out to be the same toilsome and inconclusive forms of patience which Podhoretz seems to laud in the soldiers of Korea. But in Faulkner, these virtues are not alien to those of Camus's rebel, who refuses to submit to the absurd. Podhoretz, on the other hand, seems more submissive.

In Horace Benbow, the well-intentioned, scholarly lawyer, Faulkner has shown that it is precisely the fully informed, cultured and enlightened liberal who is often the most helpless to cope with the tragic dilemmas of our time and who remains most completely "out of touch with contemporary experience" even when he pontifically defines for everyone else what that experience is.

The present collection of Faulkner criticism, *Faulkner: A Collection of Critical Essays*, edited with a long and important introductory essay by Robert Penn Warren contains most of the best positive and negative studies of his achievement. It is interesting to re-read George M. O'Donnell's essay from one of the early numbers of the *Kenyon Review*, one of the first appreciations, in depth, of Faulkner's mythology and of the fact that Faulkner is "a traditional moralist in the best sense of the word." But the essay prematurely divides Faulkner's world into Sartorises and Snopeses, so that Faulkner becomes a Sartoris artist in a Snopes world. It would not be difficult to find Snopesism in some of Faulkner's less responsible critics, but Faulkner himself is not a Sartoris; he is more a McCaslin, and even his most positive hero, Ike McCaslin, is not idealized—in spite of a mystical baptism in the forest, he is a failed saint and a fallen monk in the end.

We have delayed too much with the adverse critics of Faulkner; his serious and friendly critics are here too. Conrad Aiken, Lawrence Thompson, Irving Howe, John L. Longley, Olga Vickery, Hyatt Waggoner, Cleanth Brooks, R. W. B. Lewis, and so on. An informative "Note on *Sanctuary*" by Carvel Collins is a valuable addition to the dossier. Some of the best French criticism is here, including Sartre's study of Time in Faulkner. The French, incidentally, take Faulkner seriously as a *religious* writer. The classic preface of Malraux to the French edition of *Sanctuary* is reprinted, along with three and a half lines of Camus quoted from the *Harvard Advocate*. But a much more relevant statement of Camus on Faulkner will soon be published in a new translation of Camus's essays—the Camus preface to *Requiem for a Nun*. Unfortunately too there is nothing here by M. E. Coindreau, Faulkner's French translator and one of his best critics, whose preface to *The Wild Palms* brings out the true greatness of a neglected and misunderstood book.

What is one to conclude? This is a very important collection of reprinted essays, all of them in one way or another deeply interesting even when they are annoyingly prejudiced or unfair. Faulkner had his weaknesses, but now we can evaluate his strong points and find that he stands up very well against the strongest criticism. Time is giving us a better perspective and we are beginning to see the relative importance of the American novelists who began publishing in the twenties. There was a day when Faulkner seemed dwarfed by people like Hemingway or even Steinbeck and Caldwell. Now we can understand that he was of far greater stature: a genius comparable to Melville, Hawthorne, Dickens or Dostoyevsky. A book like this is essential at a time when Faulkner is really coming into his own.

# "The Narrators"

From *An Introduction to American Literature* (Lexington: University Press
of Kentucky, 1971), 48–49 [excerpt]. Copyright © by the translators
L. Clark Keating and Robert O. Evans.

In this chapter we have spoken of writers of unquestionable talent; now we reach a man of genius, although a willfully and per-
versely chaotic one: William Faulkner (1897–1964). He was born
in Oxford, Mississippi; in his vast work the provincial and dusty
town, surrounded by the shanties of poor whites and Negroes, is the
center of a county to which he has given the name Yoknapatawpha,
an appellation of presumably Indian origin. During the First World
War Faulkner enlisted in the Royal Canadian Air Force; then he
was a poet, a journalist connected with New Orleans publications,
and the author of famous novels and movie scenarios. In 1950 he
was awarded the Nobel Prize. Like the now forgotten Henry Timrod, Faulkner represents in American letters that feudal and agrarian
South which after so many sacrifices and so much courage was defeated in the Civil War, the most ferocious and bloody conflict of the
nineteenth century, not excepting the Napoleonic campaigns and the
Franco-Prussian War. To Timrod were given the initial hopes and
victories; Faulkner describes in an epic manner the disintegration of
the South through many generations. Faulkner's hallucinatory ten-
dencies are not unworthy of Shakespeare, but one fundamental re-
proach must be made of him. It may be said that Faulkner believes his
labyrinthine world requires a no less labyrinthine technique. Except
in *Sanctuary* (1931) his story, always a frightful one, is never told to
us directly; we must decipher it and deduce it through tortuous, in-

ward monologues, just as we do in the difficult final chapter of Joyce's *Ulysses*. Thus in *The Sound and the Fury* (1929) the degeneration and tragedy of the Compson family is provided by the slow and provocative description of four distinct hours, reflecting what is felt, seen, and remembered by three characters, one of them an idiot. Other major novels by Faulkner are *As I Lay Dying* (1930), *Light in August* (1932), *Absalom, Absalom!* (1936), and *Intruder in the Dust* (1948).

GABRIEL GARCÍA MÁRQUEZ

# "Literary Influences"

From *Seven Voices: Seven Latin American Writers Talk to Rita Guibert* (New York: Knopf, 1972), 326–27 [excerpt]. Copyright © by Rita Guibert.

Wwhat influences have you been conscious of?

The notion of influence is a problem for the critics. I'm not very clear about it, I don't know exactly what they mean by it. I think the fundamental influence on my writing has been Kafka's *Metamorphosis*, although I don't know whether the critics who analyze my work discover any direct influence in the books themselves. I remember the moment when I bought the book, and how as I read it I began to long to write. My first stories date from that time—about 1946, when I had just gotten my baccalaureate. Probably as soon as I say this to the critics—they've got no detector, they have to get certain things from the author himself—they'll discover the influence. But what sort of influence? He made me want to write. A decisive influence, which is perhaps more obvious, is *Oedipus Rex*. It's a perfect structure, wherein the investigator discovers that he is himself the assassin . . . an apotheosis of technical perfection. All the critics have mentioned Faulkner's influence. I accept that, but not in the sense they think when they see me as an author who read Faulkner, assimilated him, was impressed by him and, consciously or unconsciously, tries to write like him. That is more or less, roughly, what I understand by an influence. What I owe to Faulkner is something entirely different. I was born in Aracataca, the banana-growing country where the United Fruit Company was established. It was in this region, where the Fruit Company was building towns and hospitals

193

and draining some zones, that I grew up and received my first impressions. Then, many years later, I read Faulkner and found that his whole world—the world of the southern United States which he writes about—was very like my world, that it was created by the same people. And also, when I later traveled in the southern states, I found evidence—on those hot, dusty roads, with the same vegetation, trees, and great houses—of similarity between our two worlds. One musn't forget that Faulkner is in a way a Latin American writer. His world is that of the Gulf of Mexico. What I found in him was affinities between our experiences, which were not as different as might appear at first sight. Well, this sort of influence of course exists, but it's very different from what the critics pointed out.

# "William Faulkner"

Reprinted from *Earthly Delights, Unearthly Adornments: American Writers as Image-Makers* by Wright Morris (New York: Harper & Row, 1978), 131–40, by permission of the University of Nebraska Press. Copyright © 1978 by Wright Morris.

Through the fence, between the curling flower spaces, I could see them hitting. They were coming toward where the flag was and I went along the fence. Luster was hunting in the grass by the flower tree. They took the flag out, and they were hitting. Then they put the flag back and they went to the table, and he hit and the other hit. Then they went on, and I went along the fence. Luster came away from the flower tree and we went along the fence and they stopped and we stopped and I looked through the fence while Luster was hunting in the grass.

Will the reader of modern fiction, or the sportsman who follows golf, have the least difficulty with this passage? Only the reader, perhaps, will get the bloom of it. To see the game of golf through the eyes of the idiot Benjy is a matter of technique rather than psychology. The experiment and preparation of American writers have made this triumph possible. Technique determines the reader's first impression, as it does his first view of a Cubist painting. The reader's puzzlement, and his predictable pleasure in solving the puzzle, is a matter of technically achieved effects. The psychology takes its cues from the technical innovations. It is characteristic of Faulkner's talent to let the seeing eye determine the frame of the picture. The sentences have a visual and audible rhythm, as if the words described the movements of a half-concealed creature observed by a hunter.

> We went along the fence and came to the garden fence, where our
> shadows were. My shadow was higher than Luster's on the fence. We
> came to the broken place and went through it.

The repetition of "fence" subtly defines the limited nature of Benjy's vision. Extreme states of consciousness lend themselves, without
strain, to vernacular usage, there being little that is natural to man
that is alien to this supple language. In addition to the appropriate
extremes of emotion, Faulkner wants an effect of extravagance, of un-
bridled impressions, both expressionistic and romantic. The familiar
rhetoric of gothic horror, in its Southern branch, is charged in such a
way language crackles:

> ... a leashed turmoil of lust like so many lowering dogs after a scarce-
> fledged and apparently unawares bitch.

The master technician, Joyce, would have appreciated Faulkner's use
of the stream of consciousness where consciousness itself was felt to
be wanting.

> There was a wisteria vine blooming for the second time that summer
> on a wooden trellis before one window, into which sparrows came now
> and then in random gusts, making a dry vivid dusty sound before going
> away: and opposite Quentin, Miss Coldfield in the eternal black which
> she had worn for forty-three years now, whether for sister, father, or
> nothusband none know, sitting so bolt upright in the straight hard
> chair that was so tall for her that her legs hung straight and rigid as if
> she had iron shinbones and ankles, clear of the floor with that air of
> impotent and static rage like children's feet ...

The reader who attempts to parse this passage into sensible prose
misses the picture. It is a word construct that parallels the impressions we receive from Expressionistic painting, one of extreme hallucination. Visible objects vibrate and writhe as in the canvases of van
Gogh and Munch. Words are applied to the page like gobs of paint
to the canvas with a palette knife. The effect is that of emotions too
intense and distorted for words. Munch has a painting entitled "The

Cry." The emotion is expressed in swirls of violent, contrasting colors. We recognize that it is on the verge of madness. Munch would have been the ideal artist to have painted Miss Coldfield, in her eternal black, sitting so bolt upright that her legs hung rigid, as if she had iron shinbones and ankles. "Impotent and static rage" has compelled both artists to technical innovations in writing and painting. The discharge of this excess of emotion is usually in terms of violence. There are no Milquetoasts among the Expressionists. Trees and mountains writhe, skies flame, colors shriek and light flares, human faces are red, green, purple and yellow, objects possessed by invisible forces are twisted and contorted. Soutine has painted a strung-up plucked rooster as if it had been *lynched*. No other word is appropriate. In this manner a Russian Jew, living in Paris, combined the impotent rage of the concentration-camp survivor with the American innovation of lynching. These ultimate acts of violence, separated in space, shared in common, barbarous moments in time.

A similar sense of outrage inspired Picasso's "Guernica," where the burden of technique dominated the horror—an act of rage rather than impotence—a re-experiencing of outrage and frustration on the level of innovative image-making. Faulkner is of this breed, although his rage is both literary and highly romantic. Out of the abiding, dreamy and victorious dust he would evoke his indomitable frustration that the past is dead, long live the past. A dry, vivid, dusty sound, a grim, haggard, amazed voice, a hearing sense of self-confounded, reveals a writer, for all of his fury, sportively at play in an unexampled language. He is not so provocative as Joyce, but he, too, is an artificer and a shaman, incurably committed to innovation. Faulkner's interest in technique is exhaustive, and often at the expense of his substance. There is too much diffuse emotion, generated by verbal swagger, that strains to pass for good fiction. It is as hard for the reader as it seems to be for the writer to distinguish between the real and the bogus, the words that flow, and flow for no other reason than the spigot is open. Impotent rage, impotent outrage, impotent frustration appear as methodically as slogans, generating neither heat nor light.

The second convict was short and plump. Almost hairless, he was quite white. He looked like something exposed to light by turning over rotting logs or planks and he too carried (though not in his eyes like the first convict) a sense of burning and impotent outrage.

The colors are here, but repetition has diminished the effect. Again and again these words appear, as if part of the flooding Mississippi's burden of flotsam.

> The bow began to swing back upstream. It turned readily, it outpaced the aghast and outraged instant in which he realized it was swinging far too easily . . . his teeth bared in his bloody streaming face while his spent arms flailed the impotent paddle at the water, that innocent-appearing medium which at one time had held him in iron-like and shifting convolutions like an anaconda yet which now seemed to offer no more resistance to the thrust of his urge and need than so much air, like air; the boat . . . spinning like a wind vane while he flailed at the water and thought of, envisioned, his companion safe, inactive and at ease in the tree with nothing to do but wait, musing with impotent and terrified fury upon that arbitrariness of human affairs which had abrogated to the one the secure tree and to the other the hysterical and unmanageable boat . . .

This river is burdened not only with the usual flotsam but the flood tide of words Faulkner uses to describe it. The sheer accumulation of images diminishes the desired effect. It is technically audacious that the narrative itself should prove to be as wild and turbulent as the river, sucking the reader into its maelstrom, but the simulated literary experience is oversaturated. It is a style of narration, like that of yarn spinning, that is enhanced by the celebrated and matchless powers associated with good (and bad) bourbon whiskey.

To be free of the numberless, tiresome inhibitions associated with the choice of words, and their nuances, why not use all of them freely, in fresh combinations, and since the scene is one of disorder, not order, let it begin with the stream of disorderly impressions (we all have them) and a relaxed free-flowing syntax, in which the reader bobs up and down, like an apple: ". . . the water, that innocent-appearing medium [in a flood?] which at one time had held him in iron-like and shifting convolutions like an anaconda"—the writer swept along on his own flood of words, no small feat if it is done for hundreds of pages. There are appreciative echoes of Poe's "Into the Maelstrom" and a nod to Crane's "The Open Boat" in the "arbitrariness of human affairs" that creates such circumstances, while the river that has generated this tempest sweeps author, reader and tale along with it. The reader who snags, or backwaters, or dizzily swirls, or who chokes and goes under, should read something else.

Similar in technique, in the exuberant redundancy of words in their extravagant application to capture a bizarre, outrageous hallucination, acceptable as an image of grotesque humor or an animated cartoon of comical violence, is this scene from "Spotted Horses":

A quarter mile further on, the road gashed pallid and moony between the moony shadows of the bordering trees, the horse still galloping, galloping its shadow into the dust, the road descending now toward the creek and the bridge. It was of wood, just wide enough for a single vehicle. When the horse reached it, it was occupied by a wagon coming from the opposite direction and drawn by two mules already asleep in the harness and the soporific motion. On the seat was Tull and his wife, in splint chairs in the wagon behind them sat their four daughters, all returning belated from an all-day visit with some of Mrs. Tull's kin. The horse neither checked nor swerved. It crashed once on the wooden bridge and rushed between the two mules which waked lunging in opposite directions in the traces, the horse now apparently scrambling along the wagon-tongue itself like a mad squirrel and scrambling at the end-gate of the wagon with its forefeet as if it intended to climb into the wagon while Tull shouted at it and struck at its face with his whip. The mules were now trying to turn the wagon around in the middle of the bridge. It slewed and tilted, the bridge-rail cracked with a sharp report above the shrieks of the women; the horse scrambled at last across the back of one of the mules and Tull stood up in the wagon and kicked at its face. Then the front end of the wagon rose, flinging Tull, the reins now wrapped several times about his wrist, backward into the wagon bed among the overturned chairs and the exposed stockings and undergarments of his women. The pony scrambled free and crashed again on the wooden planking, galloping again. The wagon lurched again; the mules had finally turned it on the

bridge where there was not room for it to turn and were now kick-
ing themselves free of the traces. When they came free, they snatched
Tull bodily out of the wagon. He struck the bridge on his face and was
dragged for several feet before the wrist-wrapped reins broke. Far up
the road now, distancing the frantic mules, the pony faded on. While
the five women still shrieked above Tull's unconscious body, Eck and
the little boy came up, trotting, Eck still carrying his rope. He was pant-
ing. "Which way'd he go?" he said.

The wild humor of this scene, explicit in its exaggeration, is acceptable to the reader as a comic hallucination, the verbal rendering of an event usually reserved for cartoon animation. In his humor,
Faulkner's rage, his need of and gift for hyperbole, is most at ease with
his talent. In the context of frontier humor the bizarre is commonplace, the extravagance enhancing, the lavish rhetoric appropriate to
the occasion, the very accumulation of far-fetched images a part of
the scene's comic disorder. Imaginations schooled on the two-reel
comedies of Mack Sennett, Fatty Arbuckle, Buster Keaton and occasionally Charlie Chaplin would find little unusual in Faulkner's wildest humor except the effort to read him. If read aloud, they would be
at ease with his images.

Faulkner is as romantically ready as Fitzgerald, but the surface
violence of his landscape effectively conceals the core of sentiment.
Behind the extravagant style, beneath the ferment of events, Lena
Grove, serene and monumental, makes her way like a sleepwalker
through a gothic crackling of passions, radiant in a cloak of impenetrable sentiment.

> She begins to eat. She eats slowly, steadily, sucking the rich sardine oil
> from her fingers with slow and complete relish. Then she stops, not
> abruptly, yet with utter completeness, her jaw stilled in midchewing,
> a bitten cracker in her hand and her face lowered a little and her eyes,
> blank, as if she were listening to something very far away or so near as
> to be inside her. Her face has drained of color, of its full, hearty blood,
> and she sits quite still, hearing and feeling the implacable and imme-
> morial earth, but without fear or alarm. "It's twins at least," she says to
> herself, without lip movement, without sound.

Lena Grove is the great Mother, the abiding earth, the patient and enduring force of life itself, and sentiment saturates Faulkner's image of her. The reason we see her with such empathy, exactly as Faulkner would have us, is because she contrasts so profoundly with the turmoil of lusts, like a "howling pack of dogs," about to be released. It is this charged atmosphere that gives her serenity such depth, and veils her cloud of sentiment.

The reader swept along on the tide of words and events may hardly be aware that the situation is comic. Faulkner's accumulating rage is kept in bounds—within the scope of the rhetoric—by his humor.

> They were young voices, talking not in shouts or screams but with an unhurried profundity of volume the very apparent absence from which of any discernible human speech or language seemed but natural, as if the sound had been emitted by two enormous birds; as if the aghast and amazed solitude of some inaccessible and empty marsh or desert were being invaded and steadily violated by the constant bickering of the two last survivors of a lost species which had established residence in it—a sound which stopped short when Ratliff shouted. A moment later the two girls came to the door and stood, big, identical, like two young tremendous cows, looking at him.
>     "Morning, ladies," he said. "Where's your paw?"

A careful reading of this passage suggests that Faulkner writes with his damper wide open, sucking in more air than the occasion warrants—"aghast and amazed solitude of some inaccessible empty marsh"—but without this draft there might have been no fire, only clouds of smoke.

At the heart of this landscape of bizarre disorders and lingering odors, verbena, wisteria and bitches in heat, is a lost paradise, a flowering wilderness, a reservation where violence, the white man's noise, is either kept at bay or laughed out of existence. This landscape glows with the subdued colors appropriate to humor that dissolves rage, and sentiment that dissolves time. There is nothing in literature to compare with the courtship of David Hogganbeck and Ikkemotubbe for Herman Basket's sister, a primal and receding vision of womanliness. This tale, a stream of clear and undefiled water, winds and unwinds its way through the Faulkner wilderness. It remains pure, where others become corrupt and fouled. It never hurries toward an impending and predictable flood. Hogganbeck and Ikkemotubbe, the eternal dreamers, pursue the mystery of life, the Holy Grail, as it lures them in the form of Herman Basket's sister, the *ewige weibliche* who drew them on and on. She will become the property, predictably, of that colossal ne'er-do-well, Log in the Creek, who lies forever on the floor of the world with his harmonica cupped to his mouth. This vein of mythic humor often erupts in Faulkner, but the reader must be on the alert for it, sunny moments of clearing in a season of thunder, lightning and crackling hail.

As an image-maker, no occasion is too bizarre for the golden touch of Faulkner's imagination.

> . . . Two hours later in the twilight they saw through the streaming windows a burning plantation house. Juxtaposed to nowhere and neighbored by nothing it stood, a clear steady pyre-like flame rigidly fleeing its own reflection, burning in the dusk about the watery desolation with a quality paradoxical, outrageous and bizarre.

"Paradoxical, outrageous and bizarre" evokes the contrary and willful passions that obsess Faulkner's imagination and generate his most memorable visions. In the story "Red Leaves" there is a Negro who has come to the well to drink. "You wanted water," Basket said. "Here it is." The Negro is given a full gourd of water and attempts to drink. They stand watching his throat working, and the bright water cascading down his chin and breast.

> . . . Again they watched his throat working and the unswallowed water sheathing broken and myriad down his chin, channeling his caked chest. They waited, patient, grave, decorous, implacable; clansman and guest and kin. Then the water ceased, though still the empty gourd tilted higher and higher, and still his black throat aped the vain motion of his frustrated swallowing . . .

"Come," Basket said, taking the gourd from the Negro and hanging it back in the well.

This image of impotence and outrageous frustration gives new life to words that seemed drained of their emotion. Faulkner's thirst-crazed man who can no longer swallow, his throat working while water cascades from his chin, will speak for the writer's and the reader's accumulating frustration and impotent rage.

When dealing with horses and mules, harness, wagons and the man-worn artifacts of rural life, Faulkner is a writer of exact observation, but his inspired images are a blend of literature and imagination. "A Rose for Emily" echoes the macabre visions of Poe.

> The violence of breaking down the door seemed to fill this room with pervading dust. A thin, acrid pall as of the tomb seemed to lie everywhere upon this room decked and furnished as for a bridal: upon the valance curtains of faded rose color, upon the rose-shaded lights, upon the dressing table, upon the delicate array of crystal and the man's toilet things backed with tarnished silver, silver so tarnished that the monogram was obscured. Among them lay a collar and tie, as if they had just been removed, which, lifted, left upon the surface a pale crescent in the dust. Upon a chair hung the suit, carefully folded; beneath it the two mute shoes and the discarded socks.

The shoes and socks are Faulkner's touches to the old tableau. An avid reader, he incorporated and expanded on the technical innovations of his contemporaries, in particular the flow and rhythm of the interior monologue, the stream of consciousness, a technique that came so naturally to his gifts we recognize it as the property of the age, the consciousness to which it contributed. In one sustained effort, *The Sound and the Fury*, Faulkner was able to orchestrate the conflicting elements of his nature with his emerging and original gifts as a writer, compressing into a single volume memory, emotion and imagination. The compactness results in a tour de force, a display case of the writer at the top of his form, pulling the stops and sounding the chords that are unmistakably Faulkner. The scene of Luster driving Ben to the left of the monument, not to the right as he was accustomed, causing him to bellow with the shock and horror of all those who fear that the world has taken the wrong way, the wrong turn, forever, is an inspired and unforgettable Faulkner image.

> Ben's voice roared and roared. Queenie moved again, her feet began to clop-clop steadily again, and at once Ben hushed. Luster looked quickly back over his shoulder, then he drove on. The broken flower drooped over Ben's fist and his eyes were empty and blue and serene again as cornice and façade flowed smoothly once more from left to right, post and tree, window and doorway and signboard each in its ordered place.

ELIZABETH SPENCER

# "Emerging as a Writer in Faulkner's Mississippi"

From *Faulkner and the Southern Renaissance*, ed. Doreen Fowler and Ann J. Abadie (Jackson: University Press of Mississippi, 1982), 120–37. [Written in 1981.] Copyright © 1982 by Elizabeth Spencer. Reprinted by kind permission of Elizabeth Spencer.

Coming back to Mississippi after not so long away in terms of visiting, but a long time away in terms of living—though in another sense a real Mississippian is never really away—means the arousing of many memories, some of the most pleasant, in my case, being associated with the years I taught here in the '40s and '50s. Even if I hadn't ever taught here, it would be impossible to think of Oxford without thinking of her most famous citizen, William Faulkner.

When I was growing up in Carrollton, sixty miles west of here, where I was born, Oxford was mainly associated with the university, "Ole Miss," its various well-known professors, its law school, its football team, and several families, like the Somervilles and the Hemingways, with whom we—the Spencers, the McCains, the Youngs—were somehow "connected." Two of my uncles went here—one was to become the Admiral, John Sidney McCain, for whom the building on campus here has been named; and my brother came here also, and every one of them was Phi Delta Theta.

It was a long, twisting drive over narrow, gravel roads to get over here in the old days, but once here one immediately felt something distinguished about both town and campus, as though the cultural

205

roots were firm and strong and secure. On the campus, the lyceum, the observatory, and the grove seemed to have been created to impart a sense of the past, of classical studies, of tradition. Some campuses have this meditative quality and one need know no one ever connected with them to feel it. Others, I believe, never acquire it at all. Ole Miss had it, and Oxford itself had a serene, golden quality all its own. I would be many long years, however, in associating Oxford and Ole Miss with William Faulkner. There was, in fact, during the '30s when I was growing up, almost no importance attached to Faulkner at all. Why was this? Didn't we read books? Yes, we not only read, but some of us read extensively and intelligently. There were those, it is true, who did not read much of anything but the *Commercial Appeal* and the *Farmer's Almanac* and the *Christian Observer*, but many were very attached to books. My mother's family had a pretty large library—they would have just said that "we had a lot of books"—and most of them loved talking about their reading, comparing thoughts and impressions and judgments. The emergence of a writer of real potential in their area should have been of great interest to them, and his work should have sustained that interest. But the truth is I never remember people at home talking about Faulkner very much though it was known he was a writer who had begun to publish. One book was mentioned, *Sanctuary*. It was usually said that he had written it to make money, but the implication was that the writer and the book both were flashy, and without substance. If more was said, it was that this writer and others like him (Erskine Caldwell comes to mind) were trying to paint the South in false colors, to drag our culture through the dirt, to degrade and make fun of our ideals. To go a little further with remembering, I think I recall someone saying, "No book of his will ever be in my house." I also have a vague recollection of one of my aunts, glancing about to see that no children or men were present whispering the name of Temple Drake, but I failed to get the rest of it, and of my mother saying, "Oh, awful, just awful. How could anybody write such a thing?"

But mainly nobody spoke of Faulkner at all. When I say we had a life which made ready reference to books and literature, I feel I must back this up, as too many have fallen into the way of praising the South for its "oral tradition," letting this so-called "oral tradition" account for all we have enjoyed in the way of a literary flourishing. To me this is to simplify what our culture was like. It was no interruption in small town social life, or family life or church-going or hunting or fishing, to have your mother read to you every night out of Greek and Roman myths, the story of the Bible, Robin Hood, Arthurian legend, Uncle Remus, Hawthorne, Aesop, Grimm, Robert Louis Stevenson, George MacDonald, Louisa May Alcott, and all those others who followed naturally after Mother Goose and Peter Rabbit. Later there were Dickens, Thackery, Jane Austen, George Eliot, Victor Hugo, all of the fine Victorians. The characters in these books were often discussed as though they were live people we had all known. My uncle had a fondness for *Les Miserables* and pressed me to read it when I was about ten; too young, I got lost in all the history, French geography, manners, and characters with unpronounceable names. A cousin of mine from up the street, who often used to play with the rest of us at my house in the summer, used to quote Swinburne by the yard, and even before that, my brother, whose bent was certainly not "literary," would recite long stanzas from Macaulay along with Robert W. Service. His favorite book was *Moby Dick*; he had several copies around the house. My aunt taught Latin and relished reading fiction. Long scraps of original poems were to be found in notebooks of some of the family members. All this is to be considered, I think, as a kind of liveliness, it made life more enjoyable, expanded it, to have feelings for somebody in New England, or France or England, or for never-never characters out of myths.

I should like here to say a word about my home town of Carrollton. They have a pilgrimage there now, for people to visit its old homes and gardens. However, Carrollton never grew very much. I guess maybe it has shrunk. I recently saw it listed in a study published in one of the Mississippi quarterlies as a "dying town." My mother always said that while nobody much was left *in* Carrollton, half of the Delta was *from* Carrollton. Carrollton is a hill town, older than both Oxford and Holly Springs. It was close enough to the Delta to be a refuge place during floods and yellow fever epidemics. There was once a "female academy" there; it was the birthplace of two U.S. senators; it was considered the ideal setting for Faulkner's *The Reivers* when this book was photographed as a movie. (Oxford itself had got too modern and no longer looked like "Jefferson," or so it was judged.) Carroll County was adjacent to Leflore County, Leflore being named for Greenwood Leflore, the last of the Choctaw chiefs, part French-Canadian, whose plantation was largely in Carroll County, as was his splendid plantation home, Malmaison. My own family's plantation was neighbor to his, being called Teoc, after the Choctaw name, Teoc Tillila, meaning Tall Pines.

Carrollton was a sleepy town in the '20s and '30s, when I was growing up. It was really two towns, separated by Big Sand Creek. When this creek got up and roared after a big rain, it was always threatening to wash the bridge out. The town on the other side of the creek was called North Carrollton. North Carrollton got mad at Carrollton once, back in the mists of time, or Carrollton got mad at North Carrollton, I forget which. At any rate, we had, between us, never more than 1,000 souls, but two separate 12-year high schools, two separate post offices, two mayors and boards of aldermen, and any number of separate reasons to feel different and superior, each to the other. I think, though, that since Carrollton had the courthouse and the county records, we quite possibly were more successful snobs, if this is any distinction. There were no paved roads in the state then, except maybe one or two down around Jackson, or up near Greenville. There was one half-paved road, I remember, that is, paved on one side only. It was up near Greenville and was done so the milk wouldn't get churned on the way to town. It was difficult to go any distance by car without getting covered in dust. We usually counted on one or two flat tires on the way to Jackson, a hundred miles away. A teacher who came to our town school in the '30s from elsewhere was astonished that we had no school library. Since everybody I knew had books at home, I never thought a library was necessary in the schoolhouse, yet we were glad at the signs of progress when she raised some money to order books, stuck reference cards in a shoe box, and entered fines in a nickel notebook. Before that, a teacher I had in the fourth grade, whose home was there, had thought the textbook prescribed by the state was boring and had got us to buy copies of a book called *One Hundred and One Best Poems*. She loved reading aloud, and I can see her yet, completely wrapped up in the words and rhythm, chanting Poe's "The Bells" or "The Raven," or Bryant's "Thanatopsis," or something of Robert Browning's or Tennyson's, shaking her head until the hairpins fell out and peppered the floor. She was a grand reader named Miss Willie Kennan, really Mrs. Kennan (everybody was "Miss" something), and really a Money, one of the Senator's family. Before Miss Willie, though, there had been Miss Jennie Nelson McBride in grades one, two, and three, one of which I was let to skip, I forget which. But for two years, along with arithmetic, spelling, reading, and penmanship, I was taught the alphabet by Bible verses, committed to memory and recited daily. I remember to this day: A—A good name is rather to be chosen than riches and loving favor rather than silver and gold. B—Be ye kind one to another, tenderhearted, forgiving one another. C—Create in me a clean heart, O God, and renew a right spirit within me.

After Miss Jennie and Miss Willie, we had a teacher from Agnes Scott, who happened into our town by accident of marriage to one of the local boys and who wanted to work. She got us into Latin about grade seven, instead of waiting for grade nine; so beating ahead toward Virgil, we were reading Caesar's Gallic Wars in the eighth grade and Ovid (probably expurgated) in the ninth. A friend of hers came to Carrollton in need of work, this one being quite fond of Shakespeare. We read the plays aloud, sitting around an iron stove with our knees toasting and our backs cold and hunks of plaster threatening to fall down on our heads, taking parts in *Romeo and Juliet*, *The Merchant of Venice*, or *As You Like It*, building up to grade 12, when she moved full-scale into *Macbeth*. She had studied it in Nashville under Walter Clyde Curry, and it was her favorite play. "Life's but a walking shadow . . . a tale told by an idiot, Full of sound and fury, signifying nothing." All this was great in itself, but we studied a lot of other writers too, even though my summertime attention had gone to pot as far as literature was concerned. The boys and the cousins who played tennis at our house were hooked on Edgar Rice Burroughs and other adventure stories, so I read those, and the girls I ran around with had discovered picture shows and *Photoplay* magazine.

A mixed education, but it was much richer than statistics would lead anybody to believe. Down here we were all supposed, in little societies like mine, to have no culture at all, except possibly this famous "oral tradition." It does seem to me that every place has, in one way or another, an oral tradition. Ours, it may be, was extraordinary—varied and expansive. Our talkers were great talkers; but people do talk most everywhere. And a Southerner can be as big a bore as anybody. Evenings of swapping local stories lead to wonderful laughter and a good night's sleep, but not necessarily to literature. It was the church-going crowd who got the most out of the sermons, and the politically involved sat drinking in every word at the "speakings." So I do believe that making books springs from a love of books, and that many cultural forces, some of a literary nature, were at work around those small, dusty, obviously "backward," apparently asleep, possibly dead, little old Southern towns.

We had books by Southerners back then, too, though I have not yet mentioned any. Thomas Nelson Page was pointed out to me as a good writer; his *Red Rock* was on our shelves. There was also Stark Young, a distant cousin, whose *So Red the Rose* met with general approval as being true to the South, as so it was. It was true to what this society thought of itself. Mr. Stark had no reason even to change the names of some of his families in that novel, as he was painting them just in the way they believed themselves to be. I think quite possibly they really were this way. I see no reason to believe that Hugh McGehee and Sallie Bedford weren't as good as Stark Young makes them out to be. There were people that noble and that fine in society then; they never hesitated one minute to be as good as humanly possible. I was fortunate enough to be born when some of that generation was still around, plus any number of people who had known them, and I don't think he exaggerated. And I think *So Red the Rose* is a fine book. *Gone with the Wind* appeared and was immediately read and widely discussed. I remember long arguments. Scarlett O'Hara was not "representative of Southern womanhood." Melanie Wilkes was "representative of Southern womanhood." But just about everybody who read at all, read it, and thought it was a great story and true to "what our people had endured." This was often said.

I began to get the reasoning a little at a time. Southern writers were supposed to be "loyal to the South." It was as if we were still in a war and if you weren't loyal to the South you were a traitor, a turncoat, and should be scorned and regarded as a pariah, if not actually shot. This was a sensitive society. Proud, it had been humiliated by defeat and Reconstruction. This humiliation, it seemed to me, the more I heard people talk about it, had been the worst part of the Civil War experience. Now here was somebody, one of us, right over here at Oxford, shocking us and exposing us to people elsewhere with story after story, drawn from the South's own private skeleton closet . . . the hushed-up family secret, the nice girl who wound up in the Memphis whorehouse, the suicides, the idiot brother kept at home, the miserable poverty and ignorance of the poor whites—(Now, the truth is I never heard the term "poor white," just as I never heard the term "Deep South," until I got out of the South. But anyway, he wrote about whites who were poor)—the revenge shootings, the occasional lynchings, the real life of the blacks. What was this man trying to do? Humiliate us again? Tell on his own people in order to make money? Few people wanted to try to sort it out. Those few who did, agreed, I think, that here was great talent. Talent should be recognized and encouraged, but how were you to "encourage" William Faulkner? (He did, as we know, find encouragement with friends like Phil Stone, Ben Wasson, and perhaps others.)

I wish to say that I think the question of what Mississippi was to think about William Faulkner really was a difficult one. Now, many years later, we come to his books after a world of critical work at the very highest levels has been accomplished. We can look back on critics, not confined to the South, who misjudged, underrated, and misunderstood his amazing vision and the variety of his efforts in fiction to make it all plain. Even today, if you come to Faulkner by way of only one fragment, say, one story or one novel (I have an opportunity to do this because I live in Montreal and I teach students who have not been as widely exposed to Faulkner as we here have)—if you come to Faulkner by way of only one work, you are apt to be confused, not as to the brilliance or even value of this particular piece, if you have chosen a good one, but as to the motive for it, the writer's focus. Faulkner, of course, we know now, had read widely in modern literature from the first; there was not much he didn't know about the French writers, and a study of modern literature makes us know that the modern writer's attempt is to hide within the work. Faulkner had as much right to this method as did Flaubert, whose precise focus is also not discoverable. Looking horizontally, regarding the literary scene of his moment, which is the only moment the artist ever knows, he had every aesthetic right to mask himself. The question that arose with many Southerners was not of aesthetic but of moral right. Did Faulkner have a right to make use of his own society (that is to say by extension, his own family, as the South or Mississippi was, in those days, something like a vast family connection) to create a shocking literature?

I was sent to a small Presbyterian school in Jackson, Mississippi, Belhaven by name. There was something that met each spring among those colleges, I guess it still meets, at Millsaps, Ole Miss, Southwestern, Mississippi State, Blue Mountain, Mississippi Southern, MSCW. It was known as the Southern Literary Festival. If I'm not mistaken, Robert Penn Warren founded this. Warren taught for a time at Southwestern, and as happened everywhere he went, something positive and creative resulted. He thought that if the students in this area could get together once a year, students interested in writing, that is, and talk about what was going on in the world of writing, perhaps have writers or literary critics as speakers, then good things might happen. He was right. One thing that happened was that it came the turn of Belhaven College to have this festival and several literary people, writers and critics, were about to show up and students from the whole area were about to attend. It was then discovered that here in 1939 not a single book by the man who had become Mississippi's best-known writer was in the college library, any more than any book of his was in the Carrollton High School library, or in the Spencer residence. Yet an exhibit of Mississippi writing was being set up. A quandary. The college president, Dr. Guy Gillespie, was a very fine and learned and highly religious man. If people sometimes seem to act or think narrowly out of convictions, we have to recall the overwhelming numbers of people who have no convictions to act out of. Anyway, Dr. Gillespie had his troubles with literature. At times, he speculated that Shakespeare probably should not be taught to his girls in college, because he personally could not tell what Shakespeare's theology was. (As a matter of fact, I can't either.) Milton was all right, but he had more trouble yet with the romantic poets—Wordsworth was probably a pantheist, Coleridge undoubtedly took dope, Shelley was declared an atheist, Byron a libertine, and Keats was a pagan. Dr.

Gillespie taught the required course in philosophy himself, lest something go wrong. Now here were the college librarian and the English department wishing to acquire one or two books by the notorious William Faulkner. Fortunately, Faulkner himself had innocently furnished Dr. Gillespie with a solution, as some up-to-date person on the committee realized. He had just published *The Unvanquished*, his most gentle and loving book about the trials of the Sartoris family in War and Reconstruction times. I remember seeing this book on the display table in the library at the time of the festival and thinking I would certainly check it out and read it when the meeting was over. I did so and encountered disappointment. I was looking for sex and violence, but I found little of either. I put Faulkner aside indefinitely.

I confess with shame that it wasn't until I was in my early twenties and in graduate school at Vanderbilt that I realized I must find out more about Faulkner. I had still read very little of him, maybe an anthologized story or two. Nevertheless, in the Modern British and American Novel course under Donald Davidson, I dauntlessly picked out a book by Faulkner on which to base one of my required papers. The book was *Sartoris*. I admitted in the paper to never having read widely in the writer's work. I took it, however, from this book that Faulkner was trying to present a decadent picture of the South, especially Mississippi—a deteriorated society. Mr. Davidson did not agree with the paper or its thesis, but was intrigued by it enough to read it aloud to the class and tear it to shreds. Faulkner was not pointing the finger at a terrible place called Mississippi. He was not out to reform anybody. The secrets of his writing lay deeper than that. Davidson did not try to give them all to us at once, but he pointed the way by indicating criticism that was already beginning to outline the Sartoris-Snopes poles of character, that was probing the mystery of Quentin Compson, and suggesting how Faulkner really regarded, and meant the reader to regard, the outrageous Bundrens. Much more serious after my scolding, I began a long commitment to try to understand slowly and as thoroughly as possible the literary genius of my own locale. I had hoped to find a quick way out of doing this, but finally I was so challenged I had to go on with it, and I then read a great deal of Faulkner, all the books up through *The Hamlet*, *Go Down, Moses*, some as they were appearing, and finally *The Collected Stories*. And then I thought I understood enough, as much as I ever would, and being not so interested in the later ones, I called it as much as I could do.

But by that time I was thoroughly converted and baptized. More than baptized, I was saturated. More than converted, I was almost fanatical. If anybody said anything about Faulkner that wasn't thoroughly positive and to my mind correct, I would undertake to lecture them. I thought everyone should be enlightened about his work, read it, see it as I had come to. To discover Faulkner was a great experience, of the sort which few writers can offer a reader. In our time, Proust can offer it, as can Joyce. Who else? Perhaps others. I can think of none. The work is there, complex and difficult, but finally understandable; we read it as though we visited a new country—I should say, being from Mississippi, another county. We can read its history, meet its people, see its sights, learn its language. The characters become like people personally known, part of our acquaintance who crop up from time to time.

I saw, of course, the perils all this was letting me in for, as a young woman who had wanted to write since childhood and who, worse luck, came from what was rapidly getting to be known as "Faulkner country." Once you were in it, especially as a writer, how in the world did you get out of it? (That was the 1940s.)

I think now that writers, would-be writers, beginning writers, writers already publishing, all over the South (for the South did, as we know, experience a real flowing of literature, call it what you will) were facing the same question as I. Faulkner was a lion in the path, menacing further advance—or a bear in everybody's private wilderness, if you prefer. Maybe some of us gave up. But a lot of us didn't. Few got by without a claw mark or two. I thought my work was original, all my own, but critics inevitably compared me to Faulkner. Some of them must have been simply aware of superficial resemblances in the landscape or the architecture or the characters or the speech. I knew little about any world other than the north Mississippi world where I had been born and my parents and their parents before them. But some of the critics must have been right; perhaps resemblances are really there between my work and Faulkner's and also the work of many other Southern writers and Faulkner's. For one thing, the

Faulkner style, once it gets into your thinking, tends to want to get out on paper. Faulkner found a way of expanding the English sentence from within, elongating its rhythms so that line after line of subordinate matter could be introduced without losing or damaging the residing thought it was intended to qualify. He knew how to lay clause after clause in long, richly worded sentences, not like equal stones along a flat path, but builder's units, raising some complex image before us, involving it along the way with his story's history, feeling and character all together. All this he managed to tune into the idiom that was native to him, in all its range. Should this great gain in stylistic method then be lost to other writers because none are strong enough to use it without becoming imitative? Many writers have learned from Joyce, even though few would even covet his enormous interest in linguistics, and perhaps none, even if they wished, would have the learning to bring it into full play. Many have found in Proust the courage to let memory create symphonic fiction out of past event. Well, a good many writers have found a way to borrow from this extraordinary style of Faulkner's without sounding too much like the one who invented it. We can, of course, immediately mention William Styron and Robert Penn Warren. But every so often, these rhythms crop up in some New Englander's novel, or in a midwestern Jewish family saga, or are heard in Canada from some lonely dreamer on some of the prairies of Saskatchewan. Any day now I expect to find the Aurora Borealis—the Northern Lights—described in rolling Faulknerian rhetoric. When we run across these things, we have to wonder if new writers are catching hold, putting the style to good use, or if it has come sneaking up out of the swamps and bayous and caught them. The first way would be the right one, the second is a kind of cop-out. The question, as it says in *Alice*, is who's to be master.

I can remark on all this now, but twenty or thirty years ago for me, it was a stiff problem. I personally managed to work out the threat of the Faulkner style, by reading certain other writers I lavishly admired, who served as counter-influences, neutralizers. (It's a bit like chemistry, where the solution turns from pink to blue.) One writer I read was the Russian Turgenev. I read him, of course, in translation, yet his style got through to me as flexible, apparently simple, certainly lucid, and capable of both subtlety and feeling. There was the strong direct appeal of Chekov, also his lyrical vein; for someone writing a bit this way in English you could read Katherine Mansfield. There was also, right in our own Southern literature, the crystalline style of Katherine Anne Porter. While Willa Cather bore a creditable resemblance to Turgenev, and Hemingway's strict economies of language, though almost ballet-like in their stylization, were always a good antidote to Faulkner's baroque flamboyance. There were many ways, then, to hack your way out of the jungle, praying not to get snake bit. Another way I found to escape from the Faulkner overdose was to go back to what I knew before I ever encountered his work. The discipline of Latin phrasing, the patient diagramming of English sentences, the rhythms of the King James Bible, the plain admonitions of country teachers, to say nothing of one's parents, aunts, uncles, and grandfathers: "Say what you mean! Mean what you say!" There is no better advice for anybody, and for a writer you can't beat it.

I hadn't, until this invitation reminded me of it, read much of Faulkner in recent years. Occasionally I go through one of his wonderful stories in *The Collected Stories* with my students, in the old "creative writing" way, pointing out richness of texture, level of meaning, language, character, humor, etc. (Faulkner's humor, by the way, to people of cultures other than ours doesn't seem to travel very well. Either that or I don't know how to teach it. Sometimes they catch on to it, but often not. Seems a shame.) These stories, incidentally, seem to have been too much overlooked. They did not all fit in with the novels, and many are not even related to Jefferson and Yoknapatawpha. One is set in Hollywood, one in the Tennessee mountains, one in New York City, two in Virginia, two in the Caribbean, several marvelous ones deal with the First World War in France and postwar times in England and France. I have also reread recently several of the major Faulkner novels, only to be swept anew, like the Bundrens' mules in the flood; this old river can do it every time.

There are certain questions about Faulkner's work that to me have never been, for my personal satisfaction, adequately answered. Maybe some of the other critics here can enlighten me. Maybe they don't bother anyone but me. Since I'm not a critic, I should say they're not criticism but worries. I would like now to mention three areas.

One is Faulkner's nihilism. For there is nihilism at work here and in some of the greatest books. Mainly in *Sanctuary*, also in *The Sound and the Fury, Absalom, Absalom!, Light in August,* to some extent, and in many of the stories. We not only approach the abyss in the writer's work, we go right on over the edge. I think personally that Faulkner may have been stimulated by a nihilistic approach, finding in it that source of a feeling of danger—threat, doom, the impossible event—which informs many of his strongest works. Violence is one thing—I don't mean only violence; but beyond violence, beyond tragedy even, lies the blank-out, the complete construction, the totality of blackness, darkness, nothing, nothing. Toward this end, this writer often is prone to move. His powerful writing demands the reader move with him, experience a nothing without measure.

A second worry: Faulkner's treatment of women characters often disturbs me. Many, *if* they are sexually involved, are hysterical, violent, raving, unable to cope with desire. In fact, sexual passion in Faulkner is generally treated as disastrous rather than life-giving. This is one area where one cannot say, it ought to be this way rather than that way, because the imagined experience here relates too deeply to the writer's psyche to be anything more than remarked on by the reader. I remark on it myself now because I have found it a problem with his fiction.

A third question in my mind concerns the Snopeses: worry three. A lot of double-dealing must go on in Mississippi; I say this because it goes on everywhere in the world—in Georgia, and Tennessee, and Alabama and Texas; in Italy, France, Canada, Australia, and Mexico; in Patagonia and Madagascar, in Tahiti and Denmark, in Iceland and Portugal. If more than five or six people ever get up there for more than a week, it will go on on the moon. Even Jesus Christ couldn't pick out more than eleven honest men. What I wonder is, why does everything like this have to be put off on the Snopeses? Well, of course, you are already telling me, Jason Compson is a lot worse than any Snopes. Okay, but Faulkner didn't write whole trilogies about Jason Compson. The Snopeses have been set up for us to despise. During the Civil War they were camp followers, trying to turn a quick profit out of horse-trading; they are poor whites, they work themselves up in the world, they stand for materialism, meanness of every sort; devoid of emotion, ignorant of aristocratic feeling, they are destroying Mississippi, by extension the South, by extension the world. If we were to observe a minute of silence and cut off the air conditioning and open the windows, we could probably hear them eating out there like army worms in a field of corn.

But this is a myth, says the critic. If a myth does its work, which is to find a place for itself in the imagination, whole and alive, then to ask it to be anything else is useless. It is simply there, just as an event, or a person, is there. Does the Snopes myth, in a literary sense, succeed? It succeeds marvelously; *The Hamlet* is a great work. We cannot expect, the critic points out, that Proust's world will accurately depict Parisian society during Le Belle Epoque. Perhaps it does, perhaps it doesn't. Perhaps only a Parisian associated with those times and places would even care. The thing I find troubling here is that with the Snopeses Faulkner catches up not only the literature of myth but also the literature of social observation, one of the great traditional provinces of the novel. One remembers, as one must, Flaubert, Zola and Stendhal, Dickens and George Eliot, Henry James and Theodore Dreiser. And when I know that I must think of these, I am worried a little—like the worry from a hangnail or a sty.

I cannot call myself a critic. I remember Faulkner said once, or was quoted as saying, and I read it, when asked about a comment or article on his work which praised him for his "linear discreteness," "Look, I'm just a writer, not a literary man." Lest someone think I am a literary woman, let me put the Snopes question in more practical terms. It would not be a good idea to conduct your love affairs by what you read in D. H. Lawrence. It would not be practical to try marrying your daughter off according to Jane Austen. It might be disastrous for a young man to enter the bull ring and encounter a live bull after reading Ernest Hemingway. If you are trying to deal with business matters in Mississippi, you should not confine your wariness to Snopeses. While you are busy watching out for spotted horses, somebody with the bluest blood between the Alabama state line and the Mississippi River will sneak up behind you and take everything you've got to call your own. Literature is one thing, but let's not ask too much.

After the publication of *The Hamlet* and *Go Down, Moses*, I feel that the Faulkner I had learned to prize so highly, turned into a different writer, one who is not so interesting to read. He felt he had to choose, I believe, and he chose goodness. He was sincere about it. It was a noble, admirable decision. He came out definitely on the side of endurance, courage, honor, pride, compassion, the human heart. He was writing of the heart, not of the gland. The long work of redemption had begun. So in the context of redemption we see book after book appear. The Snopeses need it, certainly, though it's up hill all the way. Temple Drake needs it, too. These books are obviously great efforts and some day, like my late discovery of Faulkner himself, I may make a discovery of books like *Requiem for a Nun*, *The Town*, and *The Mansion*. But, I must speak in the present, and my feeling is this: I hope now that we have set up, after his death, a wonderful artist, a folk hero named William Faulkner, who loved Mississippi (he said he also hated it—but we know he felt passionately about it) and tried with compassion to bring our society his understanding as well as his genius—I hope we are not going to forget the man who shocked us, horrified us, who scared the living daylights out of us, whose books were not to be allowed in anybody's mother's house. There are many gentle and civilizing qualities about Faulkner. His compassion goes so deep sometimes it will almost hurt. We can cherish that, but let's not forget the old dangerous, complex vision, with wildeyed crazy Compsons waiting to do some desperate act; with women on quiet streets apt only to murder their faithless lovers with rat poison, but keep the corpse around for a playmate; with at least one Snopes or maybe two as unredeemable as the devil himself. In other words, let's not ever get folksy and cozy about our great writer. Let's not ever make it pure and simple. Let's keep it pure and difficult—complicated, wild, passionate, dark and dangerous—the real thing.

RICHARD FORD

# "The Three Kings: Hemingway, Faulkner, and Fitzgerald"

From *Esquire*, December 1983, pages 577–86. Copyright © 1983 by Richard Ford. Reprinted by permission of Richard Ford and with the kind assistance of Kristina Ford.

Some boys, alas, do not come to serious reading, nor God knows to serious writing, precisely like hounds to round steak. Though, then again, special boys sometimes do.

I remember a few years ago reading in *Exile's Return*, Malcolm Cowley's wonderful book on the Twenties, the teenage correspondence between Cowley and Kenneth Burke. It is pretentious, chin-pulling stuff sent from Burke's parents' apartment in Weehawken to Cowley's house in Pittsburgh, dwelling chiefly on whatever were the palmy literary aspirations just then drawing on those little book-sniffs. It was 1915. Cowley was just leaving for Harvard, having already, he boasted, banged through Kipling, Congreve, and Conrad, plus a dozen other of the greats. Burke—poet and teacher to be—was contemplating his first grand tour of France, rhapsodizing about how much he loved the moon and all those things that didn't fit him out for literature, while advertising himself as "somewhat of an authority on unpresentable French novels" and the lesser Chopin—altogether things that they must both blush at now. But still, I thought: What smart boys they were! And what remarkable letters! They had already read more, I realized, digested it better, gotten it down for quicker recall, and were putting it to fancier uses at seventeen than all I'd read, understood, remembered, or could hope to make use of to that very moment. Or maybe ever. And my hat was, and continues to be, off to them.

Until I entered college at Michigan State, where I'd come from Mississippi in 1962 to learn to be a hotel manager, my own reading had been chiefly of the casual drugstore and cereal box type. Whatever came easy. And what *I* was doing when I wasn't reading Congreve or Kipling or Faulkner, Hemingway, or Fitzgerald at an early and seasoning age was whirling crazy around Mississippi in a horrible flat-back '57 Ford Fairlane my grandparents had bought me; fecklessly swiping hubcaps and occasionally cars, going bird hunting on posted land with my buddy-pals, snarfling schoolgirls, sneaking into drive-ins, drinking, fighting, and generally entertaining myself fatherlessly in the standard American ways—ways Cowley and Burke never write about that I've seen, and so probably knew little about firsthand.

Though, in truth, my "preparation" strikes me as the more usual American one, staring off from that broad middle ground between knowing nothing and knowing a little *about* something. Conceivably it is the very plane Faulkner and Fitzgerald and Hemingway themselves started out from at my age, or a couple of years younger—not particularly proud of their ignorance, but not sufficiently daunted by it to keep them (and me) from barging off toward appealing and unfamiliar terrains. They were novelists, after all, not experts on literature. And what they wrote about was people living ordinary lives for which history had not quite readied them. And it is, I think, a large part of why we like them so much when we read them. They were like us. And what they wrote about reminded us of ourselves and sanctioned our lives.

Reading was, in truth, my very problem in Mississippi. While I always read faster and with more "comprehension" than my school grade was supposed to (I used to pride myself, in the tenth grade, that I could read as well as any Ole Miss freshman), I was still slow, slow, slow as Christmas. And I am still slow, though more practiced now. I have thought that had I been evaluated by today's standards, I'd have been deemed a special student and held back. Whereas in Mississippi, 1960, I was decidedly college prep.

I have also realized, since then, that I may well and only have changed from hotel management to the study of literature in college not so much because I loved literature—what did I know?—but because it was a discipline for the slow (i.e., careful). And I'll admit as well that at Michigan State knowing about Faulkner, Hemingway, and Fitzgerald, which I began to do that first year, was a novelty to set one comfortably and creditably apart from one's fraternity brothers from Menomonie and Ishpeming, who by that time were already sunk greedy-deep into packaging engineering, retailing theory, and hotel management—all those necessary arts and sciences for which Michigan State has become justly famous.

I remember very distinctly the fist time I read anything by F. Scott Fitzgerald. I read the story "Absolution," in my first English literature class at MSU. It was 1962. And I remember it distinctly because it was the first story assigned for class, and because I didn't understand anything that happened in it.

"Absolution" was written by Fitzgerald in 1924, when he was twenty-seven, hardly older than I was when I read it. In it, a fantasizing little Minnesota schoolboy lies in Holy Confession, then gets mistakenly forced to take Communion with an impure soul. Later, and in a state of baleful terror, the boy—Rudolph Miller—confesses what he's done to the same priest, who absolves him peevishly, only then promptly and in Rudolph's presence suffers his own spiritual crack-up, giving up his senses to a giddy rhapsody about glimmering merry-go-rounds and shining, dazzling strangers—all, we suppose, because he's done nothing more venturesome than be a priest all his life. Little Rudolph sits by horrified. But in his wretchedness he has figured out already that private acts of pride and comfort matter more than public ones of abstraction and pretense. And while the priest writhes on the floor, howling like a lunatic, Rudolph slips away, having acknowledged something mysterious and consequential that will last him all his life.

End of story.

It is one of Fitzgerald's very best; youthful innocence brought into the alembic of tawdry, usurping experience. A genuine rite of passage. Real drama.

I did not understand it because even though my mother had been a convent girl in Ft. Smith, still occasionally sat in on masses, and, I believe, wished all her life and secretly that she could be a Catholic instead of a married-over Presbyterian, I did not know what absolution meant.

That is, I did not know what the word meant, and indeed what all the trouble was about. A considerable impediment.

Nor was I about to look it up. I was not big on looking things up then. It could've been that I had heard of F. Scott Fitzgerald before. Though I don't know why I would have. He was not from Mississippi. But you could argue that Americans up to a certain age, and at that particular time, were simply born knowing who F. Scott Fitzgerald was. Ernest Hemingway and William Faulkner, too. It's possible they were just in the American air. And once we breathed that air, we knew something.

It is also true that if I knew *about* F. Scott Fitzgerald—likewise Hemingway and Faulkner—before I knew them hands-on, through direct purchase of their published work, say for instance, as I had read hungrily through some Mississippi dowager's private stacks, opened to the bookless boy who craved to read and to learn (the way it happens in French biographies, though not in mine), it is because by that time, 1961–62, all three were already fully apotheosized; brought up to a plane of importance important Americans always seem to end up on: as celebrities, estranged from the rare accomplishments that first earned them notice.

What I didn't know, though, was what absolution meant, nor anything much of what the story was about. If I had, it might've changed my life, might've signaled me how to get along better with my own devious prides and festerings. But I was just too neck-up then in my own rites of passage to acknowledge anybody else's. And while I may even have known what that expression meant, I couldn't fathom the one Fitzgerald was writing about.

So my first experience with him gave me this: Puzzlement. Backed up by a vague, free-floating, self-loathing, I was, after all, not very studious then, and I balanced that habit with a vast ignorance I was not aware of. I was pledging Sigma Chi at the same time.

I know I knew who William Faulkner was by at least 1961. He *was* from Mississippi. Though I had not read a word he'd written about it. When I got to Michigan State, though, he immediately became part of the important territory I was staking out for myself. He, and Ross Barnett, and a kind of complex, swinish liberalness I affected to keep black guys from stomping on me on general principle.

I *had* laid eyes on William Faulkner. At the alumni house at Ole Miss in the fall of 1961. Or at least I remembered thinking I had. And in any case I certainly told people at Michigan State I had—tightening my grip on things rightly mine. But I know I had never read anything of his, or even of Eudora Welty's—who lived only a few blocks from me and whom I used to see buying her lunch at the steam table at the Jitney Jungle grocery, where our families shopped, but never bothered to inquire about, though her niece, Elizabeth, was in my class.

I had, by the time I left high school, strangely enough, read Geoffrey Chaucer. He was unavoidable in senior English. I could (and still can) recite from memory the first fourteen lines of the Prologue to *The Canterbury Tales*, in Middle English, without giving one thought to what any of it signifies.

I had also "written" a term paper on Thomas Wolfe by then, though I hadn't read a word he'd written either. I had been given Andrew Turnbull's biography of Wolfe and had boosted most of my text straight from there, verbatim and unconsidered. I got a B.

I do remember, somewhere in this period, noticing that a friend of mine, Frank Newell, had a copy of *The Wild Palms*. It was on his bookshelf at home, in the old green-tinted and lurid Random House dust jacket with the pastel wild palms on it. I thought that Frank Newell's family were literary people because of that. And I thought *The Wild Palms* was probably a novel about Florida. In a year I would read my first Faulkner, in the same English class in college: "A Rose for Emily." And I liked it immensely. But I was surprised to know Faulkner wrote scary stories. Somehow I had expected something different from a man who'd won the Nobel Prize.

As for Hemingway, I remember that best of all. I knew who he was by at least 1960, when I was sixteen, because my mother liked him. That is, she liked *him*.

I, of course, had not read a word, and I can't be absolutely certain my mother had, though she was a reader. Books like *The Egg* and

*Lydia Bailey* went around our house in Mississippi, and we both had put in a lot of time in the Jackson Public Library, where it was either cold or warm at the right times of year and where I would browse in comfort through the *National Geographics*.

What she liked about Hemingway was, I think, the way he looked. His pictures had been in *Life* or *Look* in the Fifties, looking about like the Karsh photo that's still sometimes seen in magazines. A rough yet sensitive guy. A straight-talking man of letters in a fisherman's sweater. The right look.

She also liked something he'd said in public about dying, about how dying wasn't so bad but living with death till it indignified you was poison, and how he would take his own life when that happened to him, which I guess he did. That my mother liked, too. She kept the quotation on a three-by-five card, written in her own hand, stuck inside the phone book, where I would occasionally see it and feel craven embarrassment. She admired resolution and certainty about first principles. And so, I suppose, did I, though not with enough interest to hunt up a novel of Hemingway's and see what else there was to it. This was about the time my father died of a heart attack, at home, in my arms and in her presence. And we—she and I—became susceptible to certain kinds of rigor as stanches against grief and varieties of bad luck. For a while during this period she kept company with a big, burly-buff guy named Matt, who was married and drove a powerful car and carried a .45 caliber pistol strapped to the steering column (I liked him very much) and who growled when he talked and who might've seemed like Hemingway to someone who knew absolutely nothing about him, but who had a notion.

In any case, though, my mother, who was born in northwest Arkansas, in a dirt-floor cabin near the Oklahoma line and the Osage strip, and who has now died, was, importantly, the first person I knew who was truly Hemingwayesque. And that included Ernest Hemingway himself.

These, then, were the first writers' names to be chalked, if obscurely, onto my remarkably clean slate, a fact vouched true to me by my ability to remember when I knew of them and by my dead reckoning that before that time I knew of no writers at all—except Geoffrey Chaucer and a part of Andrew Turnbull that I stole. I arrived at 1962, the year I would first read William Faulkner, Scott Fitzgerald, and Ernest Hemingway, remarkably ignorant for a boy eighteen; as unlettered, in fact, as a porch monkey, and without much more sense than that idle creature of what literature was good for, or to what uses it might be put in my life. Not at all a writer. And not one bit the seasoned, reasonable, apprentice bookman customary to someone who before long would want to be a novelist.

For these three kings, then, a kingdom was vacant.

And so I read them, badly. As least at first.

It was in the dog days of the New Criticism that I read *The Sun Also Rises, Absalom, Absalom!* and *The Great Gatsby.* We were being instructed to detect literature's most intrinsic worth by holding its texts aloof from life and history, and explicating and analyzing its parts to pieces. Close reading, this was known as. And my professors—one, a bemused, ex-second-string football player from Oregon; and the other, a gentle, strange-suited, bespectacled man with the picturesque, Hemingway name of Sam Baskett—put us through our formalist/objectivist paces like dreary drill sergeants. Point of view. Dramatic structure. Image. Theme. Hemingway and Faulkner were still alive at the time, and Fitzgerald managed somehow to retain his contemporariness. And there was, among us students, a fine, low-grade brio that here we were reading new work. Probably my teachers admired these men's writing. Generationally they were much more under the thumb of their influence than I could ever be, and possibly they had wanted to be writers themselves once. (One told me that people who wanted to be writers should take jobs as fire watchers and live alone in towers.) But they still chose to teach literature to satisfy a weary system, and in any case it was in these dry classroom anatomies that I first learned exactly what meaning meant.

Symbols, I remember, were very much on my teachers' minds then, and so on mine. I was not yet *reading like a writer.* Indeed, I was just learning to read like a reader—still slowly—so that I never really got onto the symbol business as straight as I might've. But we Jessie Westoned the daylights out of poor Hemingway and Fitzgerald; unearthed wastelands, identified penises, fish, fisher kings all over everywhere. From my sad underlinings and margin notes of that time, I can see the Dr. T. J. Eckleberg, the brooding, signboard optometrist, was very important to my reading of *The Great Gatsby*. He meant God, fate, decadence, evil, and impotence, and was overlord of the wasteland—all qualities and identities I could not make fit together, since they seemed like different things, and since my sense of meaning dictated that assignments only be made one to one.

Jake Barnes's mystery war wound likewise supplied me no end of industry. For a time everyone in that book was wounded, or at least alienated very badly. Many things are marked "Ironic." Many things are marked "Imp." And everywhere I could I underlined *rod, bull, bandillera, worm,* and noted "symb."

Of course, I paid no special attention to the lovely, lyrical celebration of comradeship among Jake and Bill and the Englishman, Harris, there on the Irati—a passage I now think of as the most sweetly moving and meaningful in the novel. Nor to the passage in *Gatsby* where Nick tries to say how Gatsby must've felt at the sad end of things, when he had "paid a high price for living too long with a single dream." Suppose I was just too young for all that, too busy making things harder, getting my ducks set in a straight row.

This, as I've said, was around the time I read "Absolution," and was completely puzzled by it. I was not, however, puzzled by Faulkner, whose gravity and general profusion so daunted the Michiganders I sat beside in class, since he resisted our New Critical shakedown like a demon. There was really just too much of everything in *Absalom, Absalom!* Life, in words, geysering and eddying over each other, so that just being sure what was what and who was who became challenge enough to make you beg off choosing among what things might formally *mean*—a valuable enough lesion, certainly, for anyone who wanted to learn about anything, ever.

Faulkner dazzled me, of course, as his writing inevitably will. But being from where he was from, I was already acquainted with the way the white man's peculiar experience in that particular locale over time begot the need to tell; to rehearse, explain, twist, revise, and alibi life clear out of its own weirdness and paradox and eventually into a kind of fulgent, cumulative, and acceptable sense. Begot, in fact, so much larruping and fabricating that language somehow became paramount for its own sake (a fresh idea to me) and in turn begot its own irony, its own humors, and genealogy and provenance.

That, I came to understand, was meaning, too.

For me, reading Faulkner was like coming upon a great iridescent glacier that I had dreamed about. I may have been daunted by the largeness and gravity and variety of what he told. But he never puzzled me so as to make me feel ignorant, as I had been before I read him, or when I read "Absolution." To the contrary. When I read *Absalom, Absalom!* those years ago, everything came *in* to me. I got something. Somehow the literal sense of all I did and didn't understand lay in the caress of those words—all of it, absolutely commensurate with life— suddenly seemed a pleasure, not a task. And I loved it.

Before, I don't believe I'd known what made literature necessary; neither what quality of life required that it be represented, nor what quality in literature made such abstractings a good idea. In other words, the singular value of written words, and their benefit to lived life, had not been impressed on me. That is, until I read *Absalom, Absalom!*, which, among other things sets out to testify by act to the efficacy of telling, and to recommend language for its powers of con- solation against whatever's ailing you.

I point this out now because if anything I read influenced me to take a try at being a writer—even on a midget scale—it was this plea- sure I got from reading Faulkner. I wrote my first story about this time, a moody, inconclusive, not especially Faulkner-like domestic minidrama called "Saturday," which I liked. And putting those events together makes me understand now how much the wish to trade in language as a writer traces to a pleasure gotten from its use as a reader.

Not that it has to be that way. For some writers I'm sure ideas come first. For others, pictures. For others, probably symbols and Vico. But for me it was telling, in words. I don't think I ever read the same way after that but began to read, in my own way, like a writer. Not to sat- isfy a system, but to take whatever pleasure there was from language, no matter what I understood or could parse. And that, I am satisfied now, is the way one should always read. At least to start.

In the spring of 1964, my wife and I—barely not children and certainly not yet married—drove in an old Chrysler north from East Lansing up into the lake counties where most of Hemingway's Michigan stories are set—Charlevoix, Emmet, Mackinac. The two of us hiked around sunny days through East Jordan and Petoskey, picnicked on beaches where the rich Chicagoans used to come summers, boated on Walloon Lake, staying in a little matchstick motel across the straits in St. Ignace just to say we'd been there and seen the bridge that wasn't there when Hemingway wrote about the country.

Though I was there to get a closer, more personal lowdown on those stories; stories I had been reading that spring, had loved on instinct, felt intensely, but that had also sparked my first honest act of literary criticism: namely, that I felt they never *ever* quite said enough. They forbore too much, skimped on language, made too much of silences. As if things were said only for the gods, and the gods didn't tolerate that much. And I was there, I suppose, curious and nervous about silences, to tune in on things with some experience of my own. It seems romantic now. And it probably *was* silly. But it was my way of taking things seriously and to heart. My way of reading.

What I didn't understand, of course, and certainly didn't learn marching around those woods fifty years too late, was that these were a young man's stories. And their severe economies—I think of "Indian Camp," because it was my special favorite—were the economies and silences of a still limited experience, an intelligence that wasn't finished yet, though certainly also a talent masterful at mining feeling with words, or at least at the nervy business of stripping words in such a pattern as to strand the feelings nicely inside the limits of the story.

It was a young man's aesthetic, and ideal for impressing another young man.

But I wanted badly to know why that Indian had killed himself! And I did not understand why Nick's father wouldn't just come out, while they were heading home in the boat, and say it. Tell us. Telling was what writing did, I thought. And I wasn't savvy enough myself *not* to be told. Faulkner would've told it. He'd have had Judge Benbow or Rosa Coldfield spill it out. Fitzgerald would've had somebody try to explain, later on, in another city in the Middle West.

Hemingway, though, was after something he thought was purer. Later, I read in *Death in the Afternoon* that he aimed for the "sequence of motion and fact which made the emotion." Whereas, if you said a thing—explained it—you could lose it, which is what Jake

Barnes says. And indeed what you lost was the feeling of the thing, the feeling of awe, terror, loss. Think of "Hills Like White Elephants," a story I admire and that students love because it seems so modern. No one says abortion in it. Yet the feeling of abortion—loss, puzzlement, abstraction—informs every slender, stylized gesture and line, and the story has a wonderful effect.

But the embryo writer in me, even then, wanted more. More language spent. More told so that I could know more of what went on there and feel it in the plush of the words. A man had died. And I wanted the risk the other way, risking the "blur" Hemingway so distrusted—an effect caused by a writer who has not seem something "clearly," yet who still needs to get at a truth by telling it. The world, for me, even back in 1964, seemed too various, too full, and literature too resourceful to draw such a rigid line about life just to preserve a feeling.

To me, Hemingway kept secrets rather than discovered them. He held the overcomplex world too much at arm's length either because he wouldn't on principle or couldn't say more. And for that reason I distrusted him. He valued accuracy and precision over truth, and for that reason, despite his effects, he seemed a specialist in what he himself called "minor passions." Even today, when I am always surprised at how much broader a writer he is than I remember, he still seems like a high school team captain with codes, a man who peaked too early and never went on to greater, harder feats.

Not, of course, that I didn't take with me something valuable from Hemingway, namely a deference for genuine mystery. I may now know what absolution means and why the Indian kills himself—too many doctors, too much pain and indignity. I may know beyond much doubt what was Jake Barnes's wound, but I also learned that for anyone, at any time, some things that matter can't be told, either because they're too important or too hard to bring to words, and these things can be the subject of stories. I think I learned that first and best reading Hemingway, learned the manners and protocols and codes a story observes when it comes round something it thinks is a consequential mystery. I may still prefer that mystery, once broached, be an inducement, not a restraint, to language, a signal to imagination to begin saying whatever can be said. But to have learned of that mystery at an early age is no small thing. And my debt for it is absolute.

From this highly reactive time, my memories of Fitzgerald are, at best, indistinct. I made my way through *The Great Gatsby*, exclusively settling matters of point of view and Dr. Eckleberg's significations. Then I simply left off, my memory retaining only the faraway beacon light on Daisy Buchanan's boat dock (it was "Imp."), and Gatsby floating dead in his swimming pool, a memory I soon confused with the beginning of the movie *Sunset Boulevard*, in which the corpse played by William Holden, not Nick Carraway, tells the story.

What I *was* attentive to, though, in my bird dog's way, were the subliterate runs and drumbeats of words, their physical and auditory manifestations, the extremes of utterance and cadence, what Sartre called the outside of language. It is undoubtedly one reason I liked Faulkner best, since he offers so much to the poorly educated but overly sensitive.

And my belief was that these etherish matters were matters of literary style. And like all novices, I became preoccupied with that.

What followed, then, was a partitioning-up of literature into Faulkneresque and Hemingwayesque, leaving a kind of stylistic no-man's land for all the other people. To me, Fitzgerald, by having the softest drumbeats, the fewest linguistic extremes and quirks, the rarest ethers, didn't really seem to have much of a style, of if he did he had a poor, thin one.

It seems feasible that one could think that putting Fitzgerald midway between the great putter-inner and the great taker-outer casts a kind of convenient cosmos map of the male soul and its choices. Though what I was doing twenty years ago, when I was almost twenty, was just confusing style with idiosyncrasy and making myself its champion.

Not that it was entirely my fault.

My ex-quarterback of a professor (we'd heard he'd played behind Terry Baker, and so had had plenty of time for reading) had assigned us all to write a paragraph in either "the style of Hemingway" or "the style of Faulkner"—a miserable, treacherous task to assign any student, but particularly one who had begun to write. (Though I now understand it was assigned chiefly to kill class time.)

But we all wrote. And when we read our paragraphs aloud, mine produced the profoundest response from my instructor. He stopped me three sentences in and complained to all that my Hemingway sounded like everybody else's Faulkner, and that I clearly was not much good for this kind of thing.

I was badly stung. I liked style, whatever it was. And I believed I could be its master. Only I saw I needed to study it harder—Hemingway and Faulkner in particular, and what was odd about them that I couldn't imitate them separately.

Nobody, though, was asking me to write a paragraph in the style of Fitzgerald at this time. *Fitzgeraldian* was not a word. And so, for this reason he fell even more completely below my notice.

It is notable to me that somewhere in this period someone placed in my hands, for reasons I do not remember, a copy of Arthur Mizener's gossipy, pseudo-scholarly biography of Fitzgerald, *The Far Side of Paradise*, the edition with the Van Vechten photo on the front, a smiling, wide-faced Fitzgerald practically unrecognizable from the Princetonian-Arrow shirt profile on the Scribner's books.

Reading Mizener was a big mistake for me. His biographer's interest was the archly antinew critical one of mutually corroborating art and life. And since Fitzgerald, at least for a time, had lived a very, very *rich* life, there set on for me a long period in which I could not distinguish accurately all he'd done from all he'd written: the profligacy, the madness, the high style and helling around, ruinous wives, prep schools, the Plaza, Princeton, New York, Paris, Minnesota, Hollywood. I read the other novels, the stories and notebooks. And though I didn't exactly forget them, they just fell to his life. *He* seemed smart and too clever and poignant and overweening. But the books almost always faded back into Fitzgerald myth, into imputation, half-fact, lie, remembrance, and confession—annals where even now for me they have their truest resonance.

Today, I still believe it's as much his failure as mine that I remember as much about him as I do, but can sort out so little of his work. And that his life—vulnerable, exemplary, short writer's life—save for a brilliant novel and a few excellent short pieces, makes a better story. It is tempting to think that, like Dick Diver and Amory Blaine and Anthony Patch, he represents some promising but spoilable part of our American self-conception. And since that is not exactly tragic, it is maybe more appealing and exemplary to us as biography than illusion.

Recently I read *The Great Gatsby* again, for possibly the fourth time (I know people who brag they read it every year). Fitzgerald wrote it before he was thirty, and as I get older it only gets better. I believe it is one of the maturest, more sophisticated and seamless books I have read, and I don't fault myself for not getting it back in 1964, since it has, I think, more to teach an older man than a young one.

And I have found its style: its elegant economies and proportioning, the sleek trajectory of its complex little story, the strategy of withholding Gatsby until his place is set, Fitzgerald's certain eye for the visual detail and, once observed, for that detail's suitability as host for his wonderful, clear judgment about Americans and American life— a judgment, Wilson said, saturated with twentieth-century America.

The essence of Fitzgerald's style finally was that he itched to say something smart on the page, and made his novels accommodate that. It is why as a young man he was always better in shorter, manageable forms, and why a savvy young man might've learned plenty from him without ever having to mimic. And it is why I had such a hard time at first, my own ear then being chiefly on the ground.

Faulkner, of course, was the best of all three, and the very best of any American writing fiction this century. It is not even discredit to Hemingway and Fitzgerald to say so. Liking Faulkner or not liking him is akin to liking or not liking the climate in some great territorial expanse. It seems like tautology. Whereas Hemingway and Fitzgerald, I sense, come to our affections more like the weather does, passingly.

No writer, including Henry James, minted more robust characters freshly and indelibly into our American literary memory. All those Snopeses. Temple Drake, Thomas Sutpen, Benjy Compson, Dilsey. A bear. No writer has exceeded his own natural regionalism (that dark American literary peril), or survived the codification of his style, or confessed apparently less of his personal life as grandly as Faulkner has. No one braves as much in a sentence. No one is as consistently or boisterously funny as Faulkner while remaining serious and dramatic. And, of course, no American writer this century has been so influential—impressive is the best word—both in the restraining effects of his work on other writers, and in the most generous ways as well: his work always urges all of us if not to be more hopeful, at least to be more various, to include more, see more, say more that is hopeful and surprising and humorous and that is true.

I loved Faulkner when I read him first. He stumped the symbolizers, the mythologizers, the taxonomists, the *pov* guys dead in the brackets of East Lansing. He would not reduce so as to mean more. And that I liked.

Though it seemed to me, then, as it did ten years later when I was writing a novel set in Mississippi—my home too—that that was because he'd appropriated everything there was. It was even possible to want to write like Faulkner without showing you did; to want to put down some sense of a life there without realizing it existed first in his sentences. Until the end of the Fifties—1963—I am convinced, a large part of *everybody's* idea of the South came from William Faulkner, whether they'd read him or not. He was in the American air, as I said before. And that went for the air southerners breathed too, since we could see how right he'd gotten it, and since, of course, he was ours.

How can I measure what it was worth to read Hemingway, Fitzgerald, and Faulkner back in the Sixties? Influence on a writer is a hard business to assess, and I'm not sure I would tell the truth if I could, since real influence means being affected by the weather in another writer's sentences, sometimes so much that you can't even imagine writing except in that weather. And no one who's any good ever wants to write like anyone else.

One truth is that my generation of writers—born mostly in the Forties—has not lived "the same life, the generic one" that Lowell speaks about in his elegy for his friend John Berryman. We have not all prized or even read the same books. We have not all had or aspired to teaching jobs. We do not all know one another. Lowell, of course, was probably wrong about his generation, since, from what I can tell of his thinking, it included only about fifteen people. But of my own, I am sure we are too many, too spread out and differently inclined ever to have been influenced similarly by another generation's writers.

Another truth is that I don't remember a lot of those books anymore. And I never read them all to start with. A fellow I met recently, who had spent time in a North Vietnamese prison, asked me if I thought Francis Macomber's wife shot him on purpose. And I have no idea. In my mind I had confused that story with *The Snows of Kilimanjaro*, and when I went back to figure out the answer, I was surprised. (Of course, Hemingway being Hemingway, I'm still not 100 percent sure what happened.)

Likewise, when I began to think on this essay, I chose a Faulkner novel just to graze over for atmosphere, one I thought I hadn't read—*Sanctuary*—but knew to be easy because of what Faulkner had written about it. Only now that I've finished it, I really can't be certain if I'd read it years ago or not. Odd. But there you are.

Still, as a little group, they seem to have traversed the Sixties and Seventies intact, despite the fact of a unique and intense war being on then, and of immediate life's altering so rapidly and irrevocably. To me, they seem far away, their writing became *literature* finally. But that is only because I don't read them so much, and when I do it is usually to teach readers who were being born just when Hemingway and Faulkner were dying.

Though *their* pleasure seems certain.

I have always assigned classes to read "Babylon Revisited," Fitzgerald's bitter, touching story about Charlie Wales, the man who comes to Paris to reclaim his daughter, lost to him by the calamities of the Twenties, and the Crash, and by his own bad luck and improvidence. It is one of my favorite stories. And there is always a sentiment among students that it keeps its currency because of the Thirties' similarities—at least in my students' minds—to those years since the Sixties were over.

Faulkner still seems to excite the awe and affection he excited in me, though no one—correctly—wants to write like him. Only Hemingway, I detect, can occasionally exert a genuine and direct influence on young writers' "style." His old, dour, at-war-with-words correctness seems to ride the waves of austerity, ascending in tough, Republican times, and declining when life seems abler to support grand illusions.

As writers whose work taught me serviceable lessons about writing at a formative age, all three get high marks for mentorship—a role Hemingway cared much to fill, and that Faulkner, if we take to heart the sarcasm of his Nobel address, probably thought was ridiculous.

By 1968, when I started graduate school in California, people were still talking about Faulkner, Hemingway, and Fitzgerald, though primarily just as Dutch uncles to our own newborn artistic credos. We were all tiny savages then, trying on big boys' clothes. Though it was still good to be able to quote a particular novel—*As I Lay Dying* was popular—or to own something specific one of them had reportedly said and be able to unsheathe it fast. *The Crack-up* was highly prized as a *vade mecum*, along with the *Paris Review* interviews and *A Moveable Feast*.

Anyone who actually *wrote* like Faulkner or Hemingway was, of course, thought to be washed up from the start, but with their books, others' faults could be neatly exposed, crow and humble pie served to order. We were being read to by Richard Brautigan, taught by E. L. Doctorow, and imitating Donald Barthelme. But we were still interested in how those older men got along in the world where there were no grants or teaching jobs, and how they acted out their parts. One fellow in my class actually asked us all to call him Papa. And when I remember that, I need no better proof that they were in our lives, still behind us all, like Mount Rushmore in the Santa Ana Hills.

Speaking selectively, I know I learned from the economies of *The Great Gatsby* how to get on with things narrative; how to get people in and out of scenes and doors and sections of the country by seizing some showy detail and then going along to whatever was next.

From Hemingway I learned just how little narrative "intrusion" (we talked that way) was actually necessary to keep action going, and I also learned to value the names of things, and to try to know how things worked as a way of dominating life and perfecting its illusion. There was, as well, the old workshop rapier that said Hemingway's famous dialogue, when actually spoken aloud, sounded like nothing more than an angry robot on Valium, and not like real talk. Yet locked within is the greater lesson that the page is officially different from the life, and that in creating life's illusion, the page need not exactly mimic—need not nearly mimic, really—and, moreover, that this very discrepancy is what sets art free.

From Faulkner I'm sure I learned that in "serious" fiction it is possible to be funny at the expense of nothing—a lesson also discernable in Shakespeare; that it is sometimes profitable to take risks with syntax and diction, and bring together words that ordinarily do not seem to belong together—the world being not completely foregone—and in this small way reinvent the language and cause pleasure. And finally, from Faulkner, that in representing life one needs to remember that many, many things do not stand to reason.

They were all three dead, of course, before I had written a word. Already kings. But still, I and my generation might have learned from them just what time in life our words could start to mean something to someone else—nervy business, when you think of it. They all wrote brilliant books in their twenties. We might also have learned that great literature can sometimes be written by amateurs who are either smart enough or sufficiently miscast to need to take their personal selves very seriously. In this way we might've learned some part of what talent is.

And last, we might've learned from them that the only real *place* for a writer in this country is at the top of the heap. That the only really satisfactory sanction available, the one our parents could appreciate as happily as the occupations they wanted for us—the law and banking—is success, and the personal price for success is sometimes very high, and is almost always worth it.

What I remember of them, though, is something else again, different from what they taught me. Though by saying what I actually remember, or some of it, I may say best why for me and possibly for people like me, they are three kings.

I remember, for instance, what Nick Carraway said about all our personalities, and Gatsby's in particular: that they are only "an unbroken series of successful gestures."

I remember that Hemingway gave up his first good wife, and never forgave himself for it, and that Fitzgerald kept his until she helped ruin him. (On the eve of my marriage I remember asking my soon-to-be-wife to please read *The Beautiful and Damned*, and to promise not to ruin me in that particular way.)

I remember Hemingway saying, "It is certainly valuable to a trained writer to crash in an airplane that burns."

I remember Darl Bundren in *As I Lay Dying*, describing his sister Dewey Dell's breasts as "mammalian ludicrosities which are the horizons and valleys of the earth."

I remember Horace Benbow saying to a man already doomed, "You're not being tried by common sense . . . You're being tried by a jury."

I remember where I learned what a bota bag was and how it was used—important gear for a fraternity man.

I remember where I learned what it meant to have *repose—Tender Is the Night*—and that I didn't have it.

I remember that dead Indian very distinctly.

I remember what Fitzgerald said—sounding more like Hemingway than our version of Fitzgerald, but really speaking for all three writers—that "Life was something you dominated, if you were any good."

And last, I remember what Fitzgerald wrote in his notebook about Dick Diver: "He looked like me."

This is the important stuff of my memory: objects, snapshots, odd despairs, jokes, instructions, codes. Plain life charted through its middle grounds. Literature put to its best uses. The very thing I didn't know when I started.

These men were literalists, though they could be ironic. They were writers of reference. They were intuitors and observers of small things for larger purposes. They were not zealots, nor politicians. Not researchers nor experts nor experimenters. They seemed to come to us one to one. And though Faulkner could seem difficult, really he was not if you relented as I did.

Their work, in other words, seemed like *real* work, and we gave up disbelief without difficulty and said willingly, "This is our writing." They wrote to bring the news. And they were wondrous at that task. They wrote a serious, American literature that a boy who had read nothing could read to profit, and then read for the rest of his life.

"You've got to sell your heart," Fitzgerald said, and write "so that people can read it blind like Braille." And in a sense, with their work they sold their hearts for us, and that inspires awe and fear and even pity. Reverence suitable for kings.

KENZABURO OE

# "Reading Faulkner from a Writer's Point of View"

From *Faulkner in Japan*, ed. Thomas L. McHaney (Athens: University of Georgia Press, 1985), 62–75. [Written in 1981.] Copyright © by Kenzaburo Oe. Reprinted by permission of the University of Georgia Press.

**1**

There is a wide disparity between the specialist's and the general reader's understanding of Faulkner, and this essay is written from the point of view of a general reader and a writer. We general readers are related to the specialists in that we read for enlightenment what they have written—translations, reviews, and academic monographs. But it is nonsense for us to try to express our opinions in the same ways as those who write reviews and monographs, and as for translations, the specialist's way of reading a work of Faulkner's in the original while translating it into Japanese differs greatly from our way of reading the original as amateurs (and at present, we have to read such novels as *Mosquitoes* and *The Hamlet* in the original alone).

One of Faulkner's unique narrative techniques is called "reticence," the development of narration mainly through conversations. In Japanese translations, his reticence is often replaced by words that express specific meanings. For example, I can point out translator's bald references to sexual impotence, one of the main themes of Faulkner but often implied rather than stated. Explicit translations often simplify the multiplicity of meaning in Faulkner's work, but they must

240

do so or the translations will be too obscure for general comprehension. The reading of Faulkner by a specialist who is engaged in translation may be accompanied by quite a different mental strain from ours. The translator must decide upon meanings as he goes, while we read the English of Faulkner's work with our judgment constantly held in suspense. Therefore, when I read Faulkner's novels, I always put the translations beside the originals, whenever they are available. In short, I experience Faulkner through a triangular circuit for the transmission of verbal symbols—Faulkner; the translator, who is a specialist; and myself, a reader of the words of the other two.

When I look back on my experience of reading Faulkner, I find that I have always felt myself driven to the tempting question of how I would write if I were he. Among the modern British and American writers, Faulkner is the one whom I have the strongest impulse to challenge. It strikes me strongly that my response to his attitude toward writing novels and to his way of activating the imagination may be entirely different from the reactions of other general readers to his work. The points I am going to make with reference to the actual texts may therefore be regarded from the specialists' broader vision as betraying some biases.

**2**

The feature of Faulkner's writing that most stimulates my imagination always involves the feminine, although this may sound too simple. This feature seems to me to appear most remarkably in the Snopes trilogy.

In the chapter subtitled "Eula," in book two of *The Hamlet*, Eula Varner is a mere girl when she first appears in the world of the Yoknapatawpha saga. Although Faulkner presents her as not yet thirteen years old, her appearance is no longer that of a young girl. Eula's basic image as a woman possessing a mythical halo is already established at this point: "Her entire appearance suggested some symbology out of the old Dionysic times—honey in sunlight and bursting grapes, the writhen bleeding of the crushed fecundated vine beneath the hard rapacious trampling goathoof" (107).

Labove, who first notices her, is a law student at a college. He is supported by a scholarship for playing football and serves at the same time as a schoolteacher in Frenchman's Bend. Even after graduating with qualifications to secure a regular job, he remains in the teaching position because he is attracted to or obsessed by Eula. At least he is driven to try to embrace her, but his assault is encountered by her unexpectedly strong resistance and, being pushed away, he falls down helplessly. Expecting Eula's brother to come and punish him, he thinks afterward: "It would not be penetration, true enough, but it would be the same flesh, the same warm living flesh in which the same blood ran, under impact at least—a paroxysm, an orgasm of sorts, a katharsis, anyway—something" (139).

Before long, Eula begins to attract young men, and among them is Hoake McCarron, who comes in a buggy from a nearby village to visit her. When some village admirers of Eula attack him, she beats them back with the reversed whip. She is forced by her father, Will Varner, to marry his clerk, Flem Snopes, on mercenary terms. With this marriage, her role in *The Hamlet* ends.

In this episode about Eula, we find that a human relationship is established between an archetype of womanhood and a man who is able to devote all his heart to her and who, being rejected, is still able to experience a rush of intense emotion, a sort of orgasm or catharsis. My point is that Labove's function is to bring an archetypal woman into sharp relief against him. The role of Labove in *The Hamlet* is filled in *The Town* and *The Mansion* by Gavin Stevens, a familiar figure in Faulkner's world.

Gavin is a lawyer who was educated at Harvard and later at Heidelberg in Germany and who also obtained a law degree. Charles Mallison, his nephew, not only lives close to him in the town of Jefferson but also shares with him a similar sensitivity and disposition. Therefore, Gavin's view of womanhood—the focus of which is of course on Eula and her daughter Linda—exerts a strong influence on Charles, and here the relationship between Gavin and Charles runs parallel to that between Eula and Linda. This is a device in Faulkner's writing which aims at stratifying effects, and we can find it at the beginning of *The Town*. In Charles's narrative description of Eula we can witness again Faulkner's conscious efforts to attach mythical significance to his character:

> She wasn't too big, heroic, what they call Junoesque. It was that there was just too much of what she was for any one human female package to contain, and hold: too much of white, too much of female, too much of maybe just glory, I don't know: so that at first sight of her you felt a kind of shock of gratitude just for being alive and being male at the same instance with her in space and time, and then in the next second and forever after a kind of despair because you knew there would never be enough of any one male to match and hold and deserve her; grief forever after because forever after nothing less would ever do. (*Town*, 6)

Eula is described here as a figure of dazzling womanhood, but the image cannot be rendered effectively without the tangible presence of Charles, who is deeply fascinated by her. In the actual world, Eula has come out of Frenchman's Bend to Jefferson and works behind the counter of a restaurant owned by her husband, Flem Snopes, who has by this time risen to the position of power plant superintendent by some tricky business dealings. The narrator Charles's eyes are combined with those of Gowan, another of Gavin's nephews, and the pronoun "we" is used for the narrators. Moreover, Gavin's eyes are also superimposed on those of the young town men because he casts a large shadow of influence upon both of his younger nephews. They view Eula

> not, as far as we knew, going anywhere: just moving, walking in that aura of decorum and modesty and solitariness ten times more immodest and a hundred times more disturbing than one of the bathing suits young women would begin to wear about 1920 or so, as if in the second just before you looked, her garments had managed in one last frantic pell-mell scurry to overtake and cover her. Though only for a moment because in the next one, if only you followed long enough, they would wilt and fail from that mere plain and simple striding which would shred them away like the wheel of a constellation through a wisp and cling of trivial scud. (9–10)

Although Eula is Flem's wife, she has become at the same time Mayor de Spain's mistress. The relation between this archetypal woman and the man who performs the role of her counterpart or her "match" is perceived by the narrators as follows: "It seemed to us that we were watching Fate, a fate of which both she and Mayor de Spain were victims . . . we were simply in favor of De Spain and Eula Snopes, for what Uncle Gavin called the divinity of simple unadulterated uninhibited immortal lust which they represented; for the two people in each of whom the other had found his single ordained fate; each to have found out of all the earth that one match for his mettle; ours the pride that Jefferson would supply their battleground" (14–15).

Flem discloses her affair with De Spain so as to drive De Spain out of his bank, and Eula commits suicide. "We" remember Eula after her passing: "More than me in Jefferson that even just remembering her could feel it still and grieve. I mean, grieve because the daughter didn't have whatever it was that she had; until you realized that what you grieved for wasn't that the daughter didn't have it too; grieved not that we didn't have it anymore, but that we couldn't have it any more: that even a whole Jefferson full of little weak puny frightened men couldn't have stood more than one Mrs. Snopes inside of just one one-hundred years" (74).

When Gavin was still young, he once fought with De Spain for the honor of Eula and was knocked down. At that time Gavin was "simply defending forever with his blood the principle that chastity and virtue in women shall be defended whether they exist or not" (76). Later, as city attorney, Gavin files suit against Mayor de Spain and Flem on a charge of malfeasance about the power plant, and Eula visits Gavin's office at midnight to ask him to withdraw the suit, their first personal contact. Foretold of her visit, Gavin waits for her in terror, and he cannot comply when she artlessly offers herself to him. He refuses. After this encounter, and without touching Eula, Gavin withdraws the suit. Their second encounter takes place just before Eula's suicide. She comes to ask him to marry Linda, but he is unable to accept that offer either, making a second refusal. Yet when pressed by Eula, he swears to marry Linda if that is the only way to protect her. Following Eula's suicide, Gavin looks after everything from the arrangements for her funeral to the erection of her "monument." Only after he has asked Ratliff about her suicide and received the answer, "Maybe she was bored," does he realize the truth about Eula: "'Bored.' And that was when he began to cry, sitting there straight in the chair behind the desk with his hands folded together on the desk, not even hiding his face. 'Yes,' he said. 'She was bored. She loved, had a capacity to love, for love, to give and accept love. Only she tried twice and failed twice to find somebody not just as strong enough to deserve, earn it, match it, but even brave enough to accept it. Yes,' he said, sitting there crying, not even trying to hide his face from us, 'of course she was bored'" (359).

Eula never again appears in the Snopes trilogy and, being the archetype, she can never be replaced by anyone. Even her daughter Linda, another archetypal female character, cannot fill the vacancy after Eula's death. Eula is the larger and more perfect archetype of the female. Gavin, however, in effect supplants De Spain's role as Eula's counterpart and through his relationship with Linda reveals his characteristics more distinctly. When we regard Linda as a contrast to Gavin, we notice that she thoroughly fulfills her function as a small duplicate of Eula or Eula's repeated echo. Therefore, we may consider that both Eula and Linda constitute one and the same archetype of womanhood, while Gavin as admirer and protector of both is the passive catalyst who enables them to express their most powerful emotions.

Gavin, who says, "If I had just had sense enough to say *I am, I want, I will and so here goes*" (94), dares not hope to be a man of action even when Eula suspects him of impotence. Accordingly, he never accomplishes physical love with the woman he adores. Gavin himself is conscious of this fact; he says to Eula, "Can't you see? I wouldn't have been me then?" But as an indispensible instrument for Faulkner the writer, Gavin, without playing any active part, maintains his role as an activator of the writer's imagination. The characterization of Gavin set against the archetypal women Eula and Linda is Faulkner's artistic design. It is the basic mechanism for giving full scope to Faulkner's imagination so that the author can attempt impossible jumps over a chasm too wide for him. This contrastive device is, at the same time, the fundamental structure of his literature.

**3**

When Linda appears again in *The Mansion*, she has gone through a variety of experiences outside of Jefferson. After the funeral of her mother, Linda was sent by Gavin to Greenwich Village, married a sculptor there, served in the Spanish Civil War with her husband, who died in the war, and was herself wounded. V. K. Ratliff, Gavin's longtime friend, now becomes the narrator who relates Gavin's relationship with Linda from the past. Through Ratliff's peasantlike narrative, which is interspersed with humor and exaggerations, Eula's characterization as a mythical woman becomes more striking: "Anybody, any man, anyhow, that ever looked at Eula once couldn't help but believe that all that much woman in jest one simple normal-sized chunk couldn't a possibly been fertilized by anything as frail and puny in comparison as just one single man; that it would a taken that whole generation of young concentrated men to seeded them, as the feller says, splendid—no: he would a said magnificent—loins" (*Mansion*, 114). In Ratliff's eyes, Eula "was trouble and danger enough for every male in range," a "natural phenomenon," who is compared to Helen in Greek mythology. Gavin explains that his interest in Eula and Linda is primarily for the sake of protecting Jefferson from the evil of Flem Snopes, which is infiltrating the town. "He had to be the sole one masculine feller within [Linda's] entire possible circumambience, not jest to recognize she had a soul still capable of being saved from what he called Snopesism . . . but that couldn't nobody else in range and reach but him save it" (137).

When Linda returns to Jefferson she has lost her hearing. She speaks in a harsh, quacking voice, and people have to communicate with her by writing on a pad. But this handicap reveals a new stratum in Linda's relationship with others. It makes out of her a character who can stand in comparison with Eula in *The Town*. With the growing strain in the United States of 1940 and with the world war just ahead, Linda comes to be persecuted as a communist by the plotting of Flem Snopes, her father according to the family register. In this crisis, Gavin tries to save her, and here again Gavin takes the role of drawing out an expression of her equivocal emotions. When he refuses to marry her, she, like her mother before, offers him physical love, using the explicit vulgar word. As he had refused her mother, again Gavin refuses. He works out a plan and finds her a job in a wartime shipyard, afterward visiting her there. Their compassion for each other is deepened, and at this point her dialogue takes the same pattern as in the second scene in *The Town* in which Eula urged Gavin to marry her daughter. I call this technique "stratification through repetition."

Near the end of the novel, after Mink Snopes has killed Flem with Linda's involvement, she leaves town, and Ratliff succinctly summarizes what has happened to Gavin's life, or, in other words, the lawyer's catalytic role: "'I don't know if she's already got a daughter stashed out somewhere, or if she jest aint got around to one yet. But when she does I jest hope for Old Lang Zyne's sake she don't never bring it back to Jefferson. You done already been through two Eula Varners and I don't think you can stand another one'" (434).

### 4

As I stated earlier, Gavin's role is to sustain the archetypal woman who, possessed by passion or the daughter of passion, acts vigorously according to her magnificent nature in a place where the writer can give full play to his imagination. The creation of this role made it possible for Faulkner to establish the archetypal woman as a character with the aura of reality.

Faulkner's creation of Gavin as a device for the Snopes trilogy makes me aware of two aspects of his writing all over again. These may sound too simple to specialists, but they are crucial points for me when I am writing a novel.

I think the first one holds true for most of Faulkner's works: that is, the character who I endowed with the greatest and deepest mysteriousness—in other words, the character with bottomless darkness for the imagination—is always a female who can be called an archetype of womanhood. I once tried to analyze the female characters in Dostoyevsky's world with special reference to *Crime and Punishment*, and I felt that Faulkner and Dostoyevsky are essentially similar in that besides their male characters with various original personality traits, they have created female characters who are larger in dimension, deeper in mysteriousness, and possessed by stronger passions than the males.

My second thought concerns the special traits of male characters who are endowed with a thoroughgoing good nature, naïveté, and innocence, of which Gavin is an exemplar. Of course, this observation is based on my recognition that the catalyst—a role created out of methodical necessity—and the character with original traits are effectively combined in Gavin.

The contrast between female characters who are endowed with magnificent, profound mysteriousness and imaginative darkness and male characters who are bright and simple can be found in almost all the works of Faulkner (if the word *simple* is not suitable, we may call them bright and thin-colored male characters who make a remarkable contrast with dark and deep-colored female characters). As an example, we can think of the pair of lovers in *The Wild Palms*, a sculptress and a medical student who gives up his medical studies. At the end of the novel, when Charlotte suffers a cruel death, it becomes apparent that Harry Winbourne is made to serve as a character to express the vast, profound darkness of this mysterious woman who is possessed by a sterile passion; he serves as a springboard for Faulkner and his readers to enable their imaginations to leap up toward her. Harry's reminiscences, which close the novel, explicitly reveal that he survives only because of the agency of the imagination directed toward the dead woman. "That bastard Winbourne," as she calls him (*Wild Palms*, 21), exists here only as a takeoff point that secures and orients the light of imagination both for Faulkner the writer of the novel and for us readers:

> So it wasn't just a memory. Memory was just the half of it, it wasn't enough. *But it must be somewhere,* he thought. *There's the waste. Not just me. At least I think I dont mean just me. Hope I dont mean just me. Let it be anyone,* thinking of, remembering, the body, the broad thighs and the hands that liked bitching and making things. It seemed so little, so little to want, to ask . . . But after all memory could live in the old wheezing entrails: and now it did stand to his hand, inconvertible and plain, serene, the palm clashing and murmuring dry and wild and faint and in the night but he could face it, thinking, *No Could. Will. I want*

*to. So it is the old meat after all, no matter how old. Because if memory exists outside of the flesh it wont be memory because it wont know what it remembers so when she became not then half of memory became not and if I become not then all of remembering will cease to be.*—Yes, he thought, *between grief and nothing I will take grief.* (324)

### 5

Colonel Sutpen in *Absalom, Absalom!* is without doubt another of the original characters whom Faulkner created. But the image of Sutpen shown to Quentin Compson by Miss Rosa Coldfield is at the opposite pole from his image in the reminiscences of Quentin's grandfather, who was Sutpen's only friend. Putting the two images together on a common ground, the contrast between Rosa, a female mediator, and General Compson, a male mediator, comes to the surface. The contrast indicates, I think, a difference in Faulkner's imagination between the occasions when he uses the female as a mediator and those when he uses a male. From this supposition, we may conclude that methodologically Faulkner distinguished the direction of his imaginative development when he used a female character as a mediator from when he used a male and that he brought out the contrast between the two and gave them a dynamic interrelation when he used them together. Rosa Coldfield, who was once asked by Colonel Sutpen to be his second wife in place of her dead sister, has been nourishing a solitary rage against him for forty-three years. To her, Sutpen was *"an ogre of my childhood,"* and the outcome of the Sutpen saga is forewarned as *"that fatal snarly climax before I knew the name for murder."* Yet when *"the body, the blood, the memory which that ogre had dwelt in returned* [from the Civil War] *five years later and held out its hand and said 'Come' as you might say it to a dog . . . I came"* (*Absalom, Absalom!*, 167).

The reason Colonel Sutpen so fiercely outraged Miss Rosa was that after he had engaged himself to her, he gave up the notion of a regular marriage, but only because he was beaten with the thought that he could not restore Sutpen's Hundred after the devastation of the Civil War. He insulted her by proposing that they should be married if she should beget a male heir. In this way, Sutpen lost Miss Rosa as well, and "from abysmal and chaotic dark to eternal and abysmal dark completing his descending," at last he ended in being murdered. If I may paraphrase the closing passage from *The Wild Palms*, between rage and nothing Miss Rosa took rage and let Colonel Sutpen survive in her memory for forty-three years.

Quentin's grandfather once joined the hunting party in pursuit of the escaped French architect whom Sutpen had brought to build a mansion on his plantation. Quentin's grandfather knows well Colonel Sutpen's violent and vicious act typified in that pursuit, and yet General Compson finds "innocence" at the base of Sutpen's character. Juxtaposing Quentin's grandfather's image of Sutpen with Miss Rosa's reveals a profound significance in the structure of the novel. Note the word *innocence* in the following quotation:

> Sutpen's trouble was innocence. All of a sudden he discovered, not what he wanted to do but what he just had to do, had to do it whether he wanted to or not, because if he did not do it he knew that he could never live with himself for the rest of his life, never live with what all the men and women that had died to make him had left inside of him for him to pass on, with all the dead ones waiting and watching to see if he was going to do it right, fix things right so that he would be able to look in the face not only the old dead ones but all the living ones that would come after him when he would be one of the dead. (220)

The fourteen-year-old Sutpen, son of a drunken poor white who wanders about with his family in search of work, encounters the white plantation owner living in a big house and being waited on by Negroes, but at first he does not realize that the owner is fundamentally different from himself and his people: "'Because he had not only lost the innocence yet, he had not yet discovered that he possessed it. He no more envied the man than he would have envied a mountain man who happened to own a fine rifle'" (228). Likewise, he "didn't even know he was innocent that day when his father sent him to the big house with the message" (229). But the Negro at the door rejects Sutpen, who was so innocent as to think that the owner would be pleased to show him his possessions, and tells Sutpen to go around to the back door without informing the master of the boy's errand. "'He couldn't even realize yet that his trouble, his impediment, was innocence because he would not be able to realize that until he got it straight'" (233). Thus rejected, he thought for the first time, "'Something would have to be done about it; he would have to do something about it in order to live with himself for the rest of his life and he could not decide what it was because of that innocence which he had just discovered he had, which (the innocence, not the man, the tradition) he would have to compete with'" (234).

At this point that child Sutpen struck upon the idea that "you got to have land and niggers and a fine house to combat them with" (238) and left home for the West Indies. This discovery and conversion, and the motive of his frustrated struggle in pursuit of "land and niggers and a fine house," were all caused by his innocence, and when Sutpen became old he still remained so innocent that he could not trouble himself to be conscious of his innocence. Thus we see that Quentin's grandfather transmits the story of Sutpen to his grandson, Quentin, by frequent use of the key word *innocent.*

### 6

I have tried to make clear a couple of Faulkner's characteristics as a writer through quotations. One characteristic is the use of the two differently represented qualities, male and female, and the other is the use of two ways of representing them, both devices closely intertwined. The female character is a capacious vessel in which the writer's imagination is almost infinitely exercised, and the male character is a catalyst who helps the author round out the female character. The emotional quality of the female character is *passion* and that of the male is *innocence.* The male catalyst figure activates Faulkner's imagination. He is the character who is not able to leap over an abysmal chasm between himself and a female archetype but who can be receptive of the female archetype existing beyond the chasm. And we comprehend that the chasm itself makes it possible for Faulkner to attain the greatness and depth of the represented female passion. Only through the male character can we grasp the unattainable greatness and depth of the female archetype.

Considering this point in relation to my daily problem as a writer—that is, how shall I write a novel—I am convinced that the receptive role of the male character produces the depth and multiplicity of the female archetype. When we understand this mechanism we can appreciate Faulkner's excellent methodology as a writer without the risk of apotheosizing his genius. In addition, we will be able to appreciate Faulkner's originality as a writer if we realize that the male character is not only a well-turned figure as a medium for the understanding of the female but has his own charm. If we come to think of one of the characteristics inherent in the male character as, to use Faulkner's term, "innocence," we are sure to realize clearly that this is one of the themes that Faulkner has introduced into modern literature; we can find in Dostoyevsky a superb counterpart—for example, Prince Myshkin in *The Idiot*, an incarnation of innocence, plays the role of catalyst and stirs the author's imagination to the full for such female archetypes as Nastasya Filippovna and Aglaia Epanchin. Myshkin becomes a highly accomplished character himself, of course, through the perfect combination of this role as catalyst and as a character in the fiction. We can recognize in almost all Dostoyevsky's works such innocent male characters in their own right. Faulkner and Dostoyevsky have created in most of their works the female archetype who is capable of sustaining a writer's maximum imagination and the "innocent" male character who works as a medium through which his passions are realized on the page. This combination can be said to be a key novelistic structure, and, in fact, will possibly be the model for my next work.

The examination of Faulkner's way of manipulating his characters introduces a new tool for my future writing and makes it possible for me to read his works with a much more positive attitude. It is my long-cherished wish that the scholars of literature would show us novelists an analysis of literary works based on the methodology of actual writing. I am convinced from my experience that we all can be positive readers of a novel, the art of words, when we come to know through a methodological reading of something about a writer's tools of expression and the mechanism of his way of writing. I believe that a specialist's methodological reading has an educational and enlightening influence not only on general readers but also on writers and that it will help us writers to take a step forward in our creative work.

There are few fields today in which specialists, general consumers, and manufacturers can be happy coworkers, but I think literature can be counted as one among the few.

# "Faulkner's Mississippi"

From *National Geographic* 175 (March 1989): 312–39.

His spirit is still here, of course: in the woodsmoke of November from the forlorn country shacks, in the fireflies in driftless random in the town in June, in the summer wisteria on the greenswards and the odor of verbena, in the ruined old mansions in the Yocona bottoms, in the echoes of an ax on wood and of dogs barking far away, in the languid human commerce on the courthouse square, in the aged white and blacks bantering on the brick wall beside the jail. His niece, Dean Faulkner Wells, says that late one night in the house on South Lamar she awakened suddenly to the smell of his pipe. She knew his ghost was there.

William Faulkner's imaginative, intuitive cosmos—Yoknapatawpha County—was one of the most convincing ever conceived by a writer. His own "little postage stamp of native soil," as he called it, was a spiritual kingdom that he transmuted into a microcosm not only of the South but also of the human race. More than any other major American novelist, with the possible exception of Hawthorne, he stayed close to home. In his youth, there were a few months in the East, in New Orleans, in Europe, but in the 1920s something turned in him; he began to realize the advantages of using the place where he had been reared as the setting for much of his fiction. Despite his later sojourns in Hollywood and in Charlottesville, Virginia, his physical and emotional fidelity to Oxford and to Mississippi, to the land and the people that shaped him, was at the core of his being, so that today

Oxford and the real county—Lafayette—are the most tangibly, palpably connected to one writer's soul of any locale in America.

*In the beginning it was virgin—to the west, along the Big River, the alluvial swamps threaded by black, almost motionless bayous and impenetrable with cane and buckvine and cypress and ash and oak and gum. . . .* Words like these first drew me to Faulkner when I was a homesick Mississippi boy at the University of Texas in the 1950s. At first I was awestruck, mesmerized, then saturated. His world of Sartorises and Snopeses, Compsons and Varners, Beauchamps and Gibsons, dogs and mules and woodlands and swamp bottoms was my world too. My own Yazoo City was only 120 miles from his fictional Jefferson.

Then, after a while, I became frightened, a fear that seeped deep into my blood and left me nearly breathless with doubt. I thought I wanted to be a writer. How could one ever be as good as this man?

Finally I made my private truce with Mr. Bill. I never met him. There were too many years between us. But I know him. After a long time in the East, I now live in his town.

William Faulkner was a small man, about five feet six, but his facial expression and the set of his head and neck and shoulders, especially in his later years, gave the impression of greater size. His voice was soft and whispery but had a carrying power, and he spoke fast. His laugh was a chuckle, almost a snort. "He seemed to belong outdoors," Dean Faulkner Wells remembers. "His skin was weathered, tan, slightly wrinkled, and he smelled of horses and leather, cedars and sunshine, pipe tobacco and bourbon."

His father owned a livery stable, then a hardware store, and later was the secretary and business manager of the University of Mississippi—Ole Miss. His playmates were his brothers and cousins and neighborhood children and the black children of servants. The old black retainer, Mammy Caroline Barr, was a second mother. Billy's relationship to her was very close, a love that deepened when he was grown and that in later life was almost worshipful.

Although he read a great deal in his youth, he was not considered a bookworm. He was impatient with school. He played quarterback for Oxford High School, where he broke his nose. He was an erratic pitcher in pickup baseball games. All his life he loved to ride horses, which were always throwing him, and as a grown man he owned a sailboat and took pride in being a sailor. He was good at golf and tennis and handy with tools. He adored, of course, to hunt in the big, vanishing woods, but he was not a particularly good shot. In Virginia years later he rode to the hounds. He loved and understood them as much as he did mules.

He admired the girls of his youth but was habitually shy, then and later. Long before he became a writer, he was in love with his future wife, Estelle, a fragile, popular beauty one and a half years his senior. But her parents considered him undeserving and without promise, and she married someone else, bore two children, then eventually was divorced and married him.

He enjoyed the company of children. He relished conversational games: Who were the 12 Caesars? If you were a vegetable, which would you prefer to be, and why?

He could be curt and rude and cutting, even among his family. He had no patience with cruel buffoons in any locale. I am certain he considered himself a Sartoris, an aristocrat, a fallen patrician, striving to regain grandeur of his great-grandfather W. C. Falkner. (W. C. dropped the *u* from the surname, and William reinserted it.) But to him, I sense, manners had nothing to do with class or color but with the way people behaved—their quintessential character. When he went to the University of Virginia in his declining years, he said, with considerable irony, that he admired Virginians because they were snobs, bound by manners, tradition, reserve, and, of course, superiority.

He was a master of reverse snobbery. He deplored the radio and telephone and did not own a television. For years he drove an ancient convertible with rusted floorboards. Things kept falling out: books, shirts, toys, fishhooks, swimming suits. When he had money, he bought fine things. He took good care of his family. He was intensely loyal to those he loved.

He went on horrific binges. He could be a cruel drunk, or a totally silent one, and later contrite. Those who knew him say he would almost consciously decide: I'm going to get drunk today—and he would. His bouts of heavy drinking followed not only failures but also successes—such as the one shortly after he was told that he had won the Nobel Prize. It is likely that he drank less than is popularly rumored, but he was often treated in Memphis or at least at a sanitarium in Byhalia, 35 miles north of Oxford, and that is where he died.

He wrote and told monumental tales of being a pilot and a warrior. Sometimes you have to lie to tell the truth. When, at 21, he came home from Canada after World War I, he wore around town the uniform of a British officer, complete with pips, wings of the Royal Flying Corps, Sam Browne belt, cane, and swagger stick. He affected a limp and claimed to have a silver plate in his head from a plane crash. The truth was he had not completed flight training and had never left Canada.

People began calling him Count No 'Count. He wrote poetry and worked as a painter and carpenter. He enrolled briefly at Ole Miss, only a few blocks west of the courthouse square.

He made a D in English. One of the Ole Miss literary societies refused him membership. For a time he ran the university post office. "He was the damndest postmaster the world has ever seen," a friend said. A professor filed a bill of complaint that the only way people could get their mail was to dig it out of the trash can at the back door. The postmaster delayed delivery of magazines until he had read them himself. He and his comrades played cards in the back and closed down the post office early to play golf. When he resigned under pressure, he declared that he never again would be at the beck and call of "every S.O.B. who's got two cents for the price of a stamp." He was later dismissed as the scoutmaster of the Oxford troop when a preacher complained about his drinking.

He was frequently broke then. It was not easy. He took the odd jobs around the university and help from his mother; he painted steeples and worked in the power plant. His early books were financial failures. From 1929 to 1932, in the most extraordinarily productive period of any American writer in history, he published *Sartoris*, *The Sound and the Fury*, *As I Lay Dying*, *Sanctuary*, and *Light in August*— all written while he was almost totally neglected. Not until *Sanctuary* in 1931, which the townspeople called his "corncob book," did his work attract attention, and even then, owing to the publisher's bankruptcy, he made no money to speak of on the book. Off and on over the years Faulkner claimed that he had written *Sanctuary* only for the money, which may or may not be true but which detracts gratuitously from this powerful book.

Some people in town stood by him, foremost the lawyer Phil Stone, one of his early mentors, and his mother, Miss Maud. Stone was four years older than he, an honors graduate of both Ole Miss and Yale, a garrulous man who advised and encouraged the fledgling poet and writer. He had some of the earlier manuscripts typed in his law office and peddled them to editors.

Miss Maud was a tiny wisp of a woman of immense tenacity and pride. "Bill would have had very little," his brother, Jack, often heard her say, "had he depended on the people of our county for it." During her weekly rubber of bridge with other ladies of the town, one of them disparagingly mentioned the corncob book. "My Billy writes what he has to," Miss Maud said. She finished the rubber of bridge in silence, departed, and never played with them again.

He later called himself a farmer and seldom discussed his writing. Shelby Foote recalls driving into town as an aspiring young writer in the late 1930s to keep an appointment with him. He parked his car at the courthouse and asked a man sitting on a bench for directions to William Faulkner's house. The man looked at him, then turned his head and spit on the ground in disgust. Even when they did not read them, people naturally wondered if they were characters in his books.

There were rumors around town that he did not write the books (bringing to mind the old saw that Shakespeare did not write the plays, just some fellow with the same name). For years one personage of the town argued before anyone who cared to hear that the books were written by an erudite farmer who preferred not to sign his name, and that Bill Faulkner did not know the meaning of all the big words.

Even as recently as the early 1950s, when Evans Harrington, later the chairman of the Ole Miss English Department, was teaching English in the local high school, his students exchanged snickers and knowing glances when he assigned them "A Rose for Emily." He asked them to explain their reactions. "We know about him," one of them said. "He's just an old drunk." They told Harrington of the delivery boy who went to Faulkner's house and saw him naked in a cedar tree.

Shortly before he won the 1949 Nobel Prize in Literature, his brother, John, reported, the Ole Miss faculty considered awarding him an honorary degree, but the proposal was voted down. After he got the Nobel, the professors who previously voted against him brought him up again. The other said, "For shame. We can't afford to give him one now. It's too late."

Here was a man, the writer Elizabeth Spencer says, "one of us, right over here at Oxford, shocking us and exposing us to people elsewhere with story after story, drawn from the South's own private skeleton closet . . . the hushed-up family secret, the nice girl who wound up in the Memphis whorehouse, the suicides, the idiot brother kept at home, the miserable poverty and ignorance of the poor whites . . . the revenge shootings, the occasional lynchings, the real life of the blacks. What was this man trying to do?"

Faulkner was born September 1897, died July 1962. In the years since his death, there has been in his hometown the inevitable softening, a singular amalgam of emotions involving pride, puzzlement, fear, mystery, forgiveness, and—in some quarters—a most begrudging acceptance. Some in the town say that Oxford did not really begin to look upon him seriously until MGM arrived in 1949 to film *Intruder in the Dust*, affording the local citizens the multifold titillations of Hollywood, bit parts for homegrown characters, and outside money. The Nobel Prize, with the films and photographs of Count No 'Count beside the King of Sweden, must have had almost as salubrious an effect. "The vast majority today realize he's the biggest drawing card this town's got, even if they've only read a book or two," Evans Harrington surmises.

Prominently inscribed today on an outside wall of the Ole Miss library are the words from his Nobel Prize address: "I decline to accept the end of man . . . I believe that man will not merely endure: he will prevail." In August 1987 there was a ceremony in Oxford to celebrate the U.S. Postal Service's issuing a commemorative Faulkner stamp. There was considerable irony in this too.

Yet one can still perceive an old, smoldering animosity, the remembrance of a long-ago slight from him, a buried enmity, a pent-up bitterness never reconciled: You could walk by him on the square and say hello, and he would look right through you, although the next day he might stop for an amiable conversation. He doctored his book manuscripts at the last moment, changed his words and characters in afterthought to make as much money as possible, lied and cheated for money. Had not his own daughter said in a television documentary that he once told her in his drunkenness that no one ever remembered Shakespeare's child? Who did he think he *was*? One aged town father still says William Faulkner did not like him because he thought him a Snopes. "Well," he says, across the years, "I didn't like *him* either."

Oxford is a serene and lovely town of about 11,000 people—roughly one-fifth of them black—and were it not for Ole Miss, with its student population almost as large as the town's, it would be a more or less typically isolated northern Mississippi county seat. Faulkner himself purposefully did not place the university in his fictional Jefferson. He put it in "Oxford," 40 miles away. He did not wish to complicate his pristine southern town with a university.

This is the Deep South. The milieu is a world's, or perhaps a civilization's, remove from, let one say, Hannibal, Missouri, which has so commercialized Mark Twain. There is no Faulkner Boulevard in Oxford, although there *is* a murky little passageway named Faulkner Alley, which cuts inauspiciously between the Shine Morgan Furniture & Appliance Company and Promises & Praise Christian Book Store on the square. His portrait is on display in the local McDonald's; when the restaurant first opened, two Faulkner relatives asked that the painting be removed, and for a short while it was.

Mayor John Leslie, elected in 1973, the same year as the beer referendum (he beat beer by 24 votes), says, "The town is deliberately low-keyed on Mr. Bill, because he was an intensely private man, and we know he'd prefer it this way. Also, this is the desire of the family," meaning Jill Faulkner Summers, Faulkner's only child, who lives in Charlottesville; Dean Faulkner Wells, the only niece; and Jimmy Faulkner and Chooky Falkner (spelled without the *u*), the nephews, who live in Oxford.

Richard Howorth, the owner of Square Books across from the courthouse, agrees with the mayor about the town's subdued treatment of its most famous citizen. "The mystique shouldn't be exploited," he feels, "because then it wouldn't be a mystique."

The Faulkner visitors are a fairly sophisticated crowd. A man from the Netherlands discovered Faulkner through a lecture by the distinguished Peruvian writer Mario Vargas Llosa. The Dutchman learned that Faulkner was Mario Vargas Llosa's favorite writer, so he came to Oxford. He went to Faulkner's house, Rowan Oak, and signed the guest register. He noticed the name directly above his—Mario Vargas Llosa. And there Vargas Llosa was in the next room.

People would drift into Mayor Leslie's drugstore on the square. "My wife, Elizabeth, gets to talking with them when she hears Yankee or foreign accents. Not too long ago one woman came in from Yugoslavia. She translates Faulkner's books. Just a few seconds later, another lady came in who'd produced and directed *Requiem for a Nun* in Paris."

Every summer Ole Miss sponsors a week-long Faulkner conference, which usually comes right after the Ole Miss cheerleaders clinic and draws a large group of Americans and foreigners. The cultural hazards for visiting scholars can be unusual.

A Frenchman engaged in a monograph on Christian existentialist symbolism in the later works was taken on a tour of the countryside. "I am fascinated by your peasants!" he exclaimed. Years ago an Italian woman who had known Hemingway was taken to the old Carter-Tate house, a ruined, unpainted shell with broken windows and vines ensnarling the porch. "Such marvelous decadence!" she said. "If you just had a *preservative* for all this decadence!"

One recent summer I myself was having a literary talk at a cocktail party with an obliging Russian gentleman. I asked if there were many Snopeses in the Soviet Union. "There are none," he replied sharply. "Under the Soviet system it is impossible to have Snopeses."

Dean Faulkner Wells and her husband, Larry, live in Miss Maud's house, a block south of the square. Her father, Dean, was the youngest of the four brothers. He was an avid hunter and fisherman and played second base and outfield for Ole Miss. The bond between William and Dean was exceptionally close. William let him use his airplane, a Waco cabin cruiser, and paid for his flying lessons. When all four brothers were flying, their mother would laugh and say, "I don't have a son on earth."

At 28, shortly before his daughter, Dean, was born, Dean died in a crash in an adjoining county. William wrote the inscription for his tombstone in the old Faulkner plot in St. Peter's Cemetery, the same words as on Lieut. John Sartoris's stone in *Sartoris*: "I bare him on Eagles' Wings and brought him unto me." In his horrendous grief he moved for a time into his mother's house to help look after Dean's young widow, Louise, who was five months pregnant. During this painful time he wrote part of *Absalom, Absalom!* on the dining room table, around which some of the Faulkner family and I often gather for holiday feasts. He took care of young Dean, who was less a niece than a daughter.

Mayor Leslie would deliver a package of medicine from his drugstore to Faulkner's mother's house and find him sitting in a green glider on the front porch. "Mr. Leslie, if you have a few minutes, let's pass the time," he would say, and they would talk about what was going on in town, which interested him considerably.

He would say to Louise, "Always have $50 in the bank. You can meet any situation." Dean remembers the ghost stories he told the children of the family and the neighborhood, particularly one about the doomed Judith, who he claimed threw herself to her death off the balcony of the Sheegog-Bailey house (which he bought and named Rowan Oak) after having been jilted by her Yankee beau. He would take his niece to the Charlie Chan movies at the Lyric Theater on Saturday nights, and as they walked home he would ask her, "Dean, did you like what Number One Son did?" and they would discuss the action in earnest detail. No one was to interrupt him when he was writing, but Dean burst in one afternoon and shouted: "Pappy, I've got the best news! An Ole Miss girl has just been named Miss America!" He pulled himself up from his table, took his pipe from his mouth, and said: "Well, Missy, at last somebody's put Mississippi on the map."

He loved the playfulness of life—sipping bourbon in the chilled twilights in the big woods, playing the host in ceremonial moments. He had a profound regard for tradition. He cherished Christmas and the Fourth of July. He gave Dean's daughter, Diane, an American flag shortly before her second birthday. On New Year's Eves at Rowan Oak he invited the young people his daughter Jill's age, where before a roaring fire, as the chimes of the courthouse sounded midnight, he served them champagne and gave the toast: "Here's to the younger generation. May you profit." He enjoyed the spontaneity of the young and felt deeply the vulnerability of children; people should believe in their progeny. The women he loved the best were either very young or very old. He was not an especially good husband and had a number of affairs, often with much younger women, later chronicled by either the woman, or third parties, or both.

His firstborn child, a little girl named Alabama after his Aunt 'Bama, died when she was nine days old. He carried the tiny casket on his lap to St. Peter's Cemetery and put her in her grave.

"The cedar-bemused cemetery," as he described the one in Jefferson, is only a few blocks from the square: the stones "whiter than white itself in the warm October sun against the bright yellow and red and dark red hickories and sumacs and gums and oaks like splashes of fire itself among the dark green cedars." The living and the fictitious are not strangers here. There are surnames on the stones here that are the same as his fictional characters, giving to this terrain a poetic, unearthly ambience.

Walking among the stones, as I often do, it is not difficult to imagine the idiot Benjy on his weekly visits in *The Sound and the Fury*. The inscription from Proverbs under the marble face of Eula Varner Snopes, wife of Flem Snopes, atop one of the grandest stones in the Jefferson cemetery, is nearly the same as that to Faulkner's grandmother on an equally formidable monument in the old Falkner plot: "Her Children Rise and Call Her Blessed." In the black section, which borders upon the white and mingles here and there with it, lies the grave of Mammy Caroline Barr, the indomitable woman who raised the Falkner boys. He wrote the inscription on her tombstone: "Her white children bless her."

His own stone is a rather simple one. He lies next to his wife, Estelle, under some oaks at the foot of a hill. Bill Appleton, the former supervisor of St. Peter's, has found strange objects left here by visitors: flowers, candy kisses, pints of bourbon, and once a soggy volume of the collected poems of William Butler Yeats. Many times he has seen literary pilgrims at the grave after midnight with flashlights.

Masaru Inoue, a 41-year-old professor from Yokohama, came to

Yoknapatawpha on a year's sabbatical. He discovered *The Sound and the Fury* 20 years ago in Japan. He reread it ten times. He saw parallels between Faulkner's characters and his own ancestors.

Inoue came into the town for the first time on a bus from Memphis. "We crossed South Lamar. I saw the white building with the clock above it. I moved my eyes and there was the Confederate soldier. On the other side of the courthouse was the First National Bank, which William Faulkner's grandfather established. I saw the water tower. 'Oh, this is it! This is it!' I thought."

The convergence of fact and fiction from the Faulkner corpus is often eerie, but titillating. The Oxford telephone directory, for instance, lists 13 Varners—even including a Jody Varner—2 Hippses, 8 Ratliffs (one of them on Old Highway 6 in the mythical Frenchman's Bend vicinity), 9 Littlejohns, 2 Bundrens, 13 Carotherses, and 23 Houstons (Mink Snopes killed the intolerable Jack Houston).

The real-life Lowe twins, Ed and Eph, played the Gowrie twin brothers in the movie *Intruder in the Dust*, and one can see them to this day, older yet even more uncannily identical at 66, dressed precisely alike as they stride in exact step toward Smitty's restaurant on South Lamar, or with binoculars wordlessly looking down together from a second-floor window upon the courthouse square.

There is an aging black man here—he once served a stretch in Parchman for murder—who has sporadically and unsuccessfully been digging for gold (said to have been buried when Grant came through the county on his Vicksburg campaign) in and about the ruined plantation houses in the countryside, just as various Yoknapatawpha entrepreneurs did around the Old Frenchman's place. A couple of years ago 11-year-old Cap Henry's Uncle C. E. took him on a deer hunt, where he killed his first buck and had his face ritualistically bloodied, like young Ike McCaslin's in *Go Down, Moses*.

"Where is Temple Drake?" photographer Bill Allard kept asking himself, and me, in our peregrinations about the town, the campus, the county, the state. Temple Drake was the university coed who ended up one day with some highly disreputable characters at the ruin of the Old Frenchman's place in *Sanctuary* and got in serious trouble.

The observant eye of the photographer searched everywhere for her modern equivalent. He knew, as did I, something about her: her "taunt, toothed coquetry," "her high delicate head and her bold painted mouth and soft chin, her eyes blankly right and left looking, cool, predatory, and discreet." But where was she now?

The Mississippi Delta begins 30 miles west of Oxford; Faulkner was obsessed by it and by the violent, majestic Big River at its Western edge. Some of his finest writing is set there: *This land which man has deswamped and denuded and derivered in two generations so that white men can own plantations and commute every night to Memphis and black men own plantations and ride in Jim Crow cars to Chicago to live in millionaires' mansions on Lakeshore Drive, where white men rent farms and live like niggers and niggers crop on shares and live like animals, where cotton is planted and grows man-tall in the very cracks of the sidewalks, and usury and mortgage and bankruptcy and measureless wealth, Chinese and African and Aryan and Jew, all breed and spawn together. . . .*

Nearer home, the recognizable landmarks from the fiction still abound. The bronze plaque set in the white façade of the courthouse itself bears the words from *Requiem for a Nun:* "But above all, the courthouse: the center, the focus, the hub; sitting looming in the center of the country's circumference like a single cloud in its ring of horizon. . . ."

A block north of the courthouse was the jail, which quartered the murderers, thieves, and moonshiners from the fiction, replaced in the year of his death by a bland green-and-white concrete structure. Only a few blocks west toward the university is the old railroad depot, deserted and unused now, scene of so much feverish activity in the books. A quarter of a mile or so from this place of ghosts is the black section called Freedman Town, the unpaved roads and flimsy shacks of which have now yielded to concrete streets, federal housing projects, Martin Luther King Jr. Drive, and the town's integrated junior high school. Here, at the civic park and athletic complex, are the integrated baseball and basketball games and tennis matches. Then, back toward the square again, on the unhurried, shady streets with their antebellum houses set on broad private lawns, there will be *The Sound and the Fury* house, surrounded by magnolias, bereft now of the iron fence behind which a retarded young man similar to Benjy Compson once walked up and down, and beyond that the Neilson-Culley home, which some claim as Miss Emily Grierson's in "A Rose for Emily," and where my friend Patty Lewis, who now lives there, says she sits on the back terrace under the magnolias with a tall drink at dusk and imagines Miss Emily and Homer Barron together in the cool dark of the upstairs in the days before Miss Emily went to the store to buy the arsenic.

It is the countryside, however, even more than the town, that is the most powerful testament to the lingering fable. At the old College Hill Presbyterian Church, where William and Estelle were married in 1929 and where Sherman encamped 30,000 troops before he and Grant moved on Vicksburg, there is a solitary stone obelisk in the graveyard with the inscription "The Dead." Out at the other end of the county is the village of Taylor with its post office and galleried stores.

"Nicky, Snake, Al, and the boys," says an artist friend from the delta who bought her old farmhouse here, "hang around in front of Mary's general store and catfish place telling tales and lies at the very spot where Temple Drake stepped off the train and into trouble." Along the narrow winding roads with gullies and ravines and patchy hills of cotton and corn and soybeans and the ubiquitous kudzu vines on all sides are the little tin-roofed houses and unpainted cabins, their dusty yards full of chickens and dogs and junk and clothes drying on fences and lines.

"Dark House" was the working title for *Light in August*, and the haunted countryside around Oxford is dotted with crumbling houses darkly resonating the past and the vanished people who once lived in them. In the nearby dying community of Tula, across the river south of the Frenchman's Bend area, is a derelict old building that tilts at an angle. Surely this had to have been Varner's store! Just up the hill is a neat two-story house. Could this have been Mrs. Littlejohn's hotel? I paused at the rotted window of the store, looking into the dank shadows. I did not have to close my eyes to imagine Jody Varner and Flem Snopes holding forth there on just precisely how best to make money.

Racism and poverty had forever been his native state's twin burdens, and in his deepest soul he knew them both. In the heart of his fiction over the years it was the Snopeses and their friends who exerted the most ruinous influence on the society; it was the blacks who, through their quiet courage and dignity, endured.

In the 1950s he began speaking out publicly against racial injustice in his state: on the 1954 U.S. Supreme Court decision, the Emmett Till murder, and other things. "To live anywhere in the world of A.D. 1955," he said, "and be against equality because of race or color, is like living in Alaska and being against snow." In those trying times he was a pariah in his native land more than Count No 'Count had ever been. He would be gratified, I believe, by the remarkable racial strides in recent years in Mississippi and by the civilized public dialogue on race.

Perhaps it has finally come full circle. Unless I am mistaken, the young people of his beloved Mississippi are reading him. David Sansing, an Ole Miss professor, assigns a least one of his books to students in his Mississippi history courses. They invariably say they want to read more. "They're awed," he tells me, "that he takes a locale, places, white and black people they know and raises them to the level of great literature. It really does show something for them. It enhances their own self-esteem. He shows them that a Mississippi sharecropper or poor black man can face the same choices and mysteries as a great leader of state. He makes them aware for the first time that his people have to wrestle with the same complexities, the same inconsistencies that they do in their own lives. For the first time they realize, whether they'll be a lawyer in a small town, a doctor, a schoolteacher, a coach, that they too are in a life-and-death struggle. They tell me they're better equipped to deal with these things after reading him."

A young black woman, a Mississippian, in one of Sansing's classes had such an emotional reaction to *Absalom, Absalom!* that she was unable to write her report. Her grandfather, she told him, was white and still lived in her town. They never talked to one another. When she read about Thomas Sutpen, she said, he reminded her of her grandfather and of how evil man can be. "If Mississippians had read him 35 or 40 years ago," Sansing says, "we wouldn't have had the problems we had."

In the sweep of his work his sense of the tragedy and dishonor of even the worst of human beings gradually softened, to be replaced by compassion and pity. "Man aint really evil," the sewing machine agent V. K. Ratliff says, "he jest aint got any sense." Running through Faulkner's work is a profound recognition of the awful brevity of life, that people are only temporary tenants of the earth and at its mercy in the end.

"It was the land itself which owned them," Mink Snopes acknowledges, "and not just from a planting to its harvest but in perpetuity. . . ." We are all in it together, I believe he is saying to me, and we are all in for a difficult time: "Memory believes before knowing remembers. Believes longer than recollects, longer than knowing even wonders."

As I sit in deep orange February twilights at the kitchen table in his mother's house listening with my friends to the Ole Miss games, I hear everlastingly the chimes of the hour from the courthouse down the way. They reverberate through the town, pervading his landmarks and his people with an almost palpable transience. They curiously suffuse me with the bravery and vision and majesty of his genius. They remind me: "The past is never dead. It's not even past." He was right about this, as he was about most things.

# "The Faulkner Thing"

From *The Oxford American* 1 (Spring 1992): 8–9. Copyright © by John Grisham.

It was Dallas, or some other city. They all look the same at the end of a book tour, so it makes no difference where you are, really, you just keep telling yourself that this city, whatever it is, is one step closer to home. I was sitting on a small, creaky, makeshift throne in a corner of a quaint little bookshop. The throne was between the fishing and erotica shelves; my back was to the poetry. Before me was a table stacked with copies of *The Firm*, and beyond it a line of people waited patiently as I scribbled my name and made impossible small talk.

I heard a commotion at the front door, then saw her as she surveyed the place and headed for me. Behind her was a burly cameraman, and he followed her with great discipline as she elbowed past the others and approached me. She had plastic hair and an orange face, and I knew immediately she was another of those busy TV beat reporters scouring the street looking for holdups and housefires. Evidently, it was a slow day for Dallas (?), so she dropped by the bookstore to gather a few gems from the guy who wrote *The Firm*.

On this day, I had already suffered through three interviews, all properly arranged through my publisher, and I was in no mood for another, especially one that materialized from nowhere. I scrawled my name, thanked the person, and tried to ignore the reporter. But there she was, suddenly standing near me with a microphone.

"Are you John Grisham?" she asked loudly, waving the mike.

I did not look up, but began inscribing the next book. I wrote very slow. She was the first interviewer to ask that question.

"Of course he is," said a man waiting in line. I too thought it was rather obvious who I was.

"Is it true you live in Oxford, Mississippi?" she asked, even louder. Why would I lie about something like this? My picture is on the dust jacket, and under it is a sentence that plainly states where I live.

"Yes," I said abruptly, without looking into the orange face.

This inspired her. She came closer and stabbed the mike to within inches of my head. The bouncer with the camera hit a switch, and suddenly there was a bright light everywhere.

"How do you compare yourself with William Faulkner?" she asked.

A handful of morons have asked me this question, and nothing irritates me more. Those who ask it have read neither Faulkner nor Grisham, but are sharp enough to know Oxford is home for both of us.

"Faulkner's dead," I said, glancing in her general direction but being careful not to look at the camera.

I'm sure she knew he was dead, but she seemed a bit surprised. Undaunted, she pressed ahead. "It must be difficult to write in Oxford," she said.

It's difficult to write anywhere. I have found nothing in life more boring than staring at an empty sheet of paper and praying that something happens. But, truthfully, if you're going to write for a living, there's no better place than Oxford.

"Why?" I asked.

"Well, you know, the Faulkner thing."

There are at least half a dozen published novelists in Oxford. I know them, some better than others, and I see them occasionally at Square Books or Smitty's or at parties and we talk about books and editors and agents and deadlines and other writers, but I have yet to hear any of them discuss "the Faulkner thing." He was a literary artist of immense proportions, a genius, a writer thoroughly dedicated to his craft, the greatest American novelist of this century. He won the Nobel. He was peerless, but, bless his heart, he's dead. Life goes on for the rest of us.

I decided not to be ugly. "Do you read Faulkner?" I asked with a smile as I signed another book.

She hesitated. "Some." I knew she was lying.

"What's your favorite Faulkner novel?" I asked.

Hesitation. Everyone in line waited. Painful hesitation. I slowly signed another book as the mike stopped waving and everything was silent.

"Uh, let's see, I guess, *The Reivers,*" she said in desperation.

They made a movie out of *The Reivers* and it starred Steve Mc-Queen, who at the time was much more famous than William Faulkner. Nothing against the novel—it's a fun story—but it's not exactly his masterpiece. I figured she had seen the movie but had not read the book.

I was about to nail her and ask the titles of her second and third favorite Faulkner novels when she seized the moment and said, "I've been to Oxford, you know."

"What for?" I asked.

"I was a cheerleader, and we competed there."

Of course. I said, "It's a lovely town, isn't it?"

She slinked forward, the microphone now centimeters from my nose. "It's beautiful. I went to Rowan Oak, you know, Faulkner's place," she said. "I could almost feel his presence."

I almost asked what she had been drinking when she went to Rowan Oak and felt his presence, but again, I decided not to be ugly. She was just trying to do her job. This philistine with the mini-cam stepped on a woman's foot and the woman snapped at him, and for a second things were almost out of hand. He apologized without removing his face from the camera. The owner of the bookstore appeared at the end of the line to see what was happening.

The orange face was even closer. "Surely, it must be intimidating writing under the shadow of Faulkner."

This did it.

"I swear he's dead. I've seen his grave. Died thirty years ago when I was in the second grade."

I was clearly irritated, and this, of course, was exactly what she wanted. The camera moved closer.

"But what about the legend, the aura, the magic of Faulkner?

I read somewhere that all Southern writers labor in the shadow of Faulkner."

I had read this somewhere too. "I'm not a Southern writer," I said slowly without looking at her. She thought about this for a second.

"Then what are you?" she asked, definitely puzzled.

"I'm a commercial writer who lives in the South. I try to write commercial fiction of a high quality—no attempts at literature here—just good books that people enjoy reading. The libraries are already filled with great literature. There's no room for me."

"That's interesting," she said.

"Is that a question?" I asked.

She ignored this. "So you write for money?"

"Yes. At one time I was a lawyer, and I worked for money. When I served in the state legislature, I got paid for it. When I mowed grass as a kid, I did so for money. You wouldn't be holding that microphone if you weren't getting paid for it."

"What about writers who say they don't care if their books sell?"

"They're lying." I handed a book back to its purchaser. The line was growing longer. The proprietor was now standing nearby.

"What about Faulkner? Did he write for money?"

I honestly don't know why Faulkner wrote. His best books were written when he couldn't give them away. He spent many agonizing years in Hollywood cranking out screenplays so his family could eat. He was not well off, financially speaking, until late in life.

The owner stepped forward. "Mr. Grisham, your plane leaves in an hour."

"Thank you," I said. It was a welcome lie. My flight was three hours away. I ignored the reporter.

But she was not to be ignored. "Do you think Faulkner wrote for money?"

"Why don't you ask Faulkner?" I snapped as I took another book and scribbled in earnest. The light went off. The microphone was withdrawn. She mumbled something that sounded like "thanks" as they made a noisy retreat and left the store.

Book tours attract nosy little reporters who are completely uninhibited and will ask for all sorts of details such as, Do you write for money? How much money will you make off this book? How much money did you make off your last book? How much did you pay for your house? What kind of car do you drive? Does your wife work? Where do you vacation? What'd you sell the film rights for?

Nothing is private. They'll ask anything. Faulkner didn't like them either, and I'll bet he was never quizzed about legend or shadows.

# "History, Rooted in the Present"

This month, which marks the centennial of William Faulkner's birth, I am reminded of a dinner a couple of summers back at William Styron's house on Martha's Vineyard. The Colombian novelist Gabriel García Márquez and I were guests at the dinner Styron offered in honor of President Clinton.

After an hour or so of political talk, the president said that, finding himself surrounded by writers, he would like to know the favorite novel of each of us. Styron, expectedly and to general applause, chose Mark Twain's *Huckleberry Finn*. García Márquez's choice was far less expected: *The Count of Monte Cristo* by Alexandre Dumas. Why? Because it is the greatest novel on education, García Márquez answered. You throw a barely literate young sailor into a dungeon of the Chateau d'If, and 15 years later he comes out knowing mathematics, astronomy, physics, high finance, three dead languages and seven living ones—as well as all the gossip of the current Parisian scene.

I was about to tell the truth—*Don Quixote* by Cervantes is my favorite novel—but I bit my tongue and opted for second best, William Faulkner's *Absalom, Absalom!* I knew that we all wanted to hear Clinton speak about his own land, the South, in which, said Katherine Anne Porter, "we are children of a lost war."

Clinton then spoke with great frankness and emotion of his childhood and early youth in Arkansas. He spoke of the tensions within his family and within his society. As a teen, he told us, he took a bus to Oxford, Miss., in order to visit Faulkner's house, just to satisfy his certainty that the South was more than racism, burnt churches and the Klan. It was the land of William Faulkner. The South could also produce a great literary genius.

Clinton then went on to quote a couple of passages, not the easiest ones, from *The Sound and the Fury*. The next day, García Márquez and I hurried to Styron's library and checked out the accuracy of the quotes. They were almost verbatim.

When I myself was a young man, Faulkner was not regarded as a universal or even national author, but as a "regional" writer, dismissed as a "Dixie Góngorist." Well, for a Latin American, to be compared to Luis de Góngora, the great baroque 17th-century Spanish poet, was, even if it meant pejoratively, no mean tribute.

But then, was this what the American South and Latin America, Faulkner and we had in common? Not the culture of the North, where "nothing succeeds like success" but the culture of the South, where defeat is not unknown?

The baroque—a style marked by extravagant, complex, ambiguous and bizarre forms—is the aesthetics of the New World, the art that permits the Vanquished Indians and the enslaved Africans to recover their gods and their dreams under the domes of Christianity. It is also, thanks to Faulkner, the literary space where the South can recognize itself fully as a multiracial, modern society. History, in Faulkner's novels, is rooted in the present, where we can all come together in remembrance and desire. For, as he himself put it, "The present, you know, began 10,000 years ago, but the past began one minute ago."

# "On Coming Late to Faulkner"

If you discover the Old Man late—*discover* hardly the term: you have heard of him if you have heard of Shakespeare, if you have heard of the Civil War, and your apprehension of him will be constituted of a vague kind of hybrid of those entities grown out of more or less local soil, except that your soil will not be yet seemingly moist from the spilt blood of the War, as his was, or as he said it was, and yours will not still have the footprints of Indians on it (and not these hokey cowboy Indians but realer, stranger ones, with names like Doom and Ikkemotubbe, altogether better than Crazy Horse or Sitting Bull, which sound by contrast like names schoolchildren dreamed up, and you will be already onto a signal part of his genius, names given him by God)—

If you arrive prepared to read in the way an early writer reads, which is to steal and to love and then to repudiate and mock after stealing it from the very Old Man in question and loving it—

If you come to Faulkner late you may escape finding yourself enthralled, intoxicate, intestate. By late I mean after eighteen or so, the age about when the deep loving thefts are done and the mocking repudiations commence. If you arrive before then, in the tumescent doubt of ever finding that which you can love or be loved by, you will be forever enthralled, intoxicate, intestate, and you will have no qualm about using those three adjectives that way; you might even use them in unconscious imitation of the father. But if you come after eighteen you will use them in conscious imitation, as a small act of fond, mocking repudiation.

There will be nothing wrong with the fond mocking, because you are but a nit on the hide of the great. As Miss O'Connor put it (she is easily Artemis, if not Hera herself, to Faulkner's Zeus), you with your two-cylinder syntax are a mule and cart being borne down on by the Dixie Limited. Fond mocking is, actually, all that you can do, given the power and roar of the train that blasts you from the track. If you come late, you get off the track and hazard to throw a rock. If you don't arrive late, you get run over and are forever silenced by the presumption that you too could squall down iron like that, burning all the coal in your heart and head and blowing all the steam that an uncounted boy (called Count No 'Count by the good denizens of Oxford who today erect a statue to memorialize him) could blow.

I came late to the boy who would immortally blow by being a boy late one night at my English teacher's house and revealing—apropos of what I cannot fathom, but in the general atmosphere of my having threatened her with my being not a mere stooge of criticism under her as were my peers, who were at present not present, I was noticing; it was late and I was mixing the drinks, her sane husband had retired, and in the general atmosphere of her having promised me that she would be my mentor, then, if I would write—that I had never read Faulkner.

"What?"

She was out of her chair and gone and back, dropping in my lap a Modern Library *Absalom, Absalom!* with, I noticed, opening it, her maiden name on the flyleaf. In that mysterious sequence of events which conspires to make a boy a writer—facts and forces that are anybody's guess and are always tedious if anybody starts the guessing—this was a heavyweight moment.

"I am appalled."

I could only chuckle, because she was. Here I was, unread and unready, proclaiming I would write, and here she was read and ready to coach in a mission that was holy, and I the supplicant had not read the Scripture. What miracle prevented her throwing me out of the house? The hour, the booze, the novelty of a boy who would so presume? Was she bored by the correct boys at school? This was probably about the case for her, but it was not for me.

I was partly in love—a literary mother! but sort of not a mother! (that maiden name contained a magic suggestion—a woman was taking notice of me)—and I was in possession of The Word. It was a moment of more tumescence than doubt. The tissuey pages of the book, the tight type, the *Absalom!* whatever that meant—the gift was electrically mystified in my hand. This was as close to a religious experience as I am likely to suffer on Earth.

As had happened to me with the actual Bible, I began to try to read it, and couldn't. But I had a secular mother non-mother looking over my shoulder, not the dubious authority of Protestantism. I read to page sixty or so of *Absalom, Absalom!* four or five times, as I recall. Each time I stalled out like a car going up a hill. I had taught myself how to read by scanning Harold Robbins and Norman Mailer and Philip Roth for prurience, fashioning the not surprising conclusion that writing was celebrity; I had read Tennessee Williams, fashioning the not surprising conclusion that writing was people saying fun things about sex, mostly; I had read Miss O'Connor for the hard comedy alone, and Walker Percy for the softer comedy, happy to skip or sail over the alleged religious and philosophical concerns in both. I was therefore in no wise prepared for Faulkner.

Somehow on one of the uphill runs into *Absalom!* I made it to page one hundred or so, and then began the breathtaking downhill seduction, the rush, the delightful surrender to gravity, and I was not the same boy when I finished the book. I could not have explicated the thing (could not today), did not know who said what half the time, forgot half what mattered half the time, yet was entirely aboard the Dixie Limited. How could something so preposterously private be remotely public? How could the book-club ladies who objected to the "difficulty" be at once correct and not correct? How—alas, who cares?

I would then read about a third of the oeuvre, using as a springboard a copy of the Viking *The Portable Faulkner* which I had never returned to the local county library, and which I yet have as I negotiate an amnesty with them which will allow me to come in safely against my $3,700 fine. I stopped there (at a third of the corpus; the fine presumably mounts yet). Any more, I felt, and I would not dare presume write myself. Any more evidence of this Olympic steam a boy named Bill could learn to blow and there would be no point attempting same oneself.

Even with my post-formative arrival, the third I'd read was enough by itself to suggest one desist, because I could not see the writing as having come from a boy named Bill—I saw the shelf of books in the library as having sprung full-blown if not from the hip of Zeus then at least from the head of a non-mortal. I had encountered by that time Faulkner's irked epitaph—"He made the books"—but I did not believe it. The books were *found* made, like ancient tablets. No mere man sent Thomas Sutpen on a mission like that, wrestling in the mud his twenty wild specimens of the original domestic offender, pulling from that mud a ten-mile-square estate, confounding a dude like Quentin like that into jumping into a river like that. And got away with it—no mere man could get away with it. Miss O'Connor barely got away with a girl named Hulga neé Joy, wearing a sweatshirt with a picture of a cowboy on it, having her leg stolen by a Bible salesman.

In this period of early stultifying reverence, I had lunch in Charleston, South Carolina, with Malcolm "Buddy" Franklin, Faulkner's stepson. This was set up by another professor of English apparently taking good extracurricular care of me. I asked Buddy Franklin what was it like, being the Old Man's son in the Old Man's house. He told me that they hunted squirrel, and you had to put a quarter in a jar if you shot a squirrel in the head or if you did not shoot a squirrel in the head (one of many lacunae in the twenty-five-year memory), and the quarters so collected went to whiskey—the impression created of a community whiskey which Buddy could have partaken of, and he was partaking of now, heartily, I wish I could remember what about, and I asked how the Old Man himself was, and Buddy said perfectly okay except you did not go in his study. You drank whiskey with and sat on stumps shooting squirrels with your father but did not go in his office where the tablets were quarried. I could buy this. The Old Man Faulkner was a boy named Bill after all if what giggling Buddy Franklin was averring was true, and I had every reason to believe it was. He was enjoying a free lunch at Henry's in Charleston with a professor and two kids, what was there to misrepresent? I had it on solid, private, intimate, not altogether sober, authority that the books were made by a man. It was still improbable, but Buddy Franklin was *giggling.*

I came to be a giggler myself—at Elvis, at Marse Robert and the War, at Shelby and the Wawer, and did some writings with one arm cocked at all times to loft a fond, mocking, repudiating not rock, but sentient Earth wad, at the Old Man when I felt the need to deny him. I was in this denial until, by accident one night (I would not pay a dime to see another writer's house, and at midnight no one collects money at Rowan Oak, if they do in the day), I stepped on the porch of Caroline Barr's (clearly Dilsey's) shack and saw in the horrific lightening glare a sign on the door hand-scrawled, crayoned, not drawn but driven into the paper, or into the wood itself, the pulp of the paper not finally contra-distinct from the door into which it annealed, wed, clung—don't TELL me Faulkner ain't fun—a sign saying horribly, vitriolically, as if somehow somebody like Charles Etienne de Saint Valery Bon or Wash Jones or Wash Jones's granddaughter or Wash Jones's granddaughter's daughter lay feebly in there and had written it, KEEP OUT. Spastic, screwn, scriven notlettering that made me jump from the porch, convinced Wash with his scythe was about— my actual, and utter, fear was of the great-grandson, or thereabouts, of Jim Bond, on welfare, inside on a cot—I quit giggling.

Out of denial, I giggle no more. Not at Elvis, not at Robert, not even at Shelby. They are all reduced and enlarged to the position we who would give inadequate credit to the Old Man who phrased and it are reduced and enlarged to: Well, Kernel, they mought have kilt us, but they aint whupped us yit, air they?

That sentence is the Rosetta Stone to all the other tablets, for me. For me it alone is enough, and one other thing. There will be endless yammering this year, in these pages and in others, my own yammering included, about what we owe the Old Man and why. Some of the testimony will be as preposterously private, and folk will strain themselves carrying their utterances to the page. The bell of Human Verities will ring heavy. You will come to understand Universal Transcendence of the Mere Local. Some of it will be right, and some of it you can lob sentient Earth wads at. But Wash Jones's sentence above is large enough and meaning enough and invention enough for me, and this:

One day, sitting on a stump, or not, shooting or not, drunk or not, with Buddy or not, with a woman or not (I understand there is a woman who goes around Oxford saying she got the Old Man out in the woods and he proved impotent, and she tenders this as some kind of failure on his part, and I'd like to ask her what she thinks the woods are for—where are we?), sitting there reading *Time* magazine or not, as he was when Estelle hit him in the face with the croquet mallet, William Faulkner thunk up Flem Snopes, and then gave him his brother Mink.

As modest as he was, apparently, he had every right to stand up shaking his head at his own genius and go into the sacrosanct study to write down the names. With those two names alone—forget the exploits of their bearers and the eponymous hegemony of Snopes today, forget Doom and Ikke and Ike and the postage stamp that would be the Universe, and forget preserving by main force a disappearing world as one would desiccate a leaf to preserve a forest—the Old Man was someone you should not throw a rock at and you wouldn't hit if you did.

And yes, I have found it, Madame (cf. "Wash"): *the woods are for important and furious undefeat.*

# "Lee Smith Talks about Southern Writing"

From Kathryn B. McKee, "News of the Spirit," *The Southern Register* (Winter 1998): 15–17 [excerpt]. Reprinted by permission of Kathryn B. McKee.

*I watched you talk about the centennial of William Faulkner's birth on TV . . . and I thought we might start by going back to some of your remarks on that program. You said: "I read* Absalom, Absalom! *like some people read the Bible." Can you talk about that?*

When I first read Faulkner I was in college, and I was already trying to write things. At that point I was blown away by the language. I was just drunk on the language. I really don't think I understood a whole lot of what was going on. I think I was drawn to it because like anybody who is from the South and who would write about it, I was also alienated from it. I think I really identified with "I hate it! I hate it!" in a way that I never understood at that point. Later, I was interested in the sense of place because I come from another place that's made an indelible imprint on me and that fascinated me. Later, I think, as I was trying to write, I was interested in the writing itself and in the technique. One thing I didn't get to say on that show was that Faulkner wrote each one of his novels with a different narrative strategy. He was above all a great innovator, a totally experimental writer, the first great experimental writer I think, in this country. Those novels are all like doors that any would-be writer can walk through, and so it's exciting to read

Faulkner when you are trying to learn to write. Later, after a certain age, you discover mortality and then Faulkner makes a whole different kind of sense and you discover all kinds of things like loss and unredeemable sadness of one kind or another. Then you get to a whole bunch of things—ideas and attitudes—that I never suspected before. Faulkner is rewarding to read at whatever point you are in life.

# "Absalom, Absalom!"

*Absalom, Absalom!,* by William Faulkner

One is glad that, so far as I know, Faulkner never went and sat ringside with Joe DiMaggio as Hemingway did. Faulkner's vicarious heroic would have taken him, rather, to reunions of the American pilots who formed the Eagle Squadron of the Royal Air Force (few survivors, alas). His true heroics, visible and audible on every page, depend on fecundity, on the constant chance of saying something original by way of oratory. It is safer to count on its happening than on its not, and if this gets him a Purple Heart, then so be it, so long as we understand by that term an added intensity, an irresistible chromatic sublimity, an impenitent yen to use the full orchestra of language, indeed to create an artifact so substantial it almost supplants the world it regards. He is the auto-pilot of crescendo, the artificer of sweep, the maestro of making things thicker, the architect of density and deviance. All through he tells a straight enough story, but the entire world's howling lingers in its margins, as if narrative were being faulted for neatness, selection, symbolism even. This guarantees him as a holist, an ever-present ancient mariner who not only gives us the full tale but augments it with what one has to call the act of agile stuffing. All along, he knows and imagines more than his completed *oeuvre* could ever contain, which is a monumental feat of knowledge, to be sure, but his salient contribution is not, I think, the fabricating of Snopeses, the fleshing out of that map in the back of *Absalom, Absalom!* and those appended chronologies and gene-alogies that read like belated challenges to himself rather than aide-memories to the reader. Can these dry bones live?

They just have. Look where the east-west highway in almost Ro-man geometry intersects the north-south railroad and ringed spots like sperms with tails attaching an egg or the tadpole-like objects that astronomers call cometary knots tell us of sites: "Where Old Bayard Sartoris died in young Bayard's car," "Miss Joanna Burden's, Where Christmas killed Miss Burden & Where Lena Grove's child was born." It is the kind of map you need when recollecting emotion in tran-quility—not much use to you beforehand, of course, or even during. When he writes "William FaulkИer, Sole OwИer and Proprietor," us-ing two reversed N's perhaps in fake redneckery, he is urinating on ground already written up and dominated. This was no thing to send in to Random House as part of a book proposal, but scent-making by a literary tiger out on his own, beyond editors and Fadimans, creators of ingratiating short paragraphs and short sentences. Where Nabo-kov deals in almost scalding precision, a diagnostic triplet of definite or indefinite article, adjective and noun, Faulkner works himself up into an elephantiasis or augment, never quite sure how little to leave it at. As in this:

> He crossed that strange threshold, that irrevocable demarcation, not led, not dragged, but driven and herded by that stern implacable presence, into that gaunt and barren household where his very silken remaining clothes, his delicate shirt and stockings and shoes which still remained to remind him of what he had once been, vanished, fled from arms and body and legs as if they had been woven of chimeras or of smoke.
>
> He crossed the strange threshold, driven by that implacable presence, into the household where his remaining clothes reminded him of what he had once been.

Anyone can help the Third Reich, even the occasional half-wit, and every incompetent can crank out a tale. What Faulkner manages to do here is convey the act of dressing and undressing in the motions of the prose, the keenest of which is how the clothes themselves undress him, themselves reject him and blow away, an illusion that of course builds upon the clad quality of the narrative itself. It would have been a cliché to denude the sentences themselves to proclaim the divestment of the last two lines, and he goes nowhere near so obvious a trick. Then he resumes with an affirmative, garbing the whole mental motion anew, filling in a physique with an entire implied biography, the point of which—nothing new—is that any given detail contains the whole story if only you have the patience to draw it out and reveal it. It's a typical patch of execution, doing several things at once, as he mostly does, but it doesn't launch into the egregious kind of literate back-stammer we get elsewhere in *Absalom, Absalom!* and which makes it a visionary novel, a model of the impenitently pensive work of art:

> *He was gone; I did not even know that either since there is a metabolism of the spirit as well as of the entrails, in which the stored accumulations of long time burn, generate, create and break some maidenhead of the ravening meat; ay, in a second's time—yes, lost all the shibboleth erupting of cannot, will not, never will in one red instant's fierce obliteration.*

This is by no means the fiercest, most fluently asyntactical portion of the novel, but it does set him apart from thousands who toil to accomplish a book without mistakes in grammar, their fervent hope that the grammatically flawless *ipso facto* becomes high art. Why, you could even cobble together a sentence, a pseudo-sentence, using his most portentous words merely to evince his linguistic interest in the unlinguistic doings of humans: His metabolism had accumulated the meat of a maidenhead, at least until some shibboleth obliterated it. Free the least redneck part of his idiom from the "Hit wont need no light, honey"s, and the big words, out in the open as it were, will form uncanny relationships with one another—the latent high brow that over-animates the complete sentence or paragraph. It is as if the history of the language, there ever having been a developing language for there to be a history of, loomed up behind everything, minifying it in an erudite, fervent, un-Southern voice, all points of the compass speaking at once. That is how he works on you, doing within his pages what Proust put in the margins and in his tacked on paper wings. The vision of the All haunts them both, at their most restricted and specific, alarming them with the discovery that the minutest particular has universal force, could you but let it loose. Every mouse a rogue elephant.

Less a phrasemaker than he was a texture weaver, an apocalyptic compound voice of all the ages, Faulkner blazed the trail. Without him as forebear, some of us would never have been. He wrote in defiance, reserving the right to stylize until the "message" of his novels was that of their idiosyncratic twang. Sometimes, we are told, a surgeon works so fast, stitching, that his gloves catch fire. You sometimes sense this happens to Faulkner at his most incantatory. I am not sure his eminent performance helps me with plot or narrative line, with, for instance, what occupies me most these days: the image of the forsaken astronaut from another galaxy, perhaps a successor of Matthew Arnold's Forsaken Merman, who makes what he can of Earth, the planet he's been saddled with, thus becoming a new version of that old trope the alien observer only faintly aware of where he came from. But the furor and Dionysian tenacity of Faulkner's prose style empower me even as the fruit flies cabal and reject imagination. There's one big thing about Mr. Faulkner. He reminds you that, when the deep purple blooms, you are looking not at a posy but at a dimension.

ALICE MCDERMOTT

# "The Book That Changed My Life"

From *The Book That Changed My Life*, ed. Dianne Osen (New York: Modern Library, 2002), 115–16. Copyright © by Alice McDermott. Reprinted by permission of Alice McDermott.

**DO:** Storytellers also figure prominently in *Absalom, Absalom!*, another one of your favorite novels. When did you discover that book, and what was your initial reaction to Faulkner's storytelling?

**AM:** I discovered *Absalom, Absalom!* in college, when I was in England for my junior year. Certainly, the initial appeal to me was the onrush of language in the novel, and just like *Wuthering Heights*, the story he tells is full of passion. But there's nothing more passionate in that book than the relentless demand that the story must be told, again and again. The sentences themselves contain that passion. The breathless desperation to get it told, to pass it on, to explain it to someone else—that's the thing that caught me up. That and the sense that the telling of the story itself is of great value.

**DO:** That's a quality found in your novels, as well.

**AM:** I'm not terribly interested in plots, and am always a little skeptical of stories that are too near or too familiar. It's not surprising then that my interest most naturally goes to the "why" of the storytelling rather than the "how" or the "who" of the plot. That's the thing that *Absalom* reinforced for me—that the storyteller and the impulse to tell a story are as interesting as the plot.

**DO:** What else about Faulkner's approach to his work, or his beliefs about literature, have influenced your own writing life?

**AM:** His language—the permission he gives us to let language be lush but not wasteful, the passion for language contained in each sentence. And the idea that there are many ways to tell a story. You don't have to have a rising action and climax.

**DO:** Your own books, certainly, don't depend on that kind of structure, or even on a logical chronology.

**AM:** But in all honesty, I don't proceed with any literary theory in mind. All I have is a guess about what the story requires. There's something Eudora Welty said, about how when you're writing well you hear the sound of the next sentence before you know what the words are. In some ways there's that same sense in the structuring of a novel: before you even know exactly what the next step is, you have a full sense of what the next step is, you have a full sense of what the next step needs to be. That's not to say that your instincts are always exactly right; finally it has to come down to what the work requires. So I would never say, "Well, I don't like chronological narratives," or "I will never write a chronological narrative." I would love to write a chronological narrative; I love reading them. But the stories I've told thus far have demanded something else of me.

---

# "William Faulkner
# and His Biographers"

From *Inner Workings: Literary Essays 2000–2005* (New York: Viking, 2007), 189–206. [Written in 2005 and published in *New York Review of Books*, April 7, 2005, pages 20, 22–24.] Copyright © 2007 by J. M. Coetzee. Reprinted by permission.

"**N**ow I realize for the first time," wrote William Faulkner to a woman friend, looking back from the vantage point of his mid-fifties, "what an amazing gift I had: uneducated in every formal sense, without even very literate, let alone literary, companions, yet to have made the things I made. I don't know why God or gods or whoever it was, selected me to be the vessel."[1]

The disbelief Faulkner here lays claim to is a little disingenuous. For the kind of writer he wanted to be, he had all the education, even all the book-learning, he needed. As for company, he stood to gain more from garrulous oldsters with gnarled hands and long memories than from effete *littérateurs*. Nevertheless, a measure of astonishment is in order. Who would have guessed that a boy of no great intellectual distinction from small-town Mississippi would grow up to be not only a famous writer, celebrated at home and abroad, but the *kind* of writer he in fact became: one of the most radical innovators in the annals of American fiction, a writer to whom the avant-garde of Europe and Latin America would go to school?

Of formal education Faulkner certainly had a minimum. He dropped out of high school in his junior year (his parents seem not to have kicked up a fuss), and though he briefly attended the University of Mississippi, that was only by grace of a dispensation for returned

servicemen (of Faulkner's war service, more below). His college record was undistinguished: a semester of English (grade: D), two se-
mesters of French and Spanish. For this explorer of the mind of the
post-bellum South, no courses in history; for the novelist who would
weave Bergsonian time into the syntax of memory, no studies in philosophy or psychology.

What the rather dreamy Billy Faulkner gave himself in place of
schooling was a narrow but intense reading of *fin-de-siècle* English
poetry, notably Swinburne and Housman, and of three novelists who
had given birth to fictional worlds lively and coherent enough to rival
the real one: Balzac, Dickens, and Conrad. Add to this a familiarity
with the cadences of the Old Testament, Shakespeare, and *Moby-
Dick*, and, a few years later, a quick study of what his older contemporaries T. S. Eliot and James Joyce were up to, and he was fully armed.
As for materials, what he heard around him in Oxford, Mississippi,
turned out to be more than enough: the epic, told and retold endlessly, of the South, a story of cruelty and injustice and hope and disappointment and victimization and resistance.

Billy Faulkner had barely quit school when the First World War
broke out. Captivated by the idea of becoming a pilot and flying sor-
ties against the Hun, he applied in 1918 to be taken into the Royal Air
Force. Desperate for fresh manpower, the RAF recruiting office sent
him to Canada on a training course. Before he could make his first
solo flight, however, the war ended.

He returned to Oxford wearing an RAF officer's uniform and
sporting a British accent and a limp, the consequence, he said, of a
flying accident. To friends he also confided that he had a steel plate in
his skull.

He sustained the aviator legend for years; he began to play it down
only when he became a national figure and the risk of exposure
loomed too large. His dreams of flying were not abandoned, however. As soon as he had the money to spare, in 1933, he took flying
lessons, bought his own plane, and briefly operated a flying circus:
"WILLIAM FAULKNER'S (Famous Author) AIR CIRCUS," ran the
advertisement.[2]

Faulkner's biographers have made much of his war stories, treating them as more than just the concoctions of a puny and unprepossessing youth desperate to be admired. Frederick R. Karl believes that "the war turned [Faulkner] into a storyteller, a fictionist, which may have been the decisive turnabout in his life" (p. 111). The ease with which he duped the good people of Oxford, Karl says, proved to Faulkner that, artfully contrived and convincingly expounded, a lie can beat the truth, and thus that one can make not only a life but a living out of fantasy.

Back home, Faulkner drifted. He wrote poems about "epicene" (by which he seems to have meant narrow-hipped) women and his unrequited longings for them, poems that, even with the best will in the world, one cannot call promising; he began to sign his name not "Falkner," as he was born, but "Faulkner"; and, following the pattern of the male Falkners, he drank heavily. For some years, until he was dismissed for poor performance, he held a sinecure as postmaster of a small station, where he spent office hours reading and writing.

For someone so determined to follow his inclinations, it is odd that, rather than packing his bags and heading for the bright lights of the metropolis, he chose to remain in the town of his birth, where his pretensions were regarded with sardonic amusement. Jay Parini, his most recent biographer, suggests that he found it hard to be out of reach of his mother, a woman of some sensibility who seems to have had a deeper relation with her eldest son than with a dull and spineless husband.[3]

On forays to New Orleans, Faulkner developed a circle of bohemian friends and met Sherwood Anderson, chronicler of Winesburg, Ohio, whose influence on him he was later at pains to minimize. He began to publish short pieces in the New Orleans press; he even dipped into literary theory. Willard Huntingdon Wright, a disciple of Walter Pater, made a particular impression on him. In Wright's *The Creative Will* (1915) he read that the true artist is solitary by nature, "an omnipotent god who moulds and fashions the destiny of a new world, and leads it to an inevitable completion where it can stand alone, self-moving, independent," leaving its creator exalted of spirit.[4] The type of artist-demiurge, suggests Wright, is Balzac, much to be preferred to Émile Zola, a mere copyist of a pre-existing reality.

In 1925, Faulkner made his first trip abroad. He spent two months in Paris and liked it: he bought a beret, grew a beard, began to work on a novel—soon to be abandoned—about a painter with a war wound who goes to Paris to further his art. He hung out at James Joyce's favorite café, where he caught a glimpse of the great man but did not approach him.

All in all, nothing in the record suggests more than a would-be writer of unusual doggedness but no great gifts. Yet soon after his return to the United States, he would sit down and write a 14,000-word sketch bursting with ideas and characters which would lay the groundwork for the series of great novels of the years 1929–42. The manuscript contained, in embryo, Yoknapatawpha County.

As a child Faulkner had been inseparable from a slightly older friend named Estelle Oldham. The two were in some sense betrothed. When the time came, however, the Oldham parents, disapproving of the shiftless youth, married Estelle off to a lawyer with better prospects. Thus when Estelle returned to the parental home it was as a divorced woman of thirty-two with two small children.

Though Faulkner seems to have had doubts about the wisdom of taking up with Estelle again, he did not act on them. Before long the two were married. Estelle must have had doubts of her own. During the honeymoon she may or may not have tried to drown herself. The marriage itself turned out to be unhappy, worse than unhappy. "They were just terribly unsuited for each other," their daughter, Jill, told Parini many years later. "Nothing about the marriage was right" (Parini, p. 130). Estelle was an intelligent woman, but she was used to spending money freely and to having servants carry out her every wish. Life in a dilapidated old house with a husband who spent his mornings scribbling and his afternoons replacing rotten timbers and putting in plumbing must have come as a shock to her. A child was born but died at two weeks. Jill was born in 1933. Thereafter sexual relations between the Faulkners seem to have ceased.

Together and separately, William and Estelle drank to excess. In late middle age Estelle pulled herself right and went on the wagon; William never did. He had affairs with younger women which he was not competent or careful enough to conceal. From scenes of raging jealousy the marriage by degrees dwindled into, in the words of

Faulkner's first biographer, Joseph Blotner, "desultory domestic guerrilla warfare" (p. 537).

Nevertheless, for thirty-three years, until Faulkner's death in 1962, the marriage endured. Why? The most mundane explanation is that, until well into the 1950s, Faulkner could not afford a divorce—that is to say, could not, in addition to the troops of Faulkners or Falkners, to say nothing of Oldhams, dependent on his earnings, afford to support Estelle and three children in the style she would have demanded, and at the same time relaunch himself decently in society. Less easily demonstrable is Karl's claim that at some deep level Faulkner needed Estelle. "Estelle could never be disentangled from the deepest reaches of [Faulkner's] imagination," Karl writes. "Without Estelle . . . he could not have continued [to write]." She was his "belle dame sans merci"—"that ideal object man worships from a distance who is also . . . destructive" (p. 86).

By choosing to marry Estelle, by choosing to make his home in Oxford amid the Falkner clan, Faulkner took on a formidable challenge: how to be patron and breadwinner and paterfamilias to what he privately called "[a] whole tribe . . . hanging like so many buzzards over every penny [I] earn," while at the same time serving his inner daimon. Despite an Apollonian ability to immerse himself in his work—"a monster of efficiency," Parini calls him—the project wore him down. To feed the buzzards, the one blazing genius of American literature of the 1930s had to put aside his novel-writing, which was all that really mattered to him, first to churn out stories for popular magazines, later to write screenplays for Hollywood (Parini, pp. 319, 139).

The trouble was not so much that Faulkner was unappreciated in the community of letters as that there was no room in the economy of the 1930s for the profession of avant-garde novelist (today Faulkner would be a natural for a major fellowship). Faulkner's publishers, editors, and agents—with one miserable exception—had his interests at heart and did their best on his behalf, but that was not enough. Only after the appearance of *The Portable Faulkner*, a selection skillfully put together by Malcolm Cowley in 1945, did American readers wake up to what they had in their midst.

The time spent writing short stories was not all wasted. Faulkner was an extraordinarily tenacious reviser of his own work (in Hollywood he impressed by his ability to fix up dud scripts by other writers). Revisited and reconceived and reworked, material that made its first appearance in *The Sunday Evening Post* or *The Woman's Home Companion* resurfaced transmogrified in *The Unvanquished* (1938), *The Hamlet* (1940) and *Go Down, Moses* (1942), books that straddle the line between story collection and novel proper.

The same buried potential cannot be claimed of his screenplays. When Faulkner arrived in Hollywood in 1932, riding on his passing notoriety as the author of *Sanctuary* (1931), he knew nothing of the industry (in his private life he disdained movies as much as he disliked loud music). He had no gift for putting together snappy dialogue. Furthermore, he soon acquired a reputation as an undependable lush. From a high of $1,000 a week his salary had by 1942 dropped to $300. In the course of a thirteen-year career he worked with sympathetic directors like Howard Hawks, was friendly with celebrated actors like Clark Gable and Humphrey Bogart, acquired an attractive and attentive Hollywood mistress; but nothing that he wrote for the movies proved worth rescuing.

Worse than that: his screenwriting had a bad effect on his prose. During the war years Faulkner worked on a succession of scripts of a hortatory, uplifting, patriotic nature. It would be a mistake to load all the blame for the overblown rhetoric that mars his late prose onto these projects, but he himself came to recognize the harm Hollywood had done him. "I have realized lately how much trash and junk writing for movies corrupted into my writing," he admitted in 1947.[5]

There is nothing unusual in the story of Faulkner's struggles to balance his accounts. From the beginning he thought of himself as a *poète maudit*, and it is the lot of the *poète maudit* to be disregarded and underpaid. All that is surprising is that the burdens he took on—the high-spending wife, the impecunious relatives, the disadvantages of studio contracts—should have been borne so tenaciously (though with much griping on the side), even at the cost of his art. Loyalty is as strong a theme in Faulkner's life as in his writing, but there is such a thing as mad loyalty, mad fidelity (the Confederate South was full of it).

In effect, Faulkner spent his middle years as a migrant worker sending his pay packet home to Mississippi; the biographical record is largely a record of dollars and cents. In Faulkner's worryings over money Parini rightly discerns a deeper absorption. "Money is rarely just money," Parini writes. "The obsession with money that seems to dog Faulkner throughout his life must, I think, be regarded as a measure of his waxing and waning feelings of stability, value, purchase on the world . . . a means of calculating his reputation, his power, his reality" (pp. 295–96).

A position as a writer in residence on some quiet Southern college campus might have been the salvation of William Faulkner, giving him a steady income and demanding not much in return, allowing him time for his own work. A canny Robert Frost had since 1917 been showing that one could trade on the bardic aura to secure oneself academic sinecures. But, lacking a high-school diploma, mistrustful of talk that sounded too "literary" or "intellectual," Faulkner made no return to the groves of academe until 1946, when he was persuaded to speak to students at the University of Mississippi. The experience was not as bad as he had feared; at the age of sixty, at a more or less nominal salary, he joined the University of Virginia as writer in residence, a position he retained until his death.

One of the ironies of the life of this academic laggard is that he had probably read more widely, if less systemically, than most college professors. In Hollywood, said the actor Anthony Quinn, even though he wasn't highly rated as a screenwriter he had "a tremendous reputation as an intellectual." Another irony is that Faulkner was adopted by the New Critics as master of the kind of prose ideally suited to dissection in the college classroom. "So much to unfold that had been carefully and ingeniously folded by the author," enthused Cleanth Brooks, doyen of the New Criticism. Thus Faulkner became the darling of the New Haven formalists as he was already the darling of the French existentialists, without being quite sure what either formalism or existentialism was.[6]

The Nobel Prize for literature, awarded for 1949, presented in 1950, made Faulkner famous even in America. Tourists came from far and

wide to gawk at his home in Oxford, to his vast irritation. Reluctantly
he emerged from the shadows and began to behave like a public figure. From the State Department came invitations to travel abroad as
a cultural ambassador, which he dubiously accepted. Nervous before
the microphone, even more nervous fielding "literary" questions, he
prepared for sessions by drinking heavily. But, once he had developed
a patter to cope with journalists, he grew more comfortable with the
role. He was ill informed about foreign affairs—he did not read newspapers—but that suited the State Department well enough. His visit
to Japan was a striking public relations success; in France and Italy
he received massive attention from the press. As he remarked sar-
donically, "If they believed in my world in America the way they do
abroad, I could probably run one of my characters for President . . .
maybe Flem Snopes."[7]

Less impressive were Faulkner's interventions back home. Pressure was building on the South and its segregated institutions. In letters to editors of newspapers, he began to speak out against abuses
and to urge fellow white Southerners to accept the Negro as a social
equal.

There was a backlash. "Weeping Willie Faulkner" was denounced
as a pawn of Northern liberals, as a Communist sympathizer. Though
he was never in physical danger, he claimed (in a letter to a Swed-
ish friend) to foresee a day when he would have to flee the country
"something as the Jew had to flee from Germany during Hitler."[8]

He was of course overdramatizing. His views on race were never
radical and, as the political atmosphere grew more charged and developed states' rights overtones, descended into confusion. Segregation was an evil, he said; nevertheless, if integration were forced upon
the South, he would resist (in a rash moment he even said he would
take up arms). By the late 1950s, his position had become so out of
date as to be positively quaint. The civil rights movement should
adopt as watchwords, he said, decency, quietness, courtesy, and dignity, the Negro should learn to deserve equality.

It is easy enough to disparage Faulkner's forays into race relations.
In his personal life his behavior toward African-Americans seems
to have been generous, kindly, but, unavoidably, patronizing: he be-
longed, after all, to a *patron* class. In his political philosophy he was a

Jeffersonian individualist; it was this, rather than any residue of racism in his blood, that made him suspicious of black mass movements. If his scruples and equivocations soon rendered him irrelevant to the civil rights struggle, he was courageous in taking any stand at all the time when he did. His public statements made him somewhat of a pariah in his home town, and had more than a little to do with his decision, after his mother's death in 1960, to quit Mississippi and move to Virginia. (At the same time, it must be said, the prospect of riding to the hounds with the Albermarle County Hunt was a powerful drawcard: Faulkner in his last years regarded himself as pretty much written out, and foxhunting became the new passion of his life.)

Faulkner's interventions in public affairs were ineffectual not because he was stupid about politics but because the appropriate vehicle for his political insights was not the essay, much less the letter to the editor, but the novel, and in specific the kind of novel he invented, with its unequalled rhetorical resources for interweaving past and present, memory and desire.

The territory on which Faulkner the novelist deployed his best resources was a South that bears a strong resemblance to the real South of his day—or at least the South of his youth—but is not the whole of the South. Faulkner's South is a white South haunted by black presences. Even *Light in August*, the novel that is most clearly *about* race and racism, had at its center not a black man but rather a man whose fate it is to confront or be confronted with blackness as an interpellation, an accusation from outside himself.

A historian of the modern South, Faulkner's abiding achievement is the Snopes trilogy (*The Hamlet*, 1940; *The Town*, 1957; *The Mansion*, 1959), in which he tracks the takeover of political power by an ascendant poor white class in a revolution as quiet, implacable, and amoral as a termite invasion. His chronicle of the rise of the redneck entrepreneur is at the same time mordant and elegiac and despairing: mordant because he detests what he sees as much as he is fascinated by it; elegiac because he loves the old world that is being eaten up before his eyes; and despairing for many reasons, not least of which are, first, that the South he loves was built, as he knows better than anyone, on twin crimes of dispossession and slavery; second, that the

Snopeses are just another avatar of the Faulkners, thieves and rapists of the land in their day; and therefore, third, that as critic and judge he, William "Faulkner," has no ground to stand on.

No ground unless he falls back on the eternal verities. "Courage and honor and pride, and pity and love of justice and of liberty" is the litany of virtues recited in *Go Down, Moses* by Ike McCaslin, who is pretty much spokesman for Faulkner's wished-for, ideal self, a man who, having taken stock of his history and of the diminished and fast-diminishing world around him, renounces his patrimony, abjures fatherhood (thus putting an end to the procession of the generations), and becomes a simple carpenter.[9]

Courage and honor and pride: to his litany Ike might have added endurance, as he does elsewhere in the same story: "Endurance . . . and pity and tolerance and forbearance and fidelity and love of children . . ." (p. 225). There is a strongly moralistic strain in Faulkner's later work, a stripped-down Christian humanism stubbornly held to in a world from which God has retired. When this moralism proves unconvincing, as it often is, that is usually because Faulkner has failed to find an adequate fictional vehicle for it. The frustrations he experienced in putting together *A Fable* (written 1944–53, published 1954), which he intended to be his magnum opus, were precisely in finding a way to embody his anti-war theme. The exemplary figure in *A Fable* is Jesus reincarnated in and re-sacrificed as the unknown soldier; elsewhere in the late work he is the simple, suffering black man or, more often, black woman, who by enduring an unendurable present keeps alive the germ of a future.

For a man who lived an uneventful and largely sedentary life, William Faulkner has evoked prodigious biographical energies. The first big biographical monument was erected in 1974 by Joseph Blotner, a younger colleague from the University of Virginia whom Faulkner clearly liked and trusted, and whose two-volume *Faulkner: A Biography* provides a full and fair treatment of his subject's outward life. Even Blotner's one-volume, 400,000-word condensation (1984) may, however, prove too rich in detail for most readers.

Frederick R. Karl's huge tome *William Faulkner: An American Writer* (1989) has as its stated aim "to understand and interpret

[Faulkner's] life psychologically, emotionally, and literarily" (p. xv). There is much in Karl that is admirable, including dauntless ventures into the maze of Faulkner's compositional practices, which involved working on numbers of projects at the same time, shunting material from one to another.

As Karl justly observes, Faulkner is "the most historical of [America's] important writers"; accordingly he treats Faulkner as an American responding creatively to the historical and social forces in which he is enmeshed (p. 666). As *literary* biographer what he tries to comprehend is how a man so deeply suspicious of modernization and what it was doing to the South could at the same time in his novelistic practice have been a radical modernist.

Karl's Faulkner emerges as a figure of grandeur as well as pathos, a man who, perhaps in thrall to a Romantic image of the doomed artist, was prepared to sacrifice himself to the project of living through destiny from which any rational person would have walked away. But Karl's book is spoiled by continual reductive pyschologizing. For instance, Faulkner's neat handwriting—an editor's dream—is taken as evidence of an anal personality, his silly lies about his exploits with the RAF as a sign of a schizoid personality, his attention to detail as proof of obsessiveness, his affair with a young woman revealing of incestuous desires for his daughter.

"Often a lesser novel can provide more incisive biographical insights than a great one," says Karl (p. 75). If this is so—and not many contemporary biographers would disagree—then we confront a general problem about literary biography and the status of so-called biographical insights. May it not be that if the minor work seems to reveal more than the major work, what it reveals is worth knowing only in a minor way? Perhaps Faulkner—to whom the odes of John Keats were a poetic touchstone—was indeed what he felt himself to be: a being of negative capability, one who disappeared into, lost himself in his profoundest creations. "It is my ambition to be a private individual, abolished and voided from history, leaving it markless," he wrote to Cowley: "It is my aim . . . that the sum and history of my life . . . shall be . . . : He made the books and he died."[10]

Jay Parini is the author of biographies of John Steinbeck (1994) and

Robert Frost (1999), and of two novels with a strong biographical content: *The Last Station* (1990), about the last days of Leo Tolstoy, and
*Benjamin's Crossing* (1997), about the last days of Walter Benjamin.[11]

Parini's life of Steinbeck is solid but unremarkable. The Frost book
is more self-reflective: biography, Parini muses, may be less like his-
toriography than we like to think and more like novel-writing. Of his
own biographical novels, the one on Tolstoy is the more successful,
perhaps because there is such a multiplicity of accounts of life on Yas-
naya Polyana to draw on. In the Benjamin book Parini has to spend
too much time explaining who his self-absorbed hero is and why we
should be interested in him.

In the case of Faulkner, Parini attempts what neither Blotner nor
Karl offers: a critical biography, that is to say, a reasonably full account of Faulkner's life together with an assessment of his writings.
There is a great deal to be said for what he has produced. Though
he relies heavily on Blotner for the facts, he has gone further than
Blotner by conducting interviews with the last generation of people
to have known Faulkner personally, some of whom have interesting
things to say. He has a fellow writer's appreciation for Faulkner's
language, and expresses that appreciation vividly. Thus the prose of
"The Bear" proceeds "with a kind of inexorable ferocity, as though
Faulkner composed in excited reverie." Though by no means ha-
giography, his book pays eloquent tribute to its subject: "What
most impresses about Faulkner as writer is the sheer persistence,
the will-to-power that brought him back to the desk each day, year
after year . . . [His] grit was . . . as much physical as mental; [he]
pushed ahead like an ox through mud, dragging a whole world behind him" (pp. 261, 429).

In a non-specialist book like this, one of the first decisions the
writer has to make is whether it should reflect the critical consensus or take a strong individual line. By and large, Parini goes for a
version of the consensus option. His scheme is to follow Faulkner's
life chronologically, interrupting the narrative with short critical essays of an introductory nature on individual works. In the right hands
such a scheme could result in exemplary specimens of the critic's
art. But Parini's essays are not up to exemplary standard. Those on
Faulkner's best-known books tend to be his best; of the rest, too many

consist of not particularly deft synopsis plus summary of the critical debate, where what counts as debate tends to be rather humdrum academic inquiry.

As in Karl's book, there is also a degree of questionable pyschologism. Thus Parini offers a rather wild reading of *As I Lay Dying*—a short novel built around the grotesque trip on which the Bundren children take their mother's corpse on the way to the grave—as a symbolic act of aggression by Faulkner against his own mother as well as a "perverse" wedding present to his wife. "Does Estelle supplant Miss Maud [his mother] in Faulkner's mind?" asks Parini. "Such questions are beyond answers, but it's the province of biography to ask them, to allow them to play over the text and trouble it" (p. 151). Perhaps it is indeed the province of the biographer to trouble the text with fancies plucked from the air; perhaps not. More to the point is whether either Faulkner's mother or his wife understood the novel as a personal attack on them. There is no record that either did.

Parini's explorations of Faulkner's mind entail much talk of parts of the self, or selves within the self. Does Faulkner disapprove of the adulterous lovers in *The Wild Palms*? Answer: while "a part of his novelistic mind" condemns them, another part does not. Why does Faulkner in the late 1930s choose to focus on Flem Snopes, the beady-eyed, cold-hearted social climber of the trilogy? "I suspect it was something to do with exploring his own aggressive self," Parini writes. Having "succeeded beyond his own dreams . . . [Faulkner] wanted to think on that success and to understand the impulses that might have led him to it" (pp. 238, 232–33).

Was it really Faulkner's "aggressive self" that produced the great novels of the 1930s, achievements at which Flem would have sneered, so little money did they make for their author? Does Flem's crooked genius really resemble Faulkner's baffled relationship with money, including his naïveté in signing a contract with Warner Brothers, the most stolidly unadventurous of the studios that made him their slave for seven years?

All in all, Parini's book is a puzzling mixture: on the one hand it shows a real feel for Faulkner as a writer, on the other, a readiness to vulgarize him. The worst instance comes in his remarks on Rowan

Oak, the four-acre property that Faulkner bought in run-down state in 1929 and lived on until his death. Faulkner was prepared to spend money he did not have on renovating Rowan Oak, Parini writes, because "he had a vision of antebellum luxury and superiority that he wanted, above all else, to re-create in his daily life . . . The film *Gone with the Wind* . . . appeared [in 1939], taking the nation by storm. Faulkner didn't need to see it. It was his life's story" (p. 250). Anyone who has read Blotner on daily life at Rowan Oak will know how far it was from the fantasy of Tara.

"A book is the writer's secret life, the dark twin of a man: you can't reconcile them," says one of the characters in *Mosquitoes* (1927).[12]

Reconciling the writer with his books is a challenge that Blotner sensibly does not take on. Whether either Karl or Parini, in their different ways, brings together the man who signed his name "William Faulkner" with his dark twin is an open question.

The acid test is what Faulkner's biographers have to say about his alcoholism. This is not a subject around which one should pussyfoot. The notation on the file at the psychiatric hospital in Memphis to which Faulkner was regularly taken in a stupor was, Blotner reports, "An acute and chronic alcoholic" (p. 572). Though Faulkner in his fifties looked handsome and spry, that was only a shell. A lifetime's drinking had begun to impair his mental functioning. "This is more than a case of acute alcoholism," wrote his editor Saxe Commins in 1952. "The disintegration of the man is tragic to witness." Parini adds the chilling testimony of Faulkner's daughter: when drunk, her father could be so violent that "a couple of men" had to stand by to protect her and her mother.[13]

Blotner does not try to understand Faulkner's addiction, merely chronicles its ravages, describes its patterns, and quotes the hospital records. In Karl's reading, drinking was the form that rebellion took in Faulkner, the way in which he defended his art against the pressures of family and tradition. "Take away the alcohol and, very probably, there would be no writer; and perhaps no defined person" (pp. 130–32). Parini does not demur, but sees a therapeutic purpose to Faulkner's drinking as well. His binges were "downtime for the creative mind," he says. They were "useful in some peculiar way. They cleared away cobwebs, reset the inner clock, allowed the unconscious, like a well, to slow fill [*sic*]." Emerging from a binge was "as if he'd had a long and pleasant sleep" (p. 281).

It is in the nature of addictions to be incomprehensible to those who stand outside them. Faulkner himself is of no help here: he does not write about his addiction, does not, as far as we know, write from inside it (he was mostly sober when he sat down at his desk). No biographer has yet succeeded in making sense of it; but perhaps making sense of an addiction, finding the words to account for it, giving it a place in the economy of the self, will always be a misconceived enterprise.

*Notes*

1. Quoted in Joseph Blotner, *Faulkner: A Biography,* one-volume edition (New York: Random House, 1984), 570.

2. Frederick R. Karl, *William Faulkner: American Writer* (London: Faber, 1989), 523.

3. Jay Parini, *One Matchless Time: A Life of William Faulkner* (New York: HarperCollins, 2004), 20, 79, 141, 145. See also Karl, *William Faulkner,* 213.

4. Quoted in Blotner, *Faulkner,* 106.

5. Quoted in Karl, *William Faulkner,* 757.

6. Quinn quoted in Parini, *One Matchless Time,* 271; Brooks quoted in Parini, 292.

7. Quoted in Blotner, *Faulkner,* 611.

8. Quoted in Blotner, *Faulkner,* 599.

9. *Go Down, Moses* (Harmondsworth: Penguin, 1960), 227.

10. Quoted in Blotner, *Faulkner,* 501.

11. *John Steinbeck: A Biography* (London: Heinemann, 1994); *Robert Frost: A Life* (New York: Holt, 1999); *The Last Station: A Novel of Tolstoy's Last Year* (New York: Holt, 1990); *Benjamin's Crossing: A Novel* (New York: Holt, 1997).

12. *Mosquitoes* (London: Chatto & Windus, 1964), 209.

13. Commins quoted in Karl, *William Faulkner,* 844; Jill Faulkner quoted in Parini, *One Matchless Time,* 251.

CPSIA information can be obtained at www.ICGtesting.com
Printed in the USA
BVOW04*1803130516

447720BV00003B/6/P

9 781496 803382